Implementation of the Civil Justice Reform Act in Pilot and Comparison Districts

James S. Kakalik

Terence Dunworth

Laural A. Hill

Daniel McCaffrey

Marian Oshiro

Nicholas M. Pace

Mary E. Vaiana

RAND

The Institute for Civil Justice

Robert Mednick, Managing Partner—Professional and Regulatory Matters, Arthur Andersen LLP

Eugene I. Pavalon, Pavalon & Gifford

Jerry Reinsdorf, Chairman, Chicago White Sox, Chicago Bulls

Robert B. Shapiro, Chairman and Chief Executive Officer, Monsanto Company

Michael Traynor, Partner, Cooley Godward Castro Huddleson & Tatum

Bill Wagner, Wagner, Vaughan & McLaughlin

Paul C. Weiler, Henry J. Friendly Professor of Law, Harvard University Law School

This report is one of four RAND reports evaluating the pilot program of the Civil Justice Reform Act (CJRA) of 1990. It traces the stages in the implementation of the CJRA in the study districts: the recommendations of the advisory groups, the plans adopted by the districts, and the plans actually implemented. The study was undertaken at the request of the Judicial Conference of the United States.

The companion reports are:

Just, Speedy, and Inexpensive? An Evaluation of Judicial Case Management Under the Civil Justice Reform Act, RAND, MR-800-ICJ, by James S. Kakalik, Terence Dunworth, Laural A. Hill, Daniel McCaffrey, Marian Oshiro, Nicholas M. Pace, and Mary E. Vaiana, 1996. This executive summary provides an overview of the purpose of the CJRA, the basic design of the evaluation, the key findings, and their policy implications.

An Evaluation of Judicial Case Management Under the Civil Justice Reform Act, RAND, MR-802-ICJ, by James S. Kakalik, Terence Dunworth, Laural A. Hill, Daniel McCaffrey, Marian Oshiro, Nicholas M. Pace, and Mary E. Vaiana, 1996. This document presents the main descriptive and statistical evaluation of how the CJRA case management principles implemented in the study districts affected cost, time to disposition, and participants' satisfaction and views of fairness.

An Evaluation of Mediation and Early Neutral Evaluation Under the Civil Justice Reform Act, RAND, MR-803-ICJ, by James S. Kakalik, Terence Dunworth, Laural A. Hill, Daniel McCaffrey, Marian Oshiro, Nicholas M. Pace, and Mary E. Vaiana, 1996. This document discusses the results of an evaluation of mediation and neutral evaluation designed to supplement the alternative dispute resolution assessment contained in the main CJRA evaluation.

For more information about the Institute for Civil Justice contact:

Dr. Deborah Hensler, Director
Institute for Civil Justice
RAND
1700 Main Street, P. O. Box 2138
Santa Monica, CA 90407-2138
TEL: (310) 451-6916
FAX: (310) 451-6979
Internet: Deborah_Hensler@rand.org

A profile of the Institute for Civil Justice, abstracts of its publications, and ordering information can be found on RAND's home page on the World Wide Web at http://www.rand.org/centers/icj/.

CONTENTS

FIGURES

TABLES

The Civil Justice Reform Act (CJRA) of 1990 is rooted in more than a decade of concern that cases in federal courts take too long and cost litigants too much. As a consequence, proponents of reform argue, some litigants are denied access to justice, and many litigants incur inappropriate burdens when they turn to the courts for assistance in resolving disputes. In the late 1980s, several groups, including the Federal Courts Study Committee and the Council on Competitiveness, began formulating reform proposals. One of these—the Task Force on Civil Justice Reform, initiated by Senator Joseph Biden and convened by the Brookings Institution—produced a set of recommendations that ultimately led to legislation. The task force comprised leading litigators from the plaintiffs' and defense bar, civil and women's rights lawyers, attorneys representing consumer and environmental organizations, representatives of the insurance industry, general counsels of major corporations, former judges, and law professors.

The new legislation, the CJRA, required each federal district court to conduct a self-study with the aid of an advisory group and to develop a plan for civil case management to reduce costs and delay. To provide an empirical basis for assessing new procedures adopted under the act, the legislation also provided for an independent evaluation. It created a pilot program requiring ten districts to incorporate six principles of case management into their plans and to consider incorporating six other case management techniques. The evaluation included ten other districts to permit comparisons.

The Judicial Conference and the Administrative Office of the U.S. Courts asked RAND's Institute for Civil Justice to evaluate the implementation and the effects of the CJRA in these districts. This document describes how the CJRA was implemented. Separate RAND reports evaluate the effects of the CJRA case management principles and techniques on time to case disposition, litigation costs, and participants' satisfaction and views of fairness.[1] Following completion of the RAND reports, the Judicial Conference will prepare and submit a report to Congress.

---

[1]Kakalik et al. (1996a and 1996b).

OVERVIEW OF THE CJRA PILOT PROGRAM

The CJRA requires the ten pilot districts to adopt six case management principles:

- Differential management of cases;

- Early and ongoing judicial control of pretrial processes;

- Special monitoring and judicial control of complex cases;

- Cost-effective discovery through cooperation and voluntary exchanges of information;

- Good-faith efforts to resolve discovery disputes before filing motions; and

- Diversion of cases, when appropriate, to alternative dispute resolution (ADR) programs.

The act also directs each district to consider adopting the following six techniques:

- Require that counsel jointly present a discovery/case management plan at the initial pretrial conference, or explain the reasons for their failure to do so;

- Require that each party be represented at each pretrial conference by an attorney with authority to bind that party;

- Require the signature of the attorney and the party on all requests for discovery extensions or postponements of trial;

- Offer an early neutral evaluation program;

- Require party representatives with authority to bind to be present or available by telephone at settlement conferences; and

- Incorporate such other features as the district court considers appropriate.

Ten pilot districts were selected by the Committee on Court Administration and Case Management of the Judicial Conference of the United States: California (S), Delaware, Georgia (N), New York (S), Oklahoma (W), Pennsylvania (E), Tennessee (W), Texas (S), Utah, and Wisconsin (E).

The Judicial Conference also selected ten comparison districts: Arizona, California (C), Florida (N), Illinois (N), Indiana (N), Kentucky (E), Kentucky (W), Maryland, New York (E), and Pennsylvania (M).

The pilot districts were required to implement their plans by January 1992; the other 84 districts, including the ten comparison districts, could implement their plans any time before December 1993. All districts met their deadlines.

FEATURES OF THE RAND EVALUATION

The evaluation is designed to provide a quantitative and qualitative basis for assessing how the management principles adopted in the pilot and comparison districts affect costs to litigants, time to disposition, participants' satisfaction with the process and views of fairness of the process, and judge work time required. Comparisons are made between the ten pilot districts and the ten comparison districts, both before and after implementation of the pilot program plans. In addition, comparisons are made between cases managed in different ways to assess the costs and effects of managing cases with and without various procedures.

We use both descriptive tabulations and complex multivariate statistical techniques to evaluate the various case management policies and procedures on predicted time to disposition, litigation costs, satisfaction, and views of fairness.

Comparability of Pilot and Comparison Districts

Ideally, the pilot and comparison districts would be similar in every respect except case management policies. However, since these policies were not known at the time the pilot and comparison districts were selected, the Judicial Conference chose comparison districts using factors such as district size, workload per judge, the number of criminal and civil filings, and the time to disposition in civil cases. Judging by these features, the pilot districts appear to be comparable to the comparison districts and reasonably representative of all federal districts.[2] Together, the 20 study districts have about one-third of all federal judges and one-third of all federal case filings.

Data Sources

The evaluation is based on extensive and detailed case-level data from January 1991 through December 1995. Data sources include:

- Court records;

- Records, reports, and surveys of CJRA advisory groups;

- Districts' cost and delay reduction plans;

- Detailed case processing, docket, and outcome information on a sample of cases;

- Surveys of judicial officers about their activities, time expenditures, and views of CJRA;

- Mail surveys of attorneys and litigants about costs, time, and satisfaction with the process and case outcomes; and

- Interviews with judges, court staff, and lawyers in each of the 20 districts.

In total, more than 10,000 cases were selected for intensive study, and we attempted to survey more than 60,000 people. About two-thirds of the judges, one-half of the lawyers, and one-eighth of the litigants responded to the surveys.

---

[2]RAND's subsequent analysis of extensive survey data collected in this evaluation indicates that there were no statistically significant differences between pilot and comparison districts in 1991 before CJRA, in either the time to disposition or the cost per litigant. Refer to our separate evaluation report for details.

Similar data were collected for a special supplementary analysis of ADR programs in the six study districts with a sufficiently high volume of ADR cases to permit evaluation.

THE ADVISORY GROUP PROCESS

The CJRA required each district to appoint an advisory group; its membership was to be balanced and representative of the actors involved in litigation. The group's mandate was to assess the condition of the civil and criminal dockets, identify the principal causes of delay and excess cost, and make recommendations for dealing with these problems. The advisory group was also to monitor the implementation of the plan and provide input to an annual assessment. Each district court then could accept, modify, or reject the advisory group recommendations when the court adopted its CJRA plan. In most districts, the courts responded positively to most or all of the advisory group recommendations. Circuit and Judicial Conference review of the plans after adoption resulted in few changes. The deadline for plan adoption was January 1, 1992, for pilot districts and December 1993 for other districts.

The act calls for advisory groups to be balanced and to include attorneys and other persons who represent major categories of litigants. One interpretation of the balance requirement is that lawyers' membership on the advisory group can achieve that balance in terms of the types of clients they represent. That balance appears to have been met as far as lawyers are concerned. "Other persons" were minimally represented. Limited by their lack of familiarity with the federal district court system, lay people usually played only a very modest role in advisory group meetings.

In general, the advisory groups approached their mission with dedication and conscientiousness. They analyzed the data that courts already had regarding time to disposition but they had little information on litigation costs. Many groups supplemented court data with interviews of judges and court clerks and with surveys of attorneys and, occasionally, litigants. The advisory groups' final reports reflected considerable independence from the courts. Most courts incorporated most of their advisory group's recommendations into their plans.

The quality of the required annual reassessments varies markedly from district to district. Although the act does not require a written assessment, seven of the 20 districts in this study have written reassessments at least twice. Six of the 20 districts had no written documentation of the results of any annual assessment when we inquired in January 1996.

Whatever the content of the plans, our interviews indicate that the efforts required to generate the reports and plans have made courts more cognizant of case management problems and opportunities. Bench-bar understanding reportedly has also been improved. That benefit alone probably justifies the advisory groups' work.

Our conclusion is that the CJRA advisory group process was useful, and the great majority of advisory group members thought so too.[3]

HOW THE DISTRICTS IMPLEMENTED THEIR CJRA PLANS

The six principles and six techniques specified in the act can be usefully assigned to four categories. We use these categories in our discussion below.

Differential Case Management

This category of procedures includes differential management of cases as well as special judicial control of complex cases.

Before CJRA, all pilot and comparison districts had special procedures for processing cases that require minimal management—typically, prisoner petitions, Social Security appeals, government loan recoveries, and bankruptcy filings. For other cases, nearly all districts relied on "judicial discretion"—judges or magistrate judges making case management decisions case by case according to their own schedules and procedures. Hereinafter, we refer to this as the judicial discretion model of case management.

In response to the CJRA, six of the ten pilot district plans replaced the judicial discretion model with a track model of differential case management. Implementing a track model implies having separate tracks for different types of general civil cases, setting guidelines for managing the cases in each track, and assigning cases to each track at or near case filing. A common formulation is to have three tracks: expedited, standard, and complex. However, five of the six pilot districts whose plans contained a track model assigned 2 percent or less of their cases to the complex track. Pennsylvania (E), which assigned 7 percent of its general civil cases to the complex track, was the sole exception. In addition, most districts that included tracking in their plan actually assigned the traditional group of minimal management case types listed above to the expedited track. The consequence was that most general civil cases to which CJRA procedural principles might be relevant were placed into the standard track, if any track assignment was made. This meant that there was little actual "differential" tracking of general civil cases in most districts that adopted a track model in their CJRA plan.

Using the act's flexible definition of differential case management, four of the pilot districts interpreted the CJRA's requirement as being fulfilled by a continuation of the judicial discretion model.

Two of the comparison districts adopted a tracking system, but one of them assigned less than 2 percent of cases to the complex track.

---

[3]The appendices of this document summarize each district's advisory group recommendations, the plans adopted by the district courts, and the courts' implementation of those plans.

Interviews with judges and lawyers suggest why districts' implementation of their CJRA plans involves less tracking than might have been anticipated: (1) the difficulty in determining the correct track assignment for most civil litigation cases using data available at or soon after case filing; and (2) judges' desire to tailor case management decisions to the needs of the case and to their style of management rather than having the track assignment provide the management structure for a category of cases.

Early Judicial Case Management

Early judicial case management as defined in the act includes early and ongoing judicial control of pretrial processes as well as having counsel jointly present a discovery/case management plan at the initial pretrial conference. Related CJRA techniques include having parties represented at pretrial conferences by an attorney with authority to bind them; requiring the signature of the attorney and the party on all requests for discovery extensions or postponements of trial; and requiring party representatives with authority to bind to be present or available by telephone at settlement conferences.

All advisory group reports favored the principle of early judicial management of general civil cases, and all of the courts' plans accepted the principle of early and ongoing judicial control of the pretrial process. However, case management styles varied considerably between districts and between judges in a given district.

Before CJRA only one district in our study required that counsel jointly present a discovery/case management plan at the initial pretrial conference, although at least one other district required attorneys to confer before the first pretrial conference to attempt to agree on a scheduling order.[4] Four of the ten pilot districts adopted this technique in their plan in 1991, and nine of the other pilot and comparison districts later adopted it when the federal rules were changed in December 1993.[5]

Both before and after CJRA, all 20 districts required, or allowed judges to require, that each party be represented at each pretrial conference by an attorney with authority to bind that party.

In contrast, none of the 20 districts required the signature of the attorney and the party on all requests for discovery extensions or postponements of trial either before or after CJRA.

Finally, before CJRA, eight of the 20 districts required, upon notice by the court, that party representatives with authority to bind be present or available by telephone at settlement conferences. Five additional districts adopted this technique as part of their CJRA plan. Note that whether this technique is used depends on judges' decisions on individual cases, rather than being an automatic requirement.

---

[4]See Form 35 of F.R.Civ.P.26(f) for an example of a possible discovery/case management plan. We consider a discovery/case management plan to include more than the typical scheduling order, although in some districts they may be functionally equivalent.

[5]F.R.Civ.P. 26(f).

Discovery Management

Issues in managing discovery include how much the court, rather than lawyers, should control volume and timing of discovery, and what types of information should be voluntarily or mandatorily exchanged without formal discovery requests. The CJRA discovery policies include early and ongoing judicial control of pretrial processes, requiring good-faith efforts to resolve discovery disputes before filing motions, and voluntary exchanges of information.

Before CJRA, most districts left court control of the volume and timing of discovery to the judge in each case; CJRA had little effect on this arrangement.

However, CJRA and the December 1993 changes in the federal rules brought about substantial change in early disclosure. Only one district required it before CJRA; after CJRA, all pilot and comparison districts have adopted one of five approaches providing either voluntary or mandatory exchange of information by lawyers, sometimes only for specified types of cases.

Four pilot districts later switched from their initial disclosure procedure to follow the mandatory disclosure required by the December 1993 revised F.R.Civ.P. 26(a)(1), and six comparison districts are following the revised Rule 26(a)(1), which requires the mandatory exchange of information relevant to disputed facts alleged with particularity in the pleadings, plus information on damages and insurance. The ten other pilot and comparison districts have exercised their right to "opt out" of the revised Rule 26(a)(1); some districts that opted out have provisions in their CJRA plans that require broader disclosure than that required by Rule 26(a)(1).

The requirement that lawyers certify good-faith efforts to resolve discovery disputes before filing motions has undergone little change. All but one district had rules governing this area before CJRA; these have been continued or strengthened.

Alternative Dispute Resolution

The CJRA's ADR policies include diverting cases, when appropriate, to ADR programs and offering an early neutral evaluation program.

The plans from all 20 districts permit the use of ADR techniques. In implementation, however, two types of programs have emerged, both of which meet the loosely defined requirements of the CJRA. About half the districts have formally structured programs involving between 2 and 19 percent of all their civil case filings. And one district uses early neutral evaluation conducted by a magistrate judge on 50 percent of its cases. The other districts have unstructured programs that involve less than 2 percent participation.

ASSESSMENT OF IMPLEMENTATION

All pilot districts complied with the statutory language in the act, which provides loosely defined principles but leaves operational interpretation of them to the discretion of individual districts and judicial officers. Many pilot and comparison districts interpreted some or all of their current and past practices to be consistent with the language of the act and continued those practices unchanged. However, if the spirit of the act is interpreted to mean experimentation and change focusing on the six CJRA principles, then the pilot districts met that spirit to varying degrees. Comparison districts, which were required to consider but were not required to adopt the six CJRA principles in their plans, generally made fewer changes than pilot districts.

Even in pilot districts whose plans suggested major changes, implementation often fell short. For example, six of the ten pilot districts adopted a plan with a track model of differential case management, but only one assigned the majority of its general civil cases to tracks and had more than 2 percent of the cases in both the standard and the complex tracks. In the other districts with track models, the assignment of cases to tracks was either not often made or was almost universally made to the standard track. For another example, all ten of the pilot districts adopted a plan with provision for alternative dispute resolution, but four referred less than 2 percent of their cases to ADR.

Thus, for various reasons, in practice there was much less change in case management after CJRA than one might have expected from reading the plans. This is evident both from observations at the district court level of how the major elements of the plans were implemented and from surveys of the judges in the 1992–1993 sample of 5,000+ cases. In 85 percent of the cases surveyed after CJRA, for example, the pilot district judges said that the surveyed case was managed no differently than it would have been before CJRA.[6]

Some possible reasons why the CJRA pilot program did not result in more change are discussed in our companion evaluation report.[7] We believe that the probability of effective implementation of change could be increased by taking into account factors that appeared to impede implementation of the CJRA in some districts. These include the vague wording of the act itself, the fact that some judges, lawyers, and others viewed the procedural innovations imposed by Congress as unduly emphasizing speed and efficiency, the fact that some judges viewed the procedural innovations of the CJRA as curtailing the judicial independence accorded their office under Article III of the Constitution, and the lack of effective mechanisms for ensuring that the policies contained in district plans were carried out on an ongoing basis.

Change is not something "done" to members of an organization; rather, it is something they participate in, experience, and shape. Studies of change in the courts and in other organizations provide some guidelines for involving participants in defining, managing, and evaluating innovations. Such guidelines, which are discussed in our companion evaluation report, could substantially enhance efforts to change the federal civil justice system.

---

[6]Our sample was drawn well before eight of the comparison districts implemented their plans, and the comparable percentage for comparison districts was 92 percent "no difference."

[7]See Chapter Three in Kakalik et al. (1996a).

Districts and judges approach case management in widely varying ways. Some have been relatively aggressive; others have continued low-key approaches. For example, one district uses differential management tracks, uses early judicial management on all general civil cases, mandates early disclosure of information bearing significantly on both sides of the case, and assigns a substantial number of cases to mandatory ADR programs. This profile contrasts sharply with a district that uses individualized case management, permits voluntary early disclosure, and allows but does not require ADR.

These large differences between districts and judges in case management policies provide the opportunity to evaluate very different policies, even though the districts and judges that use them did not change substantially as a result of CJRA.

Overall, implicit policy changes may be as important as explicit ones. Many judges and lawyers commented in interviews that the process of implementing the pilot plans has raised the consciousness of judges and lawyers and has brought about some important shifts in attitude and approach to case management on the part of the bench and the bar. For example, our interviews suggested, and the case-level data we collected also indicated, that there has been an increase in the fraction of cases managed early and a shortening of discovery cutoff time.

Finally, several of the CJRA advisory group assessments noted factors beyond the courts' direct control that influence civil litigation cost and delay. Three factors predominated. First is the pressure generated by the criminal docket. Legislation creating new federal crimes, adoption of the Speedy Trial Act, and the advent of mandatory sentencing guidelines all were said to increase the burden on the federal court and provide less time for the orderly movement of civil cases. Second is the fact that judicial vacancies were being left unfilled for substantial periods of time. And the third factor is the need for better assessment of the effect of proposed legislation on the courts' workload.

We greatly appreciate the cooperation we have received from the Judicial Conference Committee on Court Administration and Case Management; from the Administrative Office of the United States Courts; from the Federal Judicial Center; and from the judges, clerks, advisory group members, and attorneys in the 20 pilot and comparison district courts. Without their cooperation and assistance, this study would not have been possible.

We are also indebted to the thousands of attorneys and litigants who responded to our surveys. They contributed a wealth of information that previously has not been available on litigation time, lawyer hours, costs, outcomes, satisfaction with the court's management, and views on fairness.

We also are grateful to Stephen B. Middlebrook, who prepared much of the material on the advisory group process that appears in this report. This work was done in conjunction with his role as a Visiting Fellow with RAND's Institute for Civil Justice in 1994. Mr. Middlebrook was a member of the Brookings Task Force whose recommendations provided part of the background for the Civil Justice Reform Act.

Many people at RAND contributed to this five-year effort. Deborah Hensler, Director of RAND's Institute for Civil Justice, provided sound advice and strong support throughout the study. Dr. Hensler was technical advisor to the Brookings Task Force. RAND's Survey Research Group conducted our surveys and coded more than 10,000 case dockets under the direction of Laural Hill; we especially thank Eva Feldman, Jo Levy, Don Solosan, and Tim Vernier for their extraordinary efforts and care. Data file design and analyses were conducted under the direction of Marian Oshiro, with timely assistance from Lori Parker and Deborah Wesley. Beth Benjamin helped to prepare the chapter on implementation of change in the court system. The insightful comments of RAND reviewers John Adams and Peter Jacobson significantly improved the final report. We received excellent secretarial support from Rosa Morinaka and Sharon Welz, especially in dealing with calls from survey recipients. Finally, we appreciate the expert assistance of Patricia Bedrosian, who edited and oversaw production of the final version of this document.

Chapter One

INTRODUCTION

RAND's Institute for Civil Justice evaluated the pilot program of the Civil Justice Reform Act of 1990 (CJRA), at the request of the Judicial Conference of the United States. The general objective of the evaluation was to identify effective approaches to cost and delay reduction for civil cases in federal district courts. The specific objective was to evaluate the implementation and effects of the CJRA case management principles and techniques in ten pilot and ten comparison districts.

This document describes the implementation of the CJRA in pilot and comparison districts.[1] It describes how the CJRA advisory groups were created and their findings and recommendations to the court. The CJRA plans adopted by the courts are reviewed, as are the differences between past practices, the court plans, and the advisory group recommendations. And the implementation of the plans is assessed to ascertain what the districts did in practice.

Separate RAND reports use the information in this report and from other sources described below to evaluate the effects of the CJRA case management principles and techniques on time to case disposition, litigation costs, and participants' satisfaction and views of fairness.[2]

BACKGROUND TO THE LEGISLATION

Perceived Problems with the Civil Justice System

Concerns that civil litigation costs too much and takes too long have been at the forefront of the civil justice reform debate for more than a decade.[3] Both federal and state courts are thought to be increasingly overburdened; as a consequence, according to the oft-heard indictment of the civil justice system, some litigants are denied access to justice, and many litigants incur inappropriate burdens when they turn to the courts for assistance in resolving disputes.

---

[1]This document incorporates portions of the authors' article "Preliminary Observations on Implementation of the Pilot Program of the Civil Justice Reform Act of 1990," *Stanford Law Review*, Vol. 46, No. 6, July 1994, © 1994 by the Board of Trustees of the Leland Stanford Junior University.

[2]Kakalik et al. (1996a and 1996b).

[3]See, for example, Chapper et al. (1984); The Brookings Institution (1989); the Federal Courts Study Committee (1990); and President's Council on Competitiveness (1991).

Actors alleged to be responsible for creating these perceived problems include:

- The U.S. Congress—by passing laws that have significantly expanded federal jurisdiction in criminal and civil matters; by adopting mandatory minimum sentences and sentencing guidelines that have increased the time that judges must spend on criminal cases; and by not filling judicial vacancies in a timely fashion.

- The executive branch of the federal government—by periodically targeting particular areas of criminal and civil litigation, thereby affecting district court caseloads in fluctuating, burdensome, and unpredictable ways; and by not filling judicial vacancies in a timely fashion.

- Lawyers—by exacerbating the already adversarial nature of litigation and abusing existing rules of litigation, especially regarding discovery, in strategic and tactical efforts to reap profits and damage opponents.

- Litigants—by increasingly seeking redress from the courts rather than considering alternative ways to settle their disputes, and by increasingly demanding compensation for even minor injuries.

- The judiciary—by not effectively managing cases and by failing to control the burdens that lawyers and litigants are imposing.

Comments and observations about all these problems are of hoary vintage. Many annual addresses by the Chief Justices of the United States have featured the complaint that federal courts have been asked to handle more cases without being given a corresponding increase in resources. The abuse of discovery, the decline of civility among lawyers, and the transformations of legal practice from profession to business have long been at the forefront of discussions about the alleged breakdown of the legal system.

All three branches of government focused on these perceived problems in the 1980s, prompting extensive and sometimes vehement political debate. In the rush to propose solutions, objective empirical research about cost and delay often took a back seat to political rhetoric. Unnoticed in the debate, for example, was research indicating that the time required to move a case through the system had changed little during the last two decades.[4] In addition, although studies had shown that the price of litigation seemed high indeed,[5] there was little or no detailed information about the costs and benefits of litigation to involved parties. And there was virtually no information that would support an assessment of how proposed reforms might affect parties' costs or time to disposition. Nevertheless, the debate continued at ever-increasing levels of intensity, until finally all three branches of the federal government began to formulate reform proposals.

---

[4]Dunworth and Pace (1990).

[5]For example, lawyers' fees and other litigation expenses roughly were equal to the net compensation received by injured parties in tort cases. See Kakalik and Pace (1986).

All Three Branches of Government Propose Reform

In 1988, Senate Judiciary Committee Chairman Joseph Biden requested that the Foundation for Change and The Brookings Institution convene a task force of authorities to recommend ways to alleviate the excessive cost and delay attending litigation. Practitioners, business representatives, public interest advocates, and academics participated in meetings, and a separate survey of judges and lawyers conducted for the foundation bolstered the belief that the federal courts urgently needed reform. In its final report, the Brookings task force made extensive recommendations for expanding federal judicial resources and for instituting procedural reform.[6]

The Federal Courts Study Committee, appointed by the Chief Justice at the behest of Congress, also began work in 1988 on a 15-month study of the problems facing the federal courts.[7] Rather than focusing on changes in the substantive law, the committee explored institutional and managerial solutions. Specifically, the committee recommended reallocating cases between the state and federal systems, creating non-judicial branch forums for business currently in the federal courts, expanding the capacity of the judicial system, dealing with the appellate caseload, reforming sentencing procedures, protecting against judicial bias and discrimination, improving federal court administration, reducing the complexity of litigation, and expediting the movement of cases through the system. To achieve the last objective, the committee recommended sustained experimentation with alternative and supplemental dispute resolution techniques. To control the pace and cost of litigation, it also encouraged early judicial involvement, phased discovery, the use of locally developed case management plans, and additional training of judges in techniques of case management.

Concurrently, President Bush created a Council on Competitiveness to propose reforms, although its formal report was not issued until after Congress enacted the Civil Justice Reform Act. That report[8] recommended reforming expert evidence procedures, creating incentives to reduce litigation, reducing unnecessary burdens on federal courts, eliminating litigation caused by poorly drafted legislation, reducing punitive damage awards, improving the use of judicial resources through efficient case management techniques, streamlining discovery, making trials more efficient, and increasing the use of voluntary alternative dispute resolution programs.

Whatever their other differences, the studies by each branch of government stood united in their emphasis on case management techniques and procedural reform. In the end, it was The Brookings Institution report, deriving from initiatives largely sponsored by Senator Biden, that detailed many of these procedural and managerial reforms and in time formed the blueprint for draft legislation. Its goal, in brief, was to prompt the federal courts to impose rules and procedures on themselves and on lawyers that would ameliorate the perceived twin problems of cost and delay.

---

[6]The Brookings Institution (1989).

[7]The Federal Courts Study Committee (1990).

[8]President's Council on Competitiveness (1991).

The ensuing debate about the draft legislation was energetic, to say the least. It resulted in a compromise under which the main themes of procedural reform were sustained but some of the detailed statutory controls contemplated by the Brookings task force were deleted. Replacing them was an agreement that each district court would accept the responsibility for developing a cost and delay reduction plan tailored to its own needs.

The new legislation, the CJRA, required each federal district court to conduct a self-study with the aid of an advisory group and to develop a plan for pretrial civil case management to reduce costs and delay. It created a pilot program requiring ten districts to incorporate six principles of pretrial case management into their plans and to consider incorporating six other case management techniques. The techniques supplemented and were more specific than the principles. Ten other districts, although they were left free to develop their own plans that did not have to contain any of the CJRA principles or techniques, were included in the program to permit comparisons.

To generate reliable information about the effects of the case management principles, Congress provided for an independent evaluation of the activities in these 20 pilot and comparison districts. The Judicial Conference and the Administrative Office of the U.S. Courts asked RAND's Institute for Civil Justice to evaluate the implementation and the effects of the CJRA in these 20 districts. Following completion of the RAND reports, the Judicial Conference will prepare and submit a report to Congress.

OVERVIEW OF THE PILOT PROGRAM

The Six Case Management Principles

The act directs each pilot district to incorporate the following principles into its plan:

1. Systematic, differential case management tailored to the characteristics of different categories of cases (the act specifies several factors, such as case complexity, that may be used to categorize cases);

2. Early and ongoing control of the pretrial process through involvement of a judicial officer in assessing and planning the progress of the case, setting an early and firm trial date, controlling the extent and timing of discovery, and setting timelines for motions and their disposition;

3. For complex and other appropriate cases, judicial case monitoring and management through one or more discovery and case management conferences (the act specifies several detailed case management policies, such as scheduling and limiting discovery);

4. Encouragement of cost-effective discovery through voluntary exchanges and cooperative discovery devices;

5. Prohibition of discovery motions until the parties have made a reasonable, good-faith effort on the matter; and

6. Referral of appropriate cases to alternative dispute resolution programs.

Pilot districts *must* incorporate these principles, while other districts *may* do so.

The Six Case Management Techniques

The act directs each district to *consider* incorporating the following techniques into its plan, but no district is *required* to incorporate them:

1. Require that counsel jointly present a discovery/case management plan at the initial pretrial conference, or explain the reasons for their failure to do so;

2. Require that each party be represented at each pretrial conference by an attorney with authority to bind that party regarding all matters previously identified by the court for discussion at the conference and all reasonably related matters;

3. Require the signature of the attorney and the party on all requests for discovery extensions or postponements of trial;

4. Offer an early neutral evaluation program;

5. Require party representatives with authority to bind to be present or available by telephone at settlement conferences;

6. Incorporate such other features as the district court considers appropriate.

Features of the RAND Evaluation

The evaluation is designed to provide a quantitative and qualitative basis for assessing how the management principles adopted in the pilot and comparison districts affect costs to litigants, time to disposition, participants' satisfaction with the process and views of fairness of the process, and judge work time required. Comparisons are made between the ten pilot districts and the ten comparison districts, both before and after implementation of the pilot program plans. In addition, comparisons are made between cases managed in different ways to assess the costs and effects of managing cases with and without various procedures.

Representativeness and Comparability of Pilot and Comparison Districts

Ten pilot districts were selected by the Committee on Court Administration and Case Management of the Judicial Conference of the United States. The committee sought to identify districts representative of the federal system. Factors such as caseload type, filing volume, and whether the district was fast or slow relative to other districts were all taken into account. The districts selected were California (S), Delaware, Georgia (N), New York (S), Oklahoma (W), Pennsylvania (E), Tennessee (W), Texas (S), Utah, and Wisconsin (E).

After recommendations from RAND, the Judicial Conference also selected the following ten comparison districts: Arizona, California (C), Florida (N), Illinois (N), Indiana (N), Kentucky (E), Kentucky (W), Maryland, New York (E), and Pennsylvania (M).

Ideally, pilot and comparison districts would be similar in every respect except case management policies—thus illuminating the contrast between districts following the six principles and those not following them. However, at the time of selection, the case management practices and CJRA plans of the comparison districts were unknown, and the six principles had not been implemented in the pilot districts. Thus, case management practices were not and could not have been a factor in the decisions. The Judicial Conference was therefore left to focus primarily on district size, workload per judge, the number of criminal and civil filings, and the time to disposition in civil cases, as points of comparison for selecting pilot and comparison districts.

Together, the 20 study districts have about one-third of all federal judges and one-third of all federal case filings. However, since the program involves only 20 of the 94 federal districts, the representativeness of the pilot and comparison districts becomes critical. Obviously, the more representative they are, the greater the likelihood that they will yield valid generalizations about the system as a whole. A second concern is whether the ten pilot and ten comparison districts are sufficiently similar to be considered comparable. Using data from Statistical Year 1990[9]—the year used to select the comparison districts—we present the characteristics of the two groups in Table 1.1.

Because no two federal districts are identical, perfect representativeness and comparability are illusory ideals. But having considered three important types of characteristics in selecting the districts—judicial resources, number of filings, and time to disposition—we found considerable similarity and representativeness.

First, consider the number of authorized judges in each of the pilot and comparison districts in 1990. The two groups had 193 authorized positions in 1990—about one-third of the 575 judgeships authorized for the entire district court system in that year.[10] There is a roughly even split between the pilot and comparison groups with respect to both the total number of positions and the variation in size between the districts in each group. The four largest districts in the federal court system are participants in the program (two pilot, two comparison, each with 19 or more positions), and smaller districts (fewer than five judges) are also represented.

On the dimension of workloads, as measured by the total number of civil and criminal cases filed in 1990, the pilot and comparison districts also look comparable to each other and to the system as a whole. The number of filings nationally was about 251,000 in FY90, of which about 32,000 were felony criminal cases. The study districts contained about one-third of the total filings, split roughly equally between

---

[9]July 1, 1989, through June 30, 1990.

[10]The CJRA of 1990 increased the number of authorized judgeships to 649. Note that there are always some authorized judgeships unfilled because of the length of time consumed in the selection and confirmation process. For example, of the 649 authorized in FY92, 109 positions remained open nationwide.

Table 1.1

Pilot and Comparison Districts for the CJRA Pilot Program

| Pilot and Comparison Districts | District | Number of Judgeships | Weighted Filings[a] | | Unweighted Cases per Judgeship | | | Median Civil Time Intervals (months) | | % of Civil Cases over 3 Yrs Old |
			Total	Per Judgeship	Civil Filings	Felony Criminal Filings	Pending Cases	Filing to Dispose	Issue to Trial[b]	
Pilot	CA(S)	7	3,080	440	275	131	591	12	18	12.7
Comparison	AZ	8	3,296	412	358	104	538	9	20	11.5
Pilot	DE	4	924	231	195	28	249	10	17	8.6
Comparison	FL(N)	3	984	328	358	70	454	9	23	7.3
Pilot	GA(N)	11	4,169	379	312	35	350	10	19	4.0
Comparison	MD	10	4,000	400	350	38	378	9	11	10.2
Pilot	NY(S)	27	11,043	409	325	29	505	9	19	12.8
Comparison	IL(N)	21	10,248	488	380	36	346	5	12	11.6
Pilot	OK(W)	5	2,220	444	458	49	287	7	11	3.2
Comparison	PA(M)	5	2,305	461	447	53	380	8	10	5.3
Pilot	PA(E)	19	12,122	638	488	26	537	7	12	2.1
Comparison	CA(C)	22	10,714	487	401	48	471	7	12	8.6
Pilot	TN(W)	4	1,408	352	325	78	514	14	30	14.5
Comparison	KY(W)	4.5	1,503	334	361	35	442	13	19	11.7
Pilot	TX(S)	13	7,631	587	460	181	816	11	23	13.2
Comparison	NY(E)	12	5,940	495	369	80	589	9	19	13.1
Pilot	UT	4	1,620	405	310	60	481	11	14	12.3
Comparison	IN(N)	5	1,530	306	277	41	325	12	15	12.0
Pilot	WI(E)	4	1,684	421	369	61	386	7	20	6.0
Comparison	KY(E)	4.5	1,606	357	385	48	389	8	18	5.0

NOTE: Data used to select districts are from Statistical Year 1990.

a "Case weights," approved by the Judicial Conference of the United States, give the relative amount of judicial work time per case of each type.

b Months from the point in the case when the issue was joined to the start of the trial.

pilot and comparison districts. Again, some of the largest and smallest districts are found in both the pilot and comparison groups. Using other workload measures—just civil filings, just criminal filings, case mixture, or filings per judgeship—the picture looks much the same.

Finally, since this study concerns itself with time to disposition, among other factors, we consider the median time to dispose of civil cases. Figure 1.1 shows the ten pilot districts on the left, and the ten comparison districts on the right. The median was nine months nationally in 1990 and was about the same for both pilot and comparison groups. But also note the wide variation among the 20 districts, ranging from a low of five months to a high of 14. This provides a range representative of the differing times to disposition in all federal districts. Using other statistics yields similar results. For example, about 10.6 percent of the civil cases pending nationally in 1990 were over three years old, and the averages for both pilot districts (9.2 percent) and comparison districts (9.7 percent) approximate the national figure.

This examination of aggregate 1990 data pertaining to judgeships, filings, and time to disposition in the 20 districts suggests that they well represent the range of districts in the United States. Furthermore, the pilot and comparison district groups are reasonably comparable to each other, at least along these dimensions.

In 1996, after all of the RAND study's survey data described below had been collected, we conducted a multivariate statistical analysis to see if pilot and comparison

RAND *MR801-1.1*

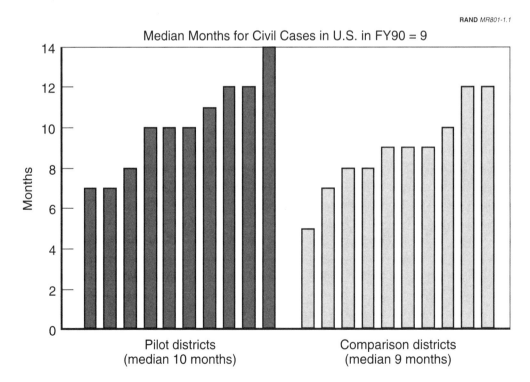

Figure 1.1—Median Time to Disposition in Pilot and Comparison Districts

districts as a group were different from one another in 1991. We controlled for differences in case characteristics among districts in the analysis. We concluded that there were no statistically significant differences between pilot and comparison districts in 1991 before CJRA, in either the time to disposition or the cost per litigant.[11]

We believe that the pilot and comparison districts represent the range of districts in the United States and are comparable to one another.

Data Sources

The evaluation is based on extensive interviews, surveys, and detailed case-level data from January 1991 through December 1995. Data sources include:

- Court records;

- Records, reports, and surveys of CJRA advisory groups;

- Districts' cost and delay reduction plans;

- Detailed case processing, docket, and outcome information on a sample of cases;

- Surveys of judicial officers about their activities, time expenditures, and views of CJRA;

- Mail surveys of attorneys and litigants about costs, time, fairness, satisfaction with the process, and case outcomes.

- Interviews with judges, court staff, and lawyers in each of the 20 districts.

We selected a stratified random sample of about 250 cases from each time period and for each district for intensive study—a total of approximately 10,000 cases.[12] To collect information on case costs and on the perceptions of lawyers and litigants on both sides, we attempted to survey the lawyers and litigants in all of the cases selected for the sample—a total of about 60,000 persons (see Table 1.2).[13]

Table 1.2

Sample Size for Pilot Program Main Survey Data Collection

Survey Type	1991 Sample Before CJRA	1992–93 Sample After CJRA Pilot Plans	Total
Cases	5,149	5,222	10,371
Judicial officers	N.A.	5,222	5,222
Lawyers	9,777	9,423	19,200
Litigants	19,949	20,272	40,221

[11]For details, see Kakalik et al. (1996a), especially Chapter Nine and Appendix D.

[12]We also conducted a supplemental alternative dispute resolution study which involved similar surveys on 1,823 additional cases. For details, see Kakalik et al. (1996b).

[13]Litigants are more numerous than lawyers because some lawyers represent more than one litigant, and some litigants have no identified lawyers (not only pro se litigants, but litigants whose case closes before they hire a lawyer or before the court is notified of the lawyer's name).

Data collection began in 1992 when the 5,000-case pre-CJRA sample was drawn from cases that terminated in the last half of 1991. Selection of the 5,000 post-CJRA cases began with cases filed in late 1992 and early 1993. We followed the 5,000+ cases filed after the CJRA became law until December 1995, as long as the Congressionally established reporting deadlines permitted. At the end of 1995, 93 percent of the main post-CJRA sample cases were closed, and only 7 percent were still open. After a case concluded and the period allowed for appeal expired, surveys were sent to judges,[14] lawyers, and litigants. For open cases, we also surveyed the lawyers in early 1996. Court dockets were analyzed for each of the sample cases.

For our companion report on the evaluation of the CJRA pilot program, we use all of the above types of data in both descriptive tabulations and complex multivariate statistical analyses to evaluate the various case management policies and procedures on predicted time to disposition, litigation costs, satisfaction, and views of fairness.

For this report on the CJRA implementation, we also used all of the above types of data except for the lawyer and litigant survey data. For example, we used court records to assess the volume and type of ADR implemented; we used CJRA advisory group reports, documents, and meeting minutes to assess the advisory group process and findings; we used the districts' plans and Local Rule changes to assess what the district said it would do under CJRA; we used the dockets for our sample of cases to help us understand what was actually done on cases (such as assignments to management tracks); we used the judicial surveys on our sample of cases to get judges' views on whether they had changed how they would have managed the case as a result of CJRA; and, most important, we used extensive semistructured interviews with judges, court staff, advisory group members, and lawyers to better understand the implementation of CJRA and case management in the districts before and after CJRA.

During each of at least three trips to each study district over a four-year period, we conducted extensive in-person interviews with the Chief Judge and several other judges (four to eight judges per district), the Clerk of Court and several other staff members (six to 12 clerks per district), the chairperson of the CJRA advisory group and usually other members (at least two other members, but sometimes we met with the entire advisory group),[15] and several representatives of the local bar (including U.S. attorneys, at least two leaders of the local bar, and at least two attorneys selected because they had several cases in our sample). In total we interviewed at least 500 people in person during this study. In addition, we have had hundreds of telephone conversations with people in the 20 pilot and comparison districts during this study (sometimes these were full interviews with people who were not available when we visited, and sometimes they were for clarification and interpretation of information that we had received from other sources). To encourage open communication, each interviewee was promised anonymity.

---

[14]Judges for the 1991 sample cases were not surveyed.

[15]We supplemented these in-person interviews of advisory group members with telephone interviews of other advisory group members whom we purposefully selected to get a range of potential viewpoints.

The semistructured interviews used extensive and lengthy interview guides that evolved over the study and covered all aspects of the CJRA process and case management in the district before and after CJRA, including but not limited to:

1. The establishment and operation of the CJRA advisory groups;

2. The interviewee's, the advisory group's and the court's assessment of causes of cost and delay;

3. The development of advisory group recommendations and their rationales;

4. The development of the district plan and the rationale for any difference between it and the advisory group recommendations;

5. Details of the implementation of each element of the plan and each aspect of case management in the district;

6. Any problems encountered and any refinements made in the implemented plans;

7. Results of annual reassessments required by CJRA;

8. Discussion of how cases were managed in practice before and after CJRA, at the district and at the individual judge level, and in great detail;

9. For each CJRA principle and technique, details on how the district and individual judges processed cases before and after CJRA;

10. Perceived problems with case management in the district and the interviewee's recommendations for improvement; and

11. The interviewee's subjective views of the effects of different case management practices implemented in the district.

RAND had full access to all official court records, personnel, and information, including the courts' full computer files.

OUTLINE OF THIS REPORT

The remainder of this report is organized as follows. Chapter Two focuses on the CJRA advisory group process, and Chapter Three traces the evolution from the advisory group recommendations through the implementation of the districts' plans. Our assessment of the implementation and conclusions appear in Chapter Four. The appendices provide a detailed summary of the advisory group recommendations, the plan adopted by the district court, and the implementation of that plan in each of the 20 districts.

Chapter Two

ADVISORY GROUPS AND THE CJRA PLAN DEVELOPMENT PROCESS[1]

INTRODUCTION

In 1990, Congress took the extraordinary step of creating a structure in which some 2,000 people across the country were empowered to take a hard look at the federal civil justice system and to prescribe ways to make it work better. These individuals were organized into advisory groups in each of the 94 federal districts and were given the responsibility of making assessments and recommendations for a plan of action to improve civil case management. The concept of using local advisory groups for matters such as local rules has been around for a long time, but the charge to these new advisory groups was significantly broader.

The Civil Justice Reform Act requires that a plan be developed (or selected if a model plan) by each district "after consideration of the recommendations of an advisory group appointed in accordance with section 478 of this title" (§472(a)). In furtherance of this goal, the advisory group "shall submit to the court a report" containing, among other items, recommended measures, rules, and programs to be incorporated into the plan. Further, the act intends that the formulation of the plan is to be made by a district court acting "in consultation" with the advisory group (§473(a)). Although a district court's chief judge and his or her fellow judges are free to adopt any plan they wish, the input of the advisory group's report clearly is intended to help shape the final plan.

The notion of using local "user" advisory groups across the country to help establish procedural reform within the federal district courts was proposed in a Brookings Institution task force report (1989).[2] The task force goal was, in essence, to recom-

---

[1] We are very grateful to Stephen B. Middlebrook, who prepared much of the material on the advisory group process that appears in this chapter. This work was done in conjunction with his role as a Visiting Fellow with the Institute for Civil Justice in 1994. In addition to reviewing the advisory group reports and the CJRA plans of each of the pilot and comparison districts, Mr. Middlebrook interviewed several members of the advisory groups in several of those districts. He also consulted, where available, written minutes of those advisory group meetings, their annual reports, and other materials prepared by these groups in the process of making their plan recommendations.

[2] In 1988, Senate Judiciary Committee Chairman Joseph Biden requested that the Foundation for Change and The Brookings Institution convene a task force of legal practitioners, judges, and representatives of different classes of users of the federal court system to recommend ways to alleviate the excessive cost and delay attending litigation.

mend a variety of possible reforms to the civil justice system, mostly focused on judicial case management. Speaking to the process for getting this done, the task force recommended that Congress authorize each federal district court, "with assistance from its local bar and client community," to develop its own reform agenda for reducing delay and litigation costs. It further recommended that such reforms be constructed within "broad parameters" as set forth in federal legislation.[3]

From the beginning, the Senate Judiciary Committee was attracted to the concept of having user groups significantly involved in the reform process. Drafts of what was to become the CJRA required that district judges work in "consultation" with their advisory groups in developing plans for managing their civil caseloads. In its final form, the act required that any plan implemented by a district court be developed after consideration of the recommendations of an advisory group. Acting on behalf of their districts, the chief judges were instructed to appoint advisory groups within 90 days of enactment of the CJRA (§478(a)).[4]

Reflecting the Brookings task force concern about involvement of the local bar and client community, the act requires the group to be "balanced and include attorneys and other persons who are representative of major categories of litigants in such [district] court as determined by the chief judge" (§478(b)).

Elsewhere in the CJRA, Congress assigns to each advisory group a number of functions, listed below:[5]

1. Assess "the state of the court's civil and criminal dockets," and, in particular:

> "determine the condition" of those dockets
>
> "identify trends in case filings"
>
> "identify . . . demands being placed on the court's resources"
>
> "identify the principal causes of cost . . . in civil litigation"[6]
>
> "identify the principal causes of . . . delay in civil litigation[7]
>
> "examine the extent to which costs and delays could be reduced by a better assessment of the impact of new legislation on the courts."

---

[3] The Brookings Institution (1989), p. 11.

[4] For a discussion of the act's legislative history, see Robel (1993).

[5] §§472, 475.

[6] The term "cost" is not defined in the act, but the following explanation appears in Senate Report 101-416: Litigation transaction costs—defined as the total costs incurred by all parties to civil litigation, excluding any ultimate liability or settlement.

[7] "Delay" is also not a statutorily defined term. Again, however, Senate Report 101-416 (p. 6) is instructive:

> [D]elays throughout the course of litigation not only often inure to the benefit of one side over the other but also increase court backlog, often inhibit the full and accurate determination of the facts, interfere with the deliberate and accurate determination of the facts, interfere with the deliberate and prompt disposition and adjudication of cases and thereby contribute to high litigation transaction costs.

2. Make recommendations to the district court as to the content of its "cost and de-lay reduction plan."

3. Consult with the district court in connection with the court's statutory mandated annual review of its cost and delay reduction plan to help determine "appropriate additional actions" that the court could take to reduce cost and delay in civil liti-gation and to improve case management.

These "assignments" cover much territory and depart significantly from the tradi-tional model of leaving the judiciary generally free to develop and revise their own procedures.[8] Why did Congress take such an approach? A variety of motivations appear to have been at play.

First, in adopting the CJRA premise that there was excessive cost and delay in the federal court system, Congress was quick to distribute the responsibility for such a result not only to all three branches of government but also to the users of that sys-tem—the litigants and their lawyers. From this, it followed that all of those players needed to be involved in "developing solutions."[9]

Second, as Senator Biden indicated, the CJRA provides a means for users of the fed-eral court system "to express their dissatisfaction with the civil justice system and to demand reform of that system."[10]

Other motivations, which the Senate Committee Report extracted from the Brook-ings task force were "to maximize the prospects that workable plans will be devel-oped," and to encourage "much needed dialogue between the bench, the bar and client communities about methods of streamlining litigation practice."[11]

We have reviewed the reports of all of the advisory groups representing the 20 pilot and comparison districts and the minutes of their meetings where available. And we have conducted in-depth, one-on-one interviews, with the chairperson of each advi-sory group, the chief judge in each district, and other judges and advisory group members to learn how this advisory process functioned.[12] Appendices to this report summarize those reports and plans and any differences between them for each of the 20 districts.

What happened in these pilot and comparison districts? How were the advisory groups appointed and organized? How did they fulfill their initial assessment, rec-ommendation, and annual reassessment roles? The remainder of this chapter ad-dresses these questions.

---

[8] See Robel (1993), p. 880.

[9] House Committee Report 101-732 (1990), p. 11.

[10] Senate Committee Report 101-416 (1990), p. 12 (quoting remarks of Chairman Joseph Biden, June 26, 1990, p. 8).

[11] Senate Committee Report 101-416, p. 14 (quoting from The Brookings Institution, 1989).

[12] To encourage candidness, and because we were evaluating processes and policies rather than people and districts, all interviews were conducted under conditions of anonymity and without attribution to the person or the district.

ADVISORY GROUP APPOINTMENTS AND ORGANIZATION

Appointments

§478 of the act provides in part:

§478. Advisory groups

"(a) Within ninety days after the date of the enactment of this chapter, the advisory group required in each United States district court in accordance with section 472 of this title shall be appointed by the chief judge of each district court, after consultation with the other judges of such court.

"(b) The advisory group shall be balanced and include attorneys and other persons who are representative of major categories of litigants in such court, as determined by the chief judge of such court . . . .

"(d) Notwithstanding subsection (c), the United States Attorney for a judicial district, or his or her designee, shall be a permanent member of the advisory group for that district court.

"(e) The chief judge of a United States district court may designate a reporter for each advisory group, who may be compensated in accordance with guidelines established by the Judicial Conference of the United States . . . ."

Other than these sections given above, the act provides no other guidance to a chief judge in deciding who should be on a district's advisory group.

The advisory groups average 21 members, plus the chair and reporter. The members are supposed to "take into account the particular needs and circumstances of the district court, litigants in such court, and the litigant's attorneys" while ensuring that each of these groups make "significant contributions" toward the task of reducing cost and delay (§472(c)(2)&(3)).

The framers of the act, aware that participants' background and profession would play a significant role in shaping their contribution to the final report, wanted a "balanced" advisory group in each district, to include "attorneys and other persons" who can speak for "major categories of litigants." For example, an advisory group member who, in day-to-day life, is a repeated litigant in the district court might well bring to the discussion table a very different perspective from one who is a practicing attorney, a sitting judge, or an average taxpayer who has never been near a courtroom. In the same vein, an advisory group whose numbers are dominated by one particular type (attorneys, judges, litigants, or others) could not help but issue reports and make recommendations that would reflect the majority's needs and desires as they concern district court business. However, the act does not specify how this balance could be achieved.

As required by the act, all groups were appointed by the chief judges of their districts. One might expect that the chief judge would, consistent with the spirit of the act and in consultation with others, pick members from a wide range of backgrounds. That expectation was met in most districts, with the exception of nonlawyer litigant representatives, who averaged only two on each advisory group. Our interviews with both lawyers and lay members suggest that it is very difficult to find nonlawyers who have sufficient expertise to contribute much. The strong tradition in procedural reform movements is to rely mostly on "expert" lawyers as outside advisors on procedural reform.[13] Given this tradition, and the lack of any specific statutory direction, it is not surprising to find relatively limited representation of lay people in the advisory groups. Minimally represented and limited by their lack of familiarity with the federal district court system, lay people played only a very modest role in advisory group meetings.

We conducted a detailed examination of the makeup of advisory groups in the 20 pilot and comparison districts.

Advisory Group Chairperson and Reporter

All 20 advisory groups followed the traditional approach of using a committee structure with a chairperson and, in most cases, a separate person as reporter.[14] The chief judge appointed the members of the group and usually the chairperson.

Current or former federal judges chaired three of the 20 advisory groups;[15] these judges' roles may raise questions about the independence of the advice provided by these groups. Most of the chairpersons were lawyers. Of these 14 lawyer-chairpersons, 12 were in private practice. Law professors chaired the other three advisory groups, including one who acted as the group's reporter but was also the de facto chairperson. Our interviews indicated that the influence of the chairperson on the thrust of the advisory group's final report varied from district to district and ranged from very strong control to group consensus building.

All but one of the districts[16] had an officially designated advisory group reporter.[17] Since the reporter is usually the one to bring a number of divergent legal and case management viewpoints into focus and summarize the advisory group's concerns, it is not surprising that almost half of the reporters were law professors. Six of the rest were clerks of court of the district or some other court administrator. Two others were practicing lawyers; the backgrounds of the remaining two were not identified in the report.

---

[13]House Committee Report 101-732 (1990), p. 11.

[14]The term "reporter" is typically used in the legal context to refer to the person who takes notes, prepares summaries of discussions for the group, and often drafts recommendations and text for consideration by the full committee based on its discussion. In IN(N), there was no formally appointed chairperson, but the reporter acted as de facto chairperson.

[15]The UT chief judge, a NY(S) senior judge, and a recently retired IL(N) chief judge.

[16]NY(S) had no official reporter.

[17]Two of the official reporters also served as chairpersons of the advisory groups (officially in MD and unofficially in IN(N)).

Advisory Group Members

Counting official and ex-officio together, there were 420 members in the 20 districts' advisory groups; 55 members were ex-officio (by virtue of holding office). All members were appointed by the chief judge, and whether the judges and court administrators on the committee were official or ex-officio members was a matter of the chief judge's choice.

Figure 2.1 shows how the total advisory group membership was distributed across lawyers, judges, court administrators, law professors, and others who were not part of the legal system.

District records show that 70 percent of these individuals (291) were lawyers. Most of these (166) were in private practice, 44 worked for public agencies, and the affiliation of the rest (81) was unclear. The largest subgroup of lawyers included 114 who were in private practice and worked for a law firm, 19 who were counsel at a corporation or other private organization, four who were identified as practicing labor law, ten who primarily did public interest work, and 19 who had an unknown type of private practice. In keeping with the act's requirement that a representative of the U.S. Attorney's office be in the group, the subgroup included 21 lawyers who worked for the federal government. State government lawyers, often active in defending prisoner and civil rights claims, constituted 12 of the public lawyers. And six public defenders made their way into a group.

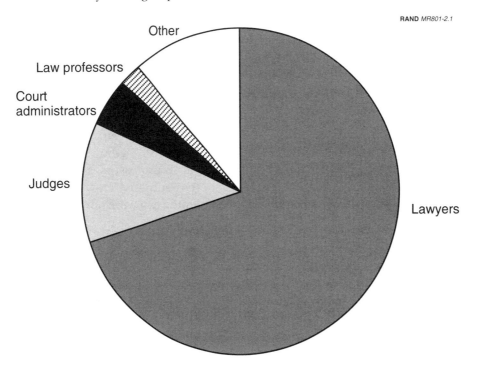

RAND MR801-2.1

Figure 2.1—Makeup of Advisory Groups

Given the large percentage of lawyers in the membership, the court-appointed advisory groups were likely to be fully conversant with the complex systems they were being asked to analyze. They were also likely to represent the best of the bar in their regions and thus, predictably, would be professional and thorough in their approach to their assignment. And, of course, they were advocates and good at their advocacy.

The groups had a contingent of judicial officers on their panels. Almost 13 percent of the total membership were judges (53). Most (38) were sitting district judges, five more had been district judges, and the current or former chief judge of the district was involved as a regular member seven times. Only three of the 20 groups had no judge as either an official or ex-officio member.

Interviews and review of the reports gives the general impression that in some districts, ex-officio participants contributed to the process only in an advisory capacity, commenting on particular issues or reviewing the draft report. However, in other districts, ex-officio participants appear to have been involved in the advisory group process every step of the way. Since we cannot distinguish the level of participation for sure, we present official and ex-officio participant numbers together. Since nearly all of the ex-officio participants were the district's own judges or clerks, it may well be that an effort was made to include the experience and viewpoint of judicial officers or court administrators on the advisory group.

Eighteen of the regular members were court administrators of some type; of these, 13 were the current clerk of the court. Staff in the clerk's office often contributed greatly to this endeavor, especially in gathering and presenting statistics and developing procedures as a part of CJRA plan development and implementation. Nine law professors also contributed to the drafting of the advisory group reports.

Only 11 percent (47) of the regular members were known not to be part of the legal system. About half were business executives, nine worked for public interest organizations, and the rest had various occupations.

Process

To assist the advisory groups, the Administrative Office of the United States Courts supplied various materials, including the CJRA itself, material describing the groups' duties, and other summarized case filings and terminations information designed to assist in the analyses. The chief judge often addressed the group at its first meeting, giving the group its charge from the viewpoint of the district court.

Most groups came to the early realization that they could perform more effectively through subcommittees, particularly in the analysis phase. However, groups treated their subcommittees quite differently. In a few instances, the parent group accepted its subcommittees' recommendations, virtually without comment. In other cases, presentation of the subcommittee report simply served to start the debate over plan recommendations. Whether because of time constraints or the need for in-depth review of selected issues, the overwhelming consensus was that the subcommittee approach made sense.

Once formed, most groups spent their initial meetings getting oriented—studying the CJRA, reviewing available statistics, and discussing the project with various judges and other members of the court system. In at least one case, the chairman took lay members of his group into the district courtroom to introduce them to court procedures. His purpose was also to reduce any possible intimidation factor for those on the advisory group not familiar with court procedures. Other groups developed bibliographies of relevant materials on case management to supplement the other available materials.

Meetings of the groups followed similar patterns. Most of their early sessions lasted 1-1/2 to 2 hours. Later, several groups held longer sessions to close out open issues and make up time (particularly in the pilot districts).

Most groups limited attendance to members, judges on the district court, the clerk of the court, and other persons who were employed by various members and had agreed to render support services pro bono. Except in a few cases where it was felt that the judicial presence may have been unwarranted or possibly intimidating, none of our interviews revealed much discomfort with either the lack of or presence of judicial officers. In some cases, when the discussion was going to be particularly sensitive, judicial officers were asked to leave.

All groups chose to advance their recommendations by group consensus, and dissenting or "minority" statements were very rare.[18]

The formats used for the reports varied considerably. As suggested by the Administrative Office, many followed a logical format in which they described their assessment process, gave their conclusion, and then listed and explained their cost and delay reduction recommendations pretty much in the order shown in the act. Others took a more free-wheeling approach; their reports read more like narratives, and it is not always easy to separate commentary from recommendations and understand how they fulfilled their statutory mandate.

Relationships between the advisory group and the court were highly varied. Again, the act offered little direction. Three major variants existed:

1. Judges were actively involved at the advisory group meetings, and in some instances acted as chair;

2. Judges played a moderate role, submitted to interviews, provided information when asked, and offered some opinions but did not work continuously and intimately with the group in its formulation of recommendations; and

3. Judges were largely passive, remaining outside the advisory process, leaving the group to work independently.

---

[18]Approximately one-quarter of the California (C) group advocated legislation providing that the prevailing party in cases litigated in the federal courts could recover its attorney fees and other costs (Smaltz et al., 1993, p. 106).

ADVISORY GROUP ASSESSMENTS

In the remainder of this chapter, we present an overview of the advisory group assessments and recommendations. These will be described in more detail in Chapter Three, where we discuss the relationship between what was recommended and what was implemented by the districts.

The act indicated that advisory groups were to assess docket conditions, trends in filings, demands on resources, and causes of cost and delay.[19] But it had little to say about how the information to do this was to be accumulated or analyzed.

The Administrative Office and the Federal Judicial Center provided summary statistics on filings and terminations to each district. Those summary statistics contained information on workload changes over time and on time to disposition of civil cases. Statistics on the cost of litigation were not available.

In general, and as expected, the groups were not fully satisfied with the information available to them. After all, if the questions could have been answered using information routinely available, there would have been no need to ask advisory groups to do the assessment. In most cases, the groups looked for other sources to supplement available data.[20] Most conducted interviews with the judges, and a majority surveyed lawyers. A minority surveyed litigants, although usually without much success because of low response rates.[21] A minority held public hearings, and some hired consultants.

The advisory groups did not have the time, money, or expertise to do extensive new research on the causes and solutions to cost and delay. Rather, their contribution was to use available statistics and to collect some subjective information from people who run and use the system. Some recurrent themes that emerged from the advisory group reports are summarized below.

Causes of Cost and Delay Beyond the Judges' Immediate Control

An item discussed in several reports was the rising pressure generated by the criminal docket. Congress's decision to create new federal crimes, adoption of the Speedy Trial Act, and the advent of mandatory sentencing guidelines, all contributed, in the view of many advisory groups, to increase the burden on the federal court and provide less time for the orderly movement of civil cases. For example, some groups believed sentencing guidelines have a tendency to increase the length of sentencing hearings because the sentences depend on a variety of factors that require factual de-

---

[19] §472(c).

[20] For a comparative analysis of how the first 34 advisory groups carried out their data collection procedures (including 12 of the pilot and comparison districts), see Segal et al. (1993), Appendix E.

[21] Litigant surveys proved to be somewhat difficult, since current procedures do not require that the litigant's address be furnished in court-filed documents. Where identifying information does appear, it is often inadequate or obsolete, thus requiring contact with the litigant's attorney, who may be reluctant to give out client addresses.

terminations by the court before actual sentencing can take place.[22] Several reports suggested that an influx of new prosecutors without an attendant increase in judgeships added to this criminal case burden.

Another problem identified by several groups was the fact that judicial vacancies were being left unfilled for substantial periods of time. Although the act does not invite specific scrutiny of judicial vacancies, it does require groups to "take into account the particular needs and circumstances" of the local court[23]—a category certainly large enough to encompass perceived shortfalls in personnel and other resources.

Several groups also suggested that cost and delay might be reduced by better assessment of the effect of proposed legislation on the civil and criminal court workload.

Causes of Cost and Delay That May Be Affected by Judicial Management

Since the advisory groups did not have objective data on costs of litigation, their analysis focused primarily on factors thought to increase time to disposition.

Advisory groups thought discovery was being abused by some lawyers in most districts, although some groups noted that the problem was confined to a small portion of the bar. Beyond opinion and anecdote, no real evidence was presented of discovery abuse or its magnitude.

Most groups pointed out some problems with judicial management of cases and recommended remedies that might shorten time to disposition. These remedies include ruling promptly on motions, setting schedules early, setting early firm trial dates, granting continuances only for good cause, and making more use of alternative dispute resolution procedures. The issue of judges' failure to efficiently manage cases was raised in interviews, public hearings, and questionnaires sent to lawyers within the district. In some cases, this was cited as an important, but not overriding, factor generally on the same plane as lawyers' failure to manage cases efficiently. Tempering these "criticisms," several groups questioned whether cost and delay problems were as serious within their district as the CJRA had implied.

Although the advisory groups did recommend significant change in case management in many of the districts, this usually was not as a result of an explicit finding of substantial problems with judicial case management. Rather, the recommendations were usually posed as ways of refining and improving the existing case management system.

We note that some districts' advisory groups made very deliberate and scholarly efforts in their analysis of specific case management questions. For example, in a thorough analysis, the NY(E) group first analyzed court-annexed arbitration already

---

[22]See, e.g., Landis et al. (1991), p. 20.

[23]28 U.S.C. §472(c)(2).

in full use within the jurisdiction. It concluded that the process worked well and suggested some fine-tuning. It then recommended that voluntary, court-annexed mediation and neutral evaluation be used as a supplementary ADR technique. It further advocated a program of publicizing ADR techniques and the assignment of an overseer for all court-annexed ADR programs.[24] The NY(S) group approached the ADR issue by analyzing ADR practices within the district and by reviewing the ADR literature to understand the tradeoff options.[25] The NY(S) group not only recommended an ADR program designed as an experiment with random assignment of cases, but suggested an evaluation and educational programs for judges, litigants, and lawyers. The PA(E) group also made diligent efforts to assess the potential of ADR. That district has an experiment using mandatory mediation with random assignment of cases. The group has been monitoring the experiment and other elements of the plan carefully, conducting follow-up surveys after the initial implementation of the CJRA plan, and doing midcourse adjustments as a result of the annual reassessments. [26]

ANNUAL REASSESSMENTS

§475 of the act requires each district court to do an annual assessment. The purpose is to keep the CJRA plans up to date and to improve "litigation management practices." Important for our purposes, and consistent with the rest of the act, §475 states that the court "shall consult with" the local advisory group when conducting the annual assessment.

The quality of the annual reassessments varies markedly from district to district. Although the act does not require a written assessment, seven of the 20 districts in this study have written reassessments at least twice. Six of the 20 districts had no written documentation of the results of any annual assessment when we inquired in January 1996.

The required annual assessments that have been prepared have been largely devoted to updating case filing and termination statistics, and often indicate that the plan seems to be functioning as intended and that it is too early to be considering change in the plan. Most of the annual reports are prepared without extensive advisory group or court effort.

It must be noted that the districts and the advisory groups asked to conduct the annual assessments usually do not have the research expertise or the time to do them well. The advisory group members work pro bono, and there is much less incentive to donate time to do a reassessment than there was to help create the initial CJRA plan.

---

[24] Wesely et al. (1991), pp. 94–104.

[25] Sweet et al. (1991), p. 35.

[26] Landis et al. (1991).

COMMENTARY BY OTHERS ON THE ADVISORY GROUP

Some people object to the concept of the CJRA advisory group process for philosophical reasons. We distinguish the several negative comments we heard about how the advisory group process was *implemented* from the comments about the *concept* of having an advisory group. Once we got beyond the philosophical objections, there seemed to be no recognizable voice that criticized the advisory group concept.

One commentator, herself a co-reporter for one of the advisory groups, exhibited strong philosophical objections to the advisory group process. Linda Mullenix put it bluntly: "Civil procedural rulemaking ought not to be in the hands of ninety-four local amateur rulemaking groups who are destined to wreak mischief, if not havoc, on the federal court system."[27] Her philosophical point is clear, but given that the courts were free to reject recommendations made by the advisory groups, and given the composition of the groups, i.e., mostly lawyers who would also be eligible to serve on more traditional local rules committees, the destiny she warned against has not been fulfilled.

More telling are Linda Mullenix's observations about the manner in which the act provided for the accumulation of cost and delay evidence within the districts.[28] She points out that the fact-gathering and assessment role imposed on the advisory groups seemed unduly restrictive, particularly with regard to the pilot districts, which were required to formulate cost and delay reduction plans within about one year after the act's passage.

Another study of the advisory group process conducted by Lauren Robel[29] produced findings that are generally consistent with ours. A mail survey was made of members of 26 advisory groups, and 86 percent responded positively to the question "Do you feel that your participation in the Civil Justice Reform Advisory Group has been a worthwhile experience?"

Robel noted that a primary benefit attributed to the CJRA process was opening a dialogue between the court and the bar. Ninety percent of respondents agreed that the process increased attorney understanding of the courts, and 81 percent believed it increased judicial understanding of attorney problems. Robel identified problems with how the advisory group process had been implemented, including the relatively small number of nonattorney members. However, the study points out "While it may be that litigants do not participate because they are unfamiliar with procedures, it is also likely that in most Groups they were so outnumbered by people with insider expertise that they cannot make a meaningful impact on the work of the Group."[30]

---

[27]Mullinex (1992), p. 375.

[28]Mullinex (1992), pp. 396–407.

[29]Robel (1993).

[30]Robel (1993), p. 897.

CONCLUSIONS

The advisory groups were created in a timely fashion by each district's chief judge. Members of the federal bar dominated the membership, and the chairperson was usually a senior member of the bar.

The act calls for advisory groups to be balanced and to include attorneys and other persons who represent major categories of litigants. One interpretation of the balance requirement is that lawyers' membership on the advisory group can achieve that balance in terms of the types of clients they represent.[31] That balance appears to have been met as far as lawyers are concerned. However, "other persons" were minimally represented. Limited by their lack of familiarity with the federal district court system, lay people usually played only a very modest role in advisory group meetings.

There was wide variation among districts in the role of judges on the advisory group. Research on court and organizational change, discussed in Chapter Three of our companion evaluation report, clearly indicates that the judges should be involved in the process. Judging by that research and our interviews, we believe the process would work best with judges playing a moderate role rather than a very active or a very passive role. If judges dominate while attending all meetings and even chair them, it may have some stifling effect on the consideration of new ideas for change and at least creates the appearance that the advisory group may not be offering independent advice. On the other hand, if the judges are almost totally uninvolved before receiving the report, then the advisory group does not get the full benefit of the wisdom of judicial officers about the practical viability of certain proposed changes, and judges do not get the full benefit of the wisdom of the advisory group members about problems and proposed solutions.

Advisory groups lacked the time, money, and expertise to conduct extensive research on the causes of and solutions to cost and delay. Their contribution was to analyze available statistics on time to disposition and assess subjective information collected in interviews and surveys of people who run and use the court system. The recommendations made generally flowed from either the identified causes of cost and delay, or from the CJRA mandate that certain principles of case management be included. When the advisory groups found causes of cost and delay unrelated to case management, they generally pointed those out and made recommendations related to those other causes. When the advisory group perceived that the court had no major cost or delay problem, or was already using a CJRA principle of case management, they said so, but usually they also made suggestions for refinements to further improve case management.

We were impressed by the dedication and conscientiousness with which the advisory groups approached developing recommendations. Advisory group members pro-

---

[31] Many of the attorneys in the groups consistently represent the same types of litigants in federal litigation. The U.S. Attorney is an obvious example, but it is also true for those who work for public interest firms and those who act as corporate or other organization counsel. In this sense, the lawyers themselves can be representative of major categories of litigants.

fessed independence from the court, indicating that they felt free to criticize when this was done on the basis of group consensus. Final reports generally reflected considerable independence from the court.

The act gives district courts the authority to accept, reject, or modify the recommendations of their advisory groups. As we will discuss in the next chapter, in most districts' CJRA plans, the courts responded positively to most or all of the advisory recommendations. Over three-quarters of the major recommendations of the pilot and comparison advisory groups were adopted into the courts' CJRA plans. Circuit and Judicial Conference review of the plans after adoption resulted in few changes.

Whatever the content of the advisory group plans, our interviews indicate that the process of generating the plans has made courts more cognizant of case management problems and opportunities. Bench-bar understanding reportedly has also been improved. That benefit alone probably justifies the advisory groups' work.

A majority of advisory group members whom we interviewed—especially the principal players among them—saw the advisory group process as valuable and believed that they had accomplished something worthwhile. A sizable minority disagreed, usually arguing either that it is inappropriate to have people outside the system interfere with a process best left to the judiciary, or that no assessment was needed because no real problem seemed to exist in the first place.

Our conclusion is that the CJRA advisory group process was useful, and the great majority of advisory group members thought so too.

In the next chapter, we turn to the content and implementation of the plans adopted by the districts.

Chapter Three

CJRA PLANS AND IMPLEMENTATION IN PILOT AND COMPARISON DISTRICTS

In this chapter we follow the evolution of case management policy in the pilot and comparison districts from pre-CJRA procedures to advisory group recommendations to district plans to actual post-CJRA implementation. The discussion is based on four major sources: a review of district CJRA plans and advisory group reports and minutes; court and case records and statistics; our surveys; and interviews with judges, clerks, lawyers, and advisory group members in each district.

CREATING AND IMPLEMENTING A PLAN

The Civil Justice Reform Act required each district, after having considered the recommendations of its advisory group, to institute a plan for reducing costs and delay. Pilot districts had to institute plans by December 31, 1991; comparison courts could adopt a plan any time before December 1993. Only two of the comparison districts adopted their plans at the same time as the pilot districts; the rest waited until late 1993 to do so.

The two-year difference in adoption dates between pilot courts and eight of the comparison courts benefits this evaluation because we selected our sample of cases for intensive study beginning in mid-1992 and had finished selecting the sample in nearly all districts by mid-1993. This means that the eight comparison districts used "status quo" pre-CJRA procedures during the critical early months of the lives of our sample of cases.

Pilot districts were required to adopt the six case management principles set forth in the act, but comparison districts were unrestricted as long as some kind of plan was developed. One comparison district that implemented at the same time as the pilot districts did not substantially change its prior case management procedures; the other adopted procedures like those of the pilot program.

Because the principles and techniques specified in the act all pertain to pretrial activities and are thus intertwined, in the discussion that follows we categorize them into four groups: differential case management, early judicial case management, discovery management, and alternative dispute resolution.

We reiterate that pilot districts had to institute plans by December 31, 1991, and comparison courts could adopt a plan any time before December 1993. Only two of the comparison districts adopted their plans at the same time as the pilot districts; the rest waited until late 1993 to do so.

DIFFERENTIAL CASE MANAGEMENT

Background

The first and third CJRA principles concern a court's responsibilities with respect to the differential pretrial management of its caseload.[1]

1. Systematic, differential treatment of civil cases that tailors the level of case-specific management to such criteria as case complexity, the amount of time reasonably needed to prepare the case for trial, and the judicial and other resources required and available for the preparation and disposition of the case;

3. For all cases a court thinks are complex and any other appropriate cases, careful and deliberate monitoring through a discovery/case management conference or a series of such conferences.

Generally speaking, these principles embody what has come to be known as Differential or Differentiated Case Management (DCM). The core of the DCM concept is the notion that some cases need different levels of judicial attention, different schedules for case events, and different treatment.[2]

One way to implement DCM is to create a number of discrete and well-structured approaches to case scheduling and management, followed by early assignment of cases to these approaches.[3] We shall call this the DCM "track model." A common formulation is to create three tracks—expedited, standard, and complex—and to establish different management procedures for each. No commonly accepted definition of these three tracks exists, and the court may assign cases to tracks according to objective criteria (such as type of case), the attorneys may choose the track into which their case will fit (subject to judicial review), or the judge may make the track assignment decision after initial case review. Within each track, judges use different case management techniques and schedules that are at least partially predetermined by the track assignment. Proponents argue that the track model of differential case management can reduce time to disposition, increase efficiency, and bring greater predictability to litigation.[4]

---

[1] 28 U.S.C. §473(a)(1)-(3). This listing extracts only a portion of the language of the act.

[2] Some practitioners view the DCM concept as inconsistent with the principle of providing a single uniform set of procedures across all federal court cases.

[3] A number of state criminal and civil courts have adopted the DCM concept in recent years—particularly those flooded with cases. For an overview of differentiated case management, see Alliegro et al. (1993).

[4] See Alliegro et al. (1993).

Before CJRA, courts were already tailoring their management of cases. All 20 districts had special differential management procedures for certain "minimal management" cases involving prisoner petitions other than death penalty cases, Social Security appeals, government loan recovery, and/or bankruptcy appeals. Frequently, these cases occupy a significant portion of a court's docket and impose special requirements. Prisoners often file petitions on a pro se basis, and they are initially processed by a pro se law clerk using standardized procedures and schedules. These cases often involve review of a request for a waiver of court fees and require some correspondence and motions activity, but few need court appearances and judicial case management in the traditional sense. Other minimal-demand cases, such as government loan collection cases and appeals from denials of Social Security benefits, often do not involve a pretrial conference between the judge and attorneys for both sides and go through the entire litigation process without much judicial management of any kind.

For cases not in the "minimal management" category, virtually all federal judges interviewed as part of the pilot program evaluation stressed that they have always managed their general civil cases individually and differentially. In support of this position, judges note that discovery is often minimal, that some cases do not require scheduling conferences, and that many lawsuits end with little or no judicial involvement. At the opposite end of the spectrum, complex cases can receive specialized management within a framework enunciated in the Federal Manual on Complex Litigation. In other words, there is a lot of intercase variation in procedure used by judges, and the variation is a manifestation of a tailored approach to case management that, in principle, is not unlike the objectives of the general differential case management concept. We shall call this approach to DCM, in which judges make case management decisions case by case for general civil cases, the "judicial discretion" model of case management.

Differential Case Management: From Advice to Implementation

For the minimal management types of cases noted above, all 20 districts used special procedures both before and after CJRA.

Before CJRA, all 20 districts used the judicial discretion model for the rest of the general civil litigation. After CJRA, six pilot and two comparison districts adopted a plan that contained the track model in one form or another. However, in practice, only three pilot districts assigned at least 1 percent of the cases to the complex track, and only one assigned more than 2 percent of cases to the complex track. The other three pilot districts either did not assign any general civil cases to tracks or assigned virtually all of them to the same standard track within which they were managed individually.

Comparison districts, which had the option of not doing DCM, were even less likely to revise their prior judicial discretion model.

Types of Differential Case Management Planned and Implemented

Table 3.1 traces the types of differential case management in the pilot and comparison districts from before CJRA to implementation of the district plans.

Seven of the 20 advisory groups recommended a change from the judicial discretion model to the track model. Only three districts adopted a model different from that recommended by the advisory group. Two added the track system when it was not recommended by the advisory group—in one district, to formalize existing practice, in the other, to provide the additional time needed to manage more difficult cases. One district rejected the track recommendation of its advisory group because the court felt these matters were better left to the discretion of individual judges to be applied case by case.

Table 3.1

Differential Case Management: From Advice to Implementation

| | Judicial Discretion Model | | Track Model | | |
Stage in Process	Standard	Magistrate Judges	Judicial-Officer-Selected	Rule-Based[a]	Attorney-Selected
			Pilot Districts		
12/91 before CJRA	10 districts				
Advisory group recommendation	TN(W), UT, WI(E), GA(N), OK(W)	CA(S)	NY(S), DE, TX(S)		PA(E)
District plan	TN(W), UT, WI(E)	CA(S)	NY(S), DE, TX(S), OK(W)	GA(N)	PA(E)
District implementation	TN(W), UT, WI(E)	CA(S)	DE, OK(W), TX(S) (each <1%)	GA(N)(2%)	NY(S) (1%), PA(E) (7%)
			Comparison Districts		
12/91 before CJRA	9 districts	NY(E)			
Advisory group recommendation	FL(N), IL(N,) IN(N), KY(E), KY(W), MD	NY(E)	AZ, PA(M)		CA(C)
District plan	CA(C), FL(N), IL(N), IN(N), KY(E), KY(W), MD	NY(E)	AZ, PA(M)		
District implementation	CA(C), FL(N), IL(N), IN(N), KY(E), KY(W), MD	NY(E)	PA(M) (4%), AZ (1%)		

NOTES: Numbers in parentheses indicate the percentage of cases assigned to the complex track. Pilot districts, IN(N), and NY(E) began implementation in 1/92; the other eight comparison districts began implementation in 12/93.

[a]Although only GA(N) uses rule-based tracking for all civil cases, other districts use hybrid systems that are partially rule-based and partially judicial-officer-selected tracking. For example, AZ uses a rule to assign cases to their expedited, prisoner pro se, and arbitration tracks, but the assignment of cases to the complex track is done by a judicial officer.

No matter what tracks are established, every DCM tracking system must overcome the hurdle of deciding how to assign particular cases to particular tracks—a decision needed early in the life of a case if cost and time to disposition are to be reduced as much as possible.

Cases at either extreme of the complexity spectrum are relatively easy to fit into a track. For example, contrast a simple personal injury suit involving an automobile accident, few questions of liability, and well-defined damage claims, with a complex patent infringement suit, involving multiple parties, many documents, and a high potential for interrogatories and depositions. For such cases, the tracking decision— expedited and complex, respectively—can be made without much confusion or risk of error. But the majority of cases are less clear cut and tend to be grouped together in a middle or "standard" track. Since some of these cases will or should actually be handled in expedited fashion and others in complex fashion, some of the potential benefits of DCM tracking may well be lost.

Most of the advisory groups struggled with this issue, and their reports reflect a fundamental dilemma. A decision to track a case made early in its life must often be made on the basis of a sparse record—perhaps resulting in an unsuitable assignment. But if the decision is delayed to allow for a full record to develop, the potential savings in time, cost, and aggravation may well be lost.

Table 3.1 summarizes how the pilot and comparison districts implemented differential case management. It identifies the case management approach implemented in each district and indicates the percentage of civil cases assigned to the complex track.

Judicial discretion means that—with the exception of the special management of prisoner petitions and minimal-demand cases—judges or magistrate judges make case management decisions case by case according to their own schedules and procedures. All 20 districts used this method of management before the CJRA. As their plans attest, four pilot districts and eight comparison districts considered the CJRA's differential case management requirement to be met by this model and continued to use it.

Pretrial management by magistrate judges refers to a system under which all cases are automatically assigned to a magistrate judge, who manages a case through all its pretrial phases and usually makes an early effort to settle, mediate, or neutrally evaluate the case. Note that this differs from the usual practice in federal district courts under which a judge delegates discrete facets of civil case pretrial processing (such as discovery motions or scheduling conferences) to a magistrate judge. One comparison district—NY(E)—uses this approach to differential case management. Though this comparison district has had magistrate judges doing pretrial management for some years, interviews suggest that it has intensified its management and early settlement efforts after implementing the CJRA plan. One pilot district—CA(S)— adopted this approach in its CJRA plan, and this district also directs the magistrate judge to conduct a neutral evaluation conference before the initial scheduling and case management conference. Two other study districts have adopted this approach for some of their cases. As of 1992 in WI(E), full-time magistrate judges are assigned a share of the cases that is 60 percent as large as a district judge's share. As of 1994 in AZ, magistrate judges in Tucson are assigned a share of the cases that is 25 percent as large as a district judge's share.

In *judicial-officer-selected tracking*, the judicial officer makes the initial track decision for a case. Although three pilot districts chose this approach in their plan, two have placed fewer than five cases per year in the complex track and a third did not implement this aspect of its plan because it did not receive funding for staff. Hence these districts are really using the judicial discretion model. Two comparison districts chose this approach in their plan, and one of them has 4 percent of cases designated to its complex track.

Rule-based tracking involves assigning a case on the basis of its objective characteristics—usually the nature of suit—known at the time of filing. One pilot district has done this using standardized discovery periods of zero, four, or eight months for different track assignments. The zero-month-discovery track contains the types of cases that were minimal management cases before CJRA. The four-month-discovery track contains the vast majority of the general civil cases, and the discovery time limit is the same as it was before CJRA. The eight-month-discovery track contains about 2 percent of civil filings (antitrust, patent, and securities/commodities cases). No comparison district chose this method of tracking.

Attorney-selected tracking usually requires the filing attorney to opt for a particular track—expedited, standard, or complex—after which the opposing attorney has an opportunity to dissent. The judge then decides. Two pilot districts have implemented this approach. One district—PA(E)—has a 12-month-to-trial schedule for standard cases and an 18-month schedule for special (complex) cases; the lawyers' choice of the track is accepted unless the judge takes action to change the track, which seldom happens. In effect, the tracking decision occurs at the time of filing for all cases, and 7 percent of the cases are in the complex track. The other district—NY(S)—has three tracks, but a judge has to act on the lawyers' request before the track assignment is accepted. In practice the track assignment occurred several months after filing for only about 15 percent of the cases, and only about 1 percent were in the complex track. The remaining 85 percent of the cases were never assigned a track, and the district eliminated the track system from its CJRA plan in mid-1995.

EARLY JUDICIAL MANAGEMENT PROCEDURES

Background

The second CJRA principle concerns a court's responsibilities with respect to the early and ongoing pretrial management of its caseload:[5]

---

[5] 28 U.S.C. §473(a)(2).

2. Early and ongoing control of the pretrial process through involvement of a judicial officer in

   a. Assessing and planning the progress of the case;

   b. Setting early, firm trial dates, such that the trial is scheduled to occur within 18 months after the filing of the complaint, unless the judicial officer certifies that

      i. The demands of the case and its complexity make such a trial date incompatible with serving the ends of justice; or

      ii. The trial cannot reasonably be held within such time because of the complexity of the case or the number or complexity of pending criminal cases;

   c. [Refers to discovery and is discussed in the next section.]

   d. Setting, at the earliest practicable time, deadlines for filing motions and a time framework for their disposition.

In addition, four of the six CJRA techniques concern early or active pretrial case management:

1. Requiring that counsel jointly present a discovery/case management plan at the initial pretrial conference, or explain the reasons for their failure to do so;

2. Requiring that all parties be represented at each pretrial conference by an attorney with authority to bind the party;

3. Requiring the signature of the party and the attorney on all requests for discovery extensions or postponements of trial; and

5. Requiring party representatives with authority to bind to be present or available by telephone at settlement conferences.

Early Judicial Management: From Advice to Implementation

The advisory groups often made recommendations for fine-tuning the scheduling, conferencing, reporting/planning, trial-setting, and motion-processing procedures. Details, too varied and numerous to recite here, are presented for each district in the appendices.

The thrust of all the advisory group reports was in favor of early judicial management of general civil cases, and all of the courts' plans accepted the principle of early judicial management. In general, most of the advisory groups' recommendations for refining the pretrial process were accepted, although sometimes with modifications. However, analysis of docket events from more than 10,000 cases indicates that early judicial management is more prevalent in some districts than in others. Interviews with judges and lawyers confirmed this and documented variation among judges in the same district.

Another aspect of differences between judges within districts is that formal procedures and standing orders may differ from judge to judge (in other words, there are "judge rules" below the "local rules"). Several advisory groups indicated that more uniformity of procedures within the district would be desirable.

CJRA technique 1 requires that counsel jointly present a discovery/case management plan at the initial pretrial conference, or explain the reasons for their failure to do so.[6] Before CJRA, only one of the 20 districts required this,[7] although at least one other district[8] required attorneys to confer before the first pretrial conference to attempt to agree on a scheduling order. Four of the ten pilot districts[9] adopted this technique in their plan, and nine of the other pilot and comparison districts adopted it later when the December 1993 F.R.Civ.P. 26(f) changes were made to require such a plan.[10]

CJRA technique 2 requires that each party be represented at conferences by an attorney with authority to bind that party. All 20 districts in the study required, or allowed judges to require, this both before and after CJRA.

CJRA technique 3 requires the signature of the attorney and the party on all requests for discovery extensions or postponements of trial. This technique does not generate enthusiasm from most lawyers, and none of the 20 districts in our study required this for all cases before or after CJRA. Although most plans were silent on why this technique was not adopted, some lawyers we interviewed felt it was unnecessary and added some cost, and others resented the implication that some clients are kept in the dark about continuance requests and that they might not approve if requested to sign.

CJRA technique 5 requires that party representatives with authority to bind be present or available by telephone at settlement conferences. Eight of the 20 districts used this technique before CJRA,[11] and five additional districts adopted it as part of their CJRA plan.[12]

DISCOVERY MANAGEMENT PROCEDURES

Background

The CJRA requires pilot districts to adopt, and other districts to consider adopting, some procedures for managing discovery. Specifically, the act mandates:

"(2) early and ongoing control of the pretrial process through involvement of a judicial officer in . . . (C) controlling the extent of discovery and the time for completion

---

[6]See Form 35 of F.R.Civ.P. 26(f) for an example of a possible discovery/case management plan. We consider a discovery/case management plan to include more than the typical scheduling order, although in some districts they may be functionally equivalent.

[7]OK(W).

[8]NY(E).

[9]OK(W), TN(W), TX(S), and UT.

[10]AZ, DE, FL(N), IL(N), IN(N), KY(E), KY(W), NY(E), and PA(M).

[11] CA(S), KY(W), MD, OK(W), PA(E), PA(M), TN(W), and UT.

[12] GA(N), IN(N), NY(E), TX(S), and WI(E).

of discovery, and ensuring compliance with appropriate requested discovery in a timely fashion . . . .

(4) encouragement of cost-effective discovery through voluntary exchange of information among litigants and their attorneys and through the use of cooperative discovery devices;

(5) conservation of judicial resources by prohibiting the consideration of discovery motions unless accompanied by a certification that the moving party has made a reasonable and good faith effort to reach agreement with opposing counsel on the matters set forth in the motion; . . . ."[13]

Two issues have arisen regarding discovery: (1) To what extent should the court control the volume, sequencing, and timing of discovery, rather than leaving this in the hands of the litigants' attorneys; and (2) what information should be voluntarily or mandatorily exchanged early in a case without a formal discovery request.

In December 1993, amendments to the Federal Rules of Civil Procedure were adopted that complicated the implementation of the CJRA discovery provisions. The CJRA directs pilot districts to develop and implement discovery control and early disclosure procedures. The new federal rules require certain changes in discovery practice and management that may conflict with the discovery programs of some pilot districts. For instance, the revised Rule 26 requires lawyers to meet and confer before the scheduling conference, to develop a proposed joint discovery plan, and to automatically disclose certain basic relevant information without awaiting a formal discovery request. And the new Rules 30, 31, and 33 place limits on depositions and interrogatories. Districts may opt out of some of the rule changes, however, as some pilot districts have done to avoid conflicts with their pilot plans.[14]

Judicial Control of Discovery Volume and Timing

All districts permit the use of judicial discretion to limit the extent of discovery case by case. Before CJRA, as shown in Table 3.2, the majority of both pilot and comparison districts also had a local rule that limited the number of interrogatories and requests for admission. The actual number varied among districts from 20 to 50. Those limits could be exceeded at the discretion of the judge for individual cases. One pilot district also placed a limit of six hours per deposition. Before CJRA, no pilot or comparison district specifically limited the number of depositions.

After adoption of the CJRA plans, local rules with respect to control of discovery volume did not change in most districts. PA(M) and WI(E) adopted a new limit on deposition length—six hours unless lawyers stipulated or the judge approved additional hours. AZ and NY(E) adopted new limits on the number of depositions—the range was eight to ten depositions per side. Two comparison districts instituted new local rules limiting the number of interrogatories or requests for admission, and

---

[13]28 U.S.C. §473(a).

[14]Stienstra (1995).

Table 3.2

Pilot and Comparison Districts with Various Types of Discovery Limitations Before and After CJRA Plan Implementation

Type of Discovery Limitation	Pilot Districts		Comparison Districts	
	Before 12/91	After 12/91	Before 12/93 (12/91 for IN(N) and NY(E))	After 12/93 (12/91 for IN(N) and NY(E))
Judicial discretion, with no prespecified limits	2 (NY(S), UT)	2 (NY(S), UT)	2 (AZ, NY(E))	0
Limitation on number of interrogatories and requests for admission (other than 12/93 F.R.Civ.P. 33 limit)	7 (CA(S), DE, GA(N), OK(W), TN(W), TX(S), WI(E))	7 (CA(S), DE, GA(N), OK(W), TN(W), TX(S), WI(E))	8 (CA(C), FL(N), IL(N), IN(N), KY(E), KY(W), MD, PA(M))	10
Limitation on number of depositions (other than 12/93 F.R.Civ.P. 30 and 31 limit)	0	0	0	2 (AZ, NY(E))
Limitation on length of depositions	1 (GA(N))	2 (GA(N), WI(E))	0	1 (PA(M))
Limitation on discovery cutoff time for certain types of cases	2 (GA(N), PA(E))	2 (GA(N), PA(E))	0	1 (MD)

NOTES: Districts with limitations may have more than one type. Pilot districts, IN(N), and NY(E) began implementation in 1/92; the other eight comparison districts began implementation in 12/93.

some other districts revised or tightened their existing local rules on the allowable number of interrogatories or requests for admission. In addition, the December 1993 revisions to F.R.Civ.P. 30, 31, and 33 limit the volume of discovery, absent leave of the court or stipulation of the parties, to ten depositions per side and 25 interrogatories per party (including subparts).

Before the CJRA, all districts allowed the establishment of discovery cutoff dates, but most left the decision to the judge in each case. However, some districts had rules allowing discovery only to a certain point in a case (usually a specified length of time before the final pretrial conference or trial date). Two pilot districts had standardized schedules limiting discovery time for cases referred to arbitration or for all cases.

The districts' CJRA plans have not changed the landscape much, except in two pilot districts and one comparison district. One pilot district has adopted a tracking system under which cases are grouped by nature of suit, and discovery is cut off after either zero, four, or eight months (instead of the pre-CJRA limit of four months for all cases). Another pilot district added to its discovery cutoff limits for arbitration cases by placing nonarbitration cases into standard or special tracks and setting trial dates within 12 or 18 months, respectively, thus automatically limiting discovery time. One comparison district limits discovery to 120 days for routine cases. Under these systems of prespecified discovery cutoff limits, judges nevertheless retain discretion to adjust discovery schedules.

Early Disclosure of Information Without Formal Discovery Requests

Pilot districts were required to encourage, though not necessarily to mandate, "cost-effective discovery" through voluntary exchange of information among litigants and their attorneys and through the use of cooperative discovery devices.

The evolution of the early disclosure procedures from advisory group advice to implementation is shown in Table 3.3.

Before the CJRA, only one comparison district required the early exchange of information without a formal discovery request for all general civil cases; two other districts required it for a limited subset of cases.

After the CJRA, the disclosure procedures changed greatly, and all pilot and comparison districts adopted one of five very different disclosure procedure models, all of which meet the requirements of the CJRA pilot program.

Three pilot and two comparison districts adopted the voluntary exchange model, which encourages lawyers to cooperate in exchanging information.[15] Judging by our interviews, lawyers do not object to this arrangement.

Table 3.3

Early Disclosure of Information: From Advice to Implementation

Stage in Process	Voluntary	Mandatory for Some Cases	Mandatory, Info on Your Side	Mandatory, Info on Both Sides	Follow 12/93 Rule 26(a)(1)
		Pilot Districts			
12/91 before CJRA	9 districts	PA(E)			
Advisory group recommendation	CA(S), TN(W), UT	DE, NY(S), TX(S)	GA(N), WI(E)	OK(W), PA(E)	
District plan	CA(S), TN(W), UT	DE, NY(S), TX(S)	GA(N), WI(E)	OK(W), PA(E)	
District implementation	CA(S)+2 before 12/93 (TN(W), UT)	NY(S) +2 before 12/93 (DE, TX(S))	GA(N), WI(E)	OK(W), PA(E)	DE, TN(W), TX(S), UT after 12/93
		Comparison Districts			
12/91 before CJRA	8 districts	AZ	CA(C)		
Advisory group recommendation	IL(N), MD, FL(N), KY(W), AZ	IN(N)	CA(C)	NY(E)	KY(E), PA(M)
District plan	IL(N), MD, AZ	IN(N)	CA(C)	NY(E)	KY(E), PA(M), FL(N), KY(W)
District implementation	IL(N), MD	+1 before 12/93 (IN(N))	CA(C)	NY(E) after 12/93	KY(E), PA(M), FL(N), KY(W), AZ, IN(N) after 12/93

NOTES: Mandatory, info on your side, requires mandatory exchange of information bearing significantly on *your* claim or defense, plus other items. Mandatory, info on both sides, requires mandatory exchange of information bearing significantly on *any* claim or defense, plus other items. Rule 26(a)(1) requires mandatory exchange of information relevant to disputed facts alleged with particularity in the pleadings, plus other items.

---

[15] Two of the three pilot districts later decided to follow the December 1993 revised F.R.Civ.P. 26(a)(1).

Three pilot districts and one comparison district followed a mandatory exchange model for a limited subset of cases and a voluntary model on other cases. Of these four districts, one required mandatory disclosure for ten or 20 cases per judge[16]; one for expedited track cases only; one for injury, medical malpractice, employment discrimination, and Racketeer Influenced and Corrupt Organizations Act (RICO) cases only; and one had different types of mandatory disclosure experiments by some of the judges (see Appendix H for details).[17]

Two pilot districts and one comparison district required lawyers to mandatorily disclose certain information, including anything bearing significantly on their sides' claims or defenses.

Two other pilot districts and one other comparison district have a similar mandatory requirement, but they apply it to all information bearing significantly on both sides' claims or defenses.[18]

Four pilot districts later switched from their initial disclosure procedure to follow the December 1993 revised F.R.Civ.P. 26(a)(1), and six comparison districts are following the revised Rule 26(a)(1). The ten other pilot and comparison districts have decided to opt out and are not following the revised Rule 26(a)(1), which requires the mandatory exchange of information relevant to disputed facts alleged with particularity in the pleadings, plus information on damages and insurance.

Early mandatory disclosure has prompted criticism on a number of grounds. Many lawyers consider it distasteful or threatening, believing it to be an assault on the adversarial model of Anglo-American litigation. Our interviews indicate that they are especially concerned about having to do the other side's work and about potential conflict of interest if they must provide everything that bears significantly on both sides of the case, even if the other side has not asked for the information or "alleged with particularity" in the pleadings.

More practically, many lawyers are not certain exactly what they must disclose, how extensively they must search to satisfy a request, how to get information from the litigant in a timely fashion, whether it is reasonable to incur the cost of disclosure for all cases when many cases never have any formal discovery, and what ancillary litigation and motion practice may arise.

When compliance is insufficient, a lawyer may ignore the problem, make a formal discovery request, or file a motion requesting the court to force compliance. According to our analysis of dockets on over 5,000 cases, and according to judges we have interviewed in pilot and comparison districts that implemented their plans in December 1991, such motions are extremely rare. Despite the dire warnings of critics of early mandatory disclosure, we did not find any explosion of ancillary litigation and

---

[16] The selection process for these cases was not clearly specified.

[17] One of the pilot and one of the comparison districts later decided to follow the December 1993 revised F.R.Civ.P. 26(a)(1).

[18] The actual wording is similar to an early draft of the December 1993 revised Rule 26 that was hotly contested by some lawyers.

motion practice related to disclosure in any of the pilot or comparison districts using mandatory disclosure.

Certification of Good-Faith Efforts

Pilot districts were required to have lawyers certify good-faith efforts to resolve discovery disputes before filing motions and have complied with the act. Before the CJRA, local rules in all pilot and nine of the ten comparison districts required the filing attorney to undertake good-faith efforts to resolve discovery disputes before filing discovery motions.[19] *Certification* of such efforts was required by local rules in nine pilot and nine comparison districts.[20] The CJRA plan slightly modified the wording of the local rule in some districts, although most retained their rules unchanged. In general, the advisory groups and the courts agreed that good-faith effort certification was desirable and should be continued.

ALTERNATIVE DISPUTE RESOLUTION PROCEDURES

Background

CJRA principle 6 requires pilot districts to adopt, and other districts to consider adopting, some type of alternative dispute resolution program. Specifically, it authorizes courts "to refer appropriate cases to alternative dispute resolution programs that—(A) have been designated for use in a district court; or (B) the court may make available, including mediation, mini-trial, and summary jury trial."[21] CJRA technique 4 requires that courts consider "a neutral evaluation program for the presentation of the legal and factual basis of a case to a neutral court representative selected by the court at a nonbinding conference conducted early in the litigation."[22] Because neutral evaluation is generally considered to be a form of ADR, we include that technique here.

The act fails to define the term "alternative dispute resolution" with specificity, and districts may therefore choose from a number of approaches such as neutral evaluation, mediation, settlement conferences, voluntary nonbinding arbitration, as well as the use of special masters, mini-trials, and summary jury trials. These ADR approaches can be designed in many different ways.[23]

Arbitration is analogous to a trial, except that a third party other than a judge or jury—usually but not necessarily selected by the parties—reviews facts and hears arguments presented by both sides and then renders a decision. Sometimes this deci-

---

[19]NY(E) did not require good-faith efforts to resolve discovery disputes before filing a motion.

[20]NY(E) and NY(S) did not require *certification* of good-faith efforts.

[21]28 U.S.C. §473(a).

[22]28 U.S.C. §473(b).

[23]For discussions of ADR programs and their design features, see, for example, Plapinger and Shaw (1992); Sander (1991); Plapinger et al. (1993); Wilkinson (1993); Hensler (1986, 1994); Resnik (1995); Lind et al. (1989); Rolph (1984); and Rolph and Moller (1995).

sion is binding by stipulation or prior contract, sometimes not. When courts *mandate* arbitration, however, it is always nonbinding unless the parties themselves agree to be bound. Like arbitration, neutral evaluation usually involves a third-party assessment of a suit; unlike arbitration, however, the third party does not render a decision and in practice may not only make an evaluation but may discuss and review ways of settling the case with the parties. In mediation, the emphasis is on helping the parties reach their own settlement of some or all the issues in the case. The third-party mediator, unlike the arbitrator, does not render a decision. The third-party mediator often does not attempt to evaluate the case, but may do so in an advisory fashion. Abbreviated mini-trials or summary jury trials, and the use of special masters to manage discovery, are relatively rare and tend to be used in complex cases only.

Judging by the CJRA plans and our interviews, some judges and attorneys consider settlement discussions with a judicial officer and requirements that lawyers certify that they have conducted private settlement efforts to be forms of ADR, although the CJRA does not include settlement conferences in its ADR language. Both before and after CJRA, at least some judges in all districts held settlement conferences. Occasionally, judges asked another judge or a magistrate judge to conduct the conference so as to avoid the risk that information presented during settlement discussions would influence decisions made at trial. In the remainder of this chapter we focus on ADR other than settlement conferences conducted by judicial officers.

Whatever form an ADR program takes, the traditional emphasis has always been on taking a dispute out of formal court litigation and at least temporarily submitting it to an independent third party. This traditional emphasis now appears to be undergoing modification, as judicial officers in some districts increasingly take on ADR-like functions. An example of this modification in judicial roles is found in CA(S), where an early neutral evaluation is conducted by a magistrate judge before the initial scheduling conference is held.

The rationale for all ADR programs is, of course, the hope that they are faster, cheaper, and/or more satisfactory than formal court adjudication. Although past research has not confirmed all these putative benefits, it does seem to suggest that litigants are more satisfied when ADR has taken place, even if they do not settle their case at that time. Perhaps this is because they feel they have had their "day in ADR court" without the expense of a formal court trial. However, because most court-connected ADR is nonbinding and because the vast majority of cases do not go to trial, ADR primarily offers an alternative mode of settlement, not trial.

Alternative Dispute Resolution Procedures: From Advice to Implementation

There was considerable debate in the advisory group and plan development process concerning alternative dispute resolution. A major issue is what type of ADR to use, since several types are mentioned in the act.[24] Another major issue raised by the act's ADR referral language is whether courts should move from the current prevalent procedure of purely "voluntary" ADR to a practice of compelling parties to participate in "mandatory," nonbinding ADR before moving to trial.[25]

The situation was complicated by an earlier effort to test mandatory ADR programs in federal court in which Congress authorized ten district courts to use mandatory arbitration methods, and ten other district courts to use voluntary arbitration methods.[26] The Federal Judicial Center evaluated the mandatory arbitration program, and because of "generally favorable findings" recommended authorizing arbitration in all federal district courts, to be mandatory or voluntary at the discretion of the court.[27] The Federal Judicial Center also studied the voluntary arbitration program and found the caseloads to be lower than for mandatory programs (programs allowing parties to opt out had caseloads comparable to the smallest mandatory arbitration programs, whereas programs in which parties had to opt in to arbitration had "almost no cases").[28] In 1994, Congress extended the court-annexed arbitration program in these 20 district courts but did not expand it to others.[29]

Both before and after CJRA, all pilot and comparison districts had ADR of one kind or another; some had only a few cases in the program, whereas others had up to 50 percent of all civil filings referred.   Table 3.4 summarizes the distribution. Pilot and comparison districts not listed in the table all permitted ADR of various types but they had less than 1 percent of their civil case filings referred to ADR.

Before CJRA, two pilot districts and one comparison district had formally structured arbitration programs involving 9 to 15 percent of their cases, requiring mandatory nonbinding early arbitration for certain cases involving only monetary damages less than $100,000. One arbitration pilot district also had a formally structured mediation program for 10 percent of the civil cases, requiring mandatory pro bono mediation for certain types of cases by a court-appointed mediator early in the life of the case. One comparison district had a voluntary mediation program involving about 4 percent of its cases, and another comparison district had one judge with a structured early neutral evaluation program involving 6 percent of the district's cases. As expected, the mandatory programs had higher volume than the voluntary programs.

---

[24]For a discussion of the pros and cons of various types of ADR in the federal courts, see Stienstra and Willging (1995).

[25]"Mandatory" ADR should not be confused with "binding" ADR. A mandatory process simply compels the parties to use the technique before continuing more traditional court procedures; a mandatory ADR process, such as mediation, supplements the courtroom process as a means of settling the case. Once the parties have used the mandatory process, however, and been unable to resolve their dispute, they are free to come back into the courtroom. Binding ADR means that an out-of-courtroom process must not only be used but must be dispositive, such as binding arbitration. A binding process cannot normally be mandated by a court, since that would interfere with the constitutional right to trial by jury. But the parties to a lawsuit may agree to be bound by an ADR process either when they enter into a contractual agreement or at the time a specific dispute arises.

[26]28 U.S.C. §651–658.

[27]Meierhoefer (1990), p. 12.

[28]Rauma and Krafka (1994), p. 3.

[29]Judicial Amendments Act of 1994, Public Law No. 103-420.

Table 3.4

ADR: From Advice to Implementation

Stage in Process	Mandatory Arbitration	Mandatory Mediation	Mandatory Early Neutral Evaluation	Voluntary Arbitration	Voluntary Mediation	Voluntary Early Neutral Evaluation
			Pilot Districts			
12/91 before CJRA	OK(W) (10); PA(E) (15)	PA(E) (10)				
Advisory group recommendation	OK(W), PA(E), GA(N)	PA(E), NY(S)	CA(S)	CA(S), UT	OK(W), TX(S)	TN(W)
District plan	OK(W), PA(E), GA(N)	PA(E), NY(S)	CA(S)	CA(S), UT	OK(W), TX(S)	TN(W)
District implementation	OK(W) (8); PA(E) (13)	PA(E) (6); NY(S) (5)	CA(S) (50)	UT (4)	OK(W) (6); TX(S) (5)	
			Comparison Districts			
12/91 before CJRA	NY(E) (9)				FL(N) (4)	IN(N) (6)
Advisory group recommendation	NY(E)			AZ	FL(N), PA(M), KY(E), KY(W), MD, NY(E)	IN(N), NY(E), CA(C), FL(N), KY(W), PA(M)
District plan	NY(E)			AZ	FL(N), PA(M), KY(E), KY(W), MD, NY(E)	IN(N), NY(E)
District implementation	NY(E) (10)			AZ (4)	FL(N) (4); PA(M) (2)	IN(N) (6); NY(E) (2)

NOTES: Numbers in parentheses indicate referrals to ADR type indicated, as a percentage of all case filings in the district during the year. Pilot districts, IN(N), and NY(E) began implementation in 1/92; the other eight comparison districts began implementation in 12/93.

After implementation of their plans, all of the pilot and comparison districts either permitted ADR referrals or had structured ADR programs. Four of the pilot and five of the comparison districts permitted individual judges to refer cases to some type of ADR on a voluntary basis but did not have a more formally structured ADR program, and the number of referrals in those districts was always very low—1 percent of civil filings or less. The remainder of the districts had more structured ADR programs and usually had a higher, but still small, percentage of their cases referred to ADR.

Following implementation of their CJRA plans, two pilot districts continued mandatory arbitration involving 8 to 13 percent of their cases. Two have early mandatory pro bono mediation involving 5 to 6 percent of their cases. Two have voluntary paid mediation involving 5 to 6 percent of their cases. One has voluntary arbitration for 4 percent. And one requires mandatory neutral evaluation efforts by a magistrate judge early in a case, coupled with early pretrial management by the same magistrate judge, involving 50 percent of all civil filings.[30]

Following implementation of its CJRA plan, one comparison district continued its mandatory arbitration program involving 10 percent of civil filings and supplemented it with a voluntary early neutral evaluation program involving 2 percent of filings. One comparison district continued its voluntary mediation program involving 4 percent of filings. One continued its early neutral evaluation program involving 6 percent of filings, and one continued a voluntary arbitration program that was implemented in 1992 involving 4 percent of civil filings. One comparison district began a structured voluntary mediation program involving about 2 percent of filings.

The federal court arbitration programs have been extensively described elsewhere,[31] but since the mediation and neutral evaluation programs are relatively new in federal court, we describe them below.

Mandatory mediation programs. Two pilot districts have mandatory mediation programs—NY(S) and PA(E). Being mandatory, they both involve hundreds of cases per year and provide a rich source of data for analysis. Still better from an evaluation standpoint, both have an experimental design in which cases are randomly assigned to mediation or not, thus creating experimental mediation and nonmediation comparison groups.

In the PA(E) mediation program, implemented in mid-1991 just before the CJRA, a case is referred to mediation if (1) the case does not qualify for mandatory arbitration, (2) it is a type of case found on the mediation list,[32] (3) the case is still open a month after appearance of all parties, and (4) it has an odd docket number. The mediation takes place before a single pro bono mediator that the court selects from a list of approved mediators, all of whom have been members of the bar for at least 15 years. It typically lasts one hour and is held three or four months after filing.

In the NY(S) mandatory mediation program, all "expedited" track cases and a two-thirds random sample of the "standard" and "complex" track cases are flagged for referral to mediation. During the study period, the referral did not take place until after the formal track assignment had been made by the judge responsible for the case. However, because 85 percent of the cases were never assigned to a track, the mediation program did not proceed as originally envisioned. The referrals were later in the life of the cases than expected and the volume of cases in the program was much lower than it otherwise would have been.[33]

---

[30] We supplemented our primary CJRA evaluation with an in-depth look at the ADR programs in five of the pilot districts that use ADR for at least 5 percent of their civil filings. We have similarly undertaken an in-depth study of one comparison district that has a substantial number of cases in a magistrate-judge-administered ADR program. See Kakalik et al. (1996a).

[31] See, for example, Meierhoefer (1990); and Rauma and Krafka (1994).

[32] The following types of cases are excluded from the PA(E) program by local rule: Social Security cases, cases in which a prisoner is a party, cases eligible for arbitration, asbestos cases, and any other case a judge may decide to exclude.

[33] NY(S) eliminated its track program in 1995 and is establishing a different mediation referral process.

Voluntary mediation programs. OK(W) and TX(S) have voluntary mediation programs that involve at least 5 percent of the cases. In contrast to the low volume programs in other districts, these programs are formally structured and administered. Both courts actively solicit volunteers and help facilitate participation by the litigants. Moreover, both mediation programs are in states with established mediation programs in the state court system and thus enjoy the advantage of a bar experienced with ADR.

In the OK(W) voluntary mediation program, a local rule provides for certification of trained mediators, the maintenance of an annotated list of mediators, a mediation clerk to administer the program, and payment of the mediator by the parties. Among other things, the local rule also provides for discussion of referral to mediation at the initial scheduling conference, the method of selecting the mediator, mediation "at the earliest practical time," confidentiality, and a notice to the court of the results of the mediation. The average session lasts about five hours, with parties splitting payment of the mediator's typical fee of $500 to $750.

The TX(S) district's voluntary mediation program handles about 300 cases per year. It, too, provides that ADR be discussed at the initial pretrial conference and allows a judge to refer a case to mediation, mini-trial, summary jury trial, arbitration, or any other ADR program. Although the program permits any type of ADR, over 98 percent of the referred cases went to mediation. The plan also provides for the certification of trained providers, the maintenance of lists of providers with information about each, a clerk to administer the program, confidentiality, and a notice to the court of the results of the ADR. The typical session lasts between a half day and a full day, and the parties split the mediator's fee.

In contrast, districts with voluntary ADR programs that have only a few cases typically have an authorizing rule that is not supported by any formal structure. In addition, there are no lists of certified ADR providers, and the clerk's office does not administer the program. Hence, judges and lawyers must find their own ADR providers, a process poorly suited to encourage volunteers.

Magistrate judge early evaluation/mediation/settlement efforts. In CA(S) and NY(E), magistrate judges actively manage all aspects of the pretrial process. This style of case management differs significantly from the traditional approach, as well as from the four mediation programs discussed above, because it is done by a judicial officer rather than by a neutral lawyer. One might hypothesize that such a program would involve more settlements than one handled by a neutral lawyer, since the magistrate judge is a member of the court and is more likely to be viewed as an authoritative source of information about probable case outcomes.

Chapter Four

ASSESSMENT OF IMPLEMENTATION

The previous chapter provided details of the implementation of the CJRA in pilot and comparison districts. Here we provide some general observations and conclusions.

DIFFERENTIAL CASE MANAGEMENT

In their CJRA plans, most pilot and comparison districts adhered to their pre-CJRA judicial discretion model of differential case management, although some adopted new track approaches.

Continuation of pre-CJRA judicial discretion model policies include the following:

1. Using special procedures for certain types of cases that have traditionally required only minimal management—typically prisoner petitions, Social Security appeals, government loan recovery cases, and bankruptcy appeals.

2. Using judicial discretion and individualized case management for all other cases. One pilot and one comparison district have modified the traditional judicial discretion model by delegating all pretrial management to a magistrate judge, with early settlement efforts.

Pilot districts were required to adopt the differential case management principle. Four of them—CA(S), TN(W), UT, and WI(E)—decided that the judicial discretion model was a valid manifestation of the DCM principle that met the act's mandate. The other six pilot districts adopted a track model. Comparison districts, which were not required to adopt differential case management, were even less likely to revise their prior judicial discretion model. Only two comparison districts—AZ and PA(M)—adopted a track system.

Both the judicial discretion approach and the new track approaches meet the CJRA's loosely defined statutory requirements for differential case management, since all districts employ special procedures for certain types of minimal management cases and at least provide individualized tailoring of management for the rest of the general civil cases.

From the perspective of evaluation, the pilot program looked promising at the plan stage because six of the ten pilot districts planned to adopt a tracking model for their general civil cases instead of retaining the judicial discretion model. However, because only the PA(E) pilot district implemented its tracks for all cases and had over 2 percent of the cases assigned to the complex or special track, we really have only one district in which to evaluate tracking. That district also implemented other changes; consequently, separating the effects of the track system from the effect of the other changes is problematic.

The lack of experimentation with and successful implementation of a tracking system for general civil litigation is probably due to a combination of factors, including: (1) the difficulty in determining the correct track assignment for most civil litigation cases using data available at or soon after case filing; and (2) judges' desire to tailor case management to the needs of the case and to their style of management rather than having the track assignment provide the management structure for a category of cases.

EARLY JUDICIAL CASE MANAGEMENT

With respect to early and ongoing control of the pretrial process by a judicial officer, the advisory groups often made recommendations for fine-tuning the scheduling, conferencing, status-reporting, case-planning, trial-setting, and motion-processing procedures. All the advisory group reports favored early judicial management of general civil cases. Although all of the courts' plans accepted the principle of early and ongoing judicial control of the pretrial process, in practice, case management styles vary substantially between districts and between judges within a district.

CJRA technique 1 requires counsel to jointly present a discovery/case management plan at the initial pretrial conference, or to explain the reasons for their failure to do so. Before CJRA, only one district in the study required this, although at least one other district required attorneys to confer before the first pretrial conference to attempt to agree on a scheduling order. Four of the ten pilot districts adopted this technique in their plan, and nine of the other pilot and comparison districts later adopted it when the December 1993 F.R.Civ.P. 26(f) changes were made to require such a plan.

CJRA technique 2 requires each party to be represented at each pretrial conference by an attorney with authority to bind that party. All 20 districts in our study required, or allowed judges to require, this both before and after CJRA.

CJRA technique 3 requires the signature of the party's attorney and the party on all requests for discovery extensions or postponements of trial. This technique does not generate enthusiasm from most lawyers, and none of the 20 districts in our study required it for all cases before or after CJRA.

CJRA technique 5 requires party representatives with authority to bind to be present or available by telephone at settlement conferences. Eight of the 20 districts used this technique before CJRA, and five additional districts adopted it as part of their CJRA plan.

DISCOVERY MANAGEMENT

The requirement that lawyers certify good-faith efforts to resolve discovery disputes before filing motions has undergone little or no change. All but one district had pre-CJRA local rules covering this area, and these have either been continued or strengthened.

All districts permit the use of judicial discretion to limit the extent of discovery case by case. Before CJRA, most pilot and comparison districts also had a local rule that placed a prespecified limit on the number of interrogatories and requests for admission, but none had a prespecified limit on the number of depositions and only one placed a limit on the time per deposition.

After adoption of the CJRA plans, local rules with respect to control of discovery volume did not change in most districts. One pilot and one comparison district adopted a new limit on deposition length, and two comparison districts adopted new limits on the number of depositions. Although the CJRA did not result in much explicit local rule change in this area, the December 1993 revisions to F.R.Civ.P. 30, 31, and 33 limit the volume of discovery, absent leave of the court or stipulation of the parties, to ten depositions per side and 25 interrogatories per party (including subparts).

All districts allowed the establishment of discovery cutoff dates before the CJRA, but most left the decision to the judge in each case. The districts' CJRA plans have not changed the landscape much, except in two pilot districts and one comparison district that established prespecified limits for certain types of cases.

With respect to early disclosure without formal discovery, we note substantial changes in local rules, since only one comparison district required this for all general civil cases before CJRA. After the CJRA, the disclosure procedures changed greatly, and all pilot and comparison districts have adopted one of five different disclosure procedure models. All of these approaches meet the statutory requirements of the CJRA pilot program. Our interviews and our analysis of dockets from a random sample of over 7,000 cases show that predictions of greatly increased ancillary litigation and motions practice have not come to pass.

Four pilot districts later switched from their initial disclosure procedure to follow the December 1993 revised F.R.Civ.P. 26(a)(1), and six comparison districts are following the revised Rule 26(a)(1), which requires the mandatory exchange of information relevant to disputed facts alleged with particularity in the pleadings, plus information on damages and insurance. The ten other pilot and comparison districts have decided to opt out and are not following the revised Rule 26(a)(1).

ALTERNATIVE DISPUTE RESOLUTION

The three pilot and comparison districts that used mandatory arbitration before CJRA have continued to do so, and two of the three pilot and comparison districts authorized to use voluntary arbitration have started doing so. However, there has been a marked trend in half of the pilot districts toward addition of other formally structured ADR programs—especially mandatory or voluntary mediation and early neutral evaluation.

Voluntary ADR that requires lawyer/party approval for participation has not attracted extensive usage when compared with mandatory ADR, probably due in part to some lawyers' unfamiliarity with ADR and in part to some lawyers' feeling that agreement to an ADR process might be viewed as a "sign of weakness" in their cases. Neither lawyers nor judges have used ADR extensively when its use is voluntary. Not all district courts feel that they can or should order unwilling parties to ADR because ADR costs the parties money. Even if the ADR provider works for free, the parties must still spend their own time and pay their own lawyers to prepare for and participate in the ADR. Nevertheless, advocates hope that ADR can reduce litigation costs by inducing early settlements or, at least, by leading to more focused (and thus more cost efficient) discovery.

All of these 20 pilot and comparison districts permit the use of ADR techniques in their CJRA plans. However, as the districts have implemented their plans, two very different groups of programs have emerged. About half the districts (six pilot and five comparison) have formally structured programs. The other half have unstructured programs that permit some sort of ADR but do not generate much ADR activity. Both groups appear to meet the loosely defined requirements of the CJRA.

Some districts with structured programs have only 2 to 4 percent of their cases referred to ADR, so structure appears to be a necessary but not sufficient feature for a volume ADR program. However, districts that permit ADR of some kind without a formally structured program have attracted few cases.

The volume of an ADR program depends greatly on the details of how it is designed and implemented. Programs that permit ADR, but are not structured or administratively supported, generate low volume and have low costs and few effects. Where participation is voluntary rather than mandatory, even structured programs generate a relatively low volume of ADR. In terms of applying ADR research results to help determine future ADR policy, this means one must get beyond generic labels like "arbitration" and "neutral evaluation" and into the principal design features of the programs (e.g., whether they are voluntary or mandatory, early or later in the case, with paid or pro bono ADR providers, primarily evaluative or facilitative, and whether they are administratively supported or not).

CONCLUSIONS

All pilot districts adopted a plan by the act's December 31, 1991, deadline. Eight of the ten comparison districts adopted their plans near the December 1, 1993, deadline; two adopted their plans at the same time as the pilot districts. The district plans usually accepted the major case management recommendations of the CJRA advisory groups, although sometimes with modification. Over three-quarters of the major recommendations of the pilot and comparison advisory groups were adopted into the courts' CJRA plans.

All pilot districts complied with the statutory language in the act, which provides loosely defined principles but leaves operational interpretation of them to the discretion of individual districts and judicial officers. Many pilot and comparison districts interpreted some or all of their current and past practices to be consistent with the language of the act and continued those practices unchanged. However, if the spirit of the act is interpreted to mean experimentation and change focusing on the six CJRA principles, then the pilot districts met that spirit to varying degrees. Comparison districts, which were required to consider but were not required to adopt the six CJRA principles in their plans, generally made fewer changes than pilot districts.

Even in pilot districts whose plans suggested major changes, implementation often fell short. For example, six of the ten pilot districts adopted a plan with a track model of differential case management, but only one assigned the majority of its general civil cases to tracks and had more than 2 percent of the cases in both the standard and the complex tracks; in the other districts with track models, the assignments of cases to tracks were either not often made or were almost universally made to the standard track. For another example, all ten of the pilot districts adopted a plan with provision for alternative dispute resolution, but four referred less than 2 percent of their cases to ADR.

Thus, in practice there was much less change in case management after CJRA than one might have expected from reading the plans. This is evident both from observations at the district court level of how the major elements of the plans were implemented and from surveys of the judges in the 1992–1993 sample of 5,000+ cases. In 85 percent of the cases surveyed after CJRA, for example, the pilot district judges said that the surveyed case was managed no differently than it would have been before CJRA.[1]

Some possible reasons why the CJRA pilot program did not result in more change are discussed in our companion evaluation report.[2] We believe that the probability of effective implementation of change could be increased by taking into account factors that appeared to impede implementation of the CJRA in some districts. These include the vague wording of the act itself, the fact that some judges, lawyers, and others viewed the procedural innovations imposed by Congress as unduly emphasizing speed and efficiency, the fact that some judges viewed the procedural innovations of the CJRA as curtailing the judicial independence accorded their office under Article III of the Constitution, and the lack of effective mechanisms for ensuring that the policies contained in district plans were carried out on an ongoing basis.

Change is not something "done" to members of an organization; rather, it is something they participate in, experience, and shape. Studies of change in the courts and in other organizations provide some guidelines for involving participants in defining, managing, and evaluating innovations. Such guidelines, which are discussed in our

---

[1] Our sample was drawn well before eight of the comparison districts implemented their plans, and the comparable percentage for comparison districts was 92 percent "no difference."

[2] See Chapter Three in Kakalik et al. (1996a).

companion evaluation report, could substantially enhance efforts to change the federal civil justice system.

Districts and judges vary widely in how they approach case management. Some have been relatively aggressive, and others have continued low-key approaches. For example, one district uses differential management tracks, uses early judicial management on all general civil cases, mandates early disclosure of information bearing significantly on both sides of the case, and assigns a substantial number of cases to mandatory ADR programs. This profile contrasts sharply with a district that uses individualized case management, permits voluntary early disclosure, and allows but does not require ADR.

These large differences between districts and judges in case management policies provide the opportunity to evaluate very different policies, even though the districts and judges that use them did not change substantially as a result of CJRA.

Overall, implicit policy changes may be as important as explicit ones. Many judges and lawyers have commented in interviews that the process of implementing the pilot plans has raised the consciousness of judges and lawyers and has brought about some important shifts in attitude and approach to case management on the part of the bench and bar. For example, our interviews suggested, and the case-level data we collected also indicated, that there has been an increase in the fraction of cases managed early and a shortening of discovery cutoff time.[3]

Several of the CJRA advisory group assessments noted factors beyond the courts' direct control that influence civil litigation cost and delay. Three factors predominated: First they cited the pressure generated by the criminal docket. Legislation creating new federal crimes, adoption of the Speedy Trial act, and the advent of mandatory sentencing guidelines all were said to increase the burden on the federal court and provide less time for the orderly movement of civil cases. Second, they cited the fact that judicial vacancies were being left unfilled for substantial periods of time. And third, the need for better assessment of the effect of proposed legislation on the courts' workload was cited.

Ultimately, of course, the questions of greatest significance are whether the case management procedures make any difference to the factors of most interest to the CJRA—cost, time to disposition, satisfaction with the process, and views on fairness of the process. Our analyses and findings on these questions are contained in our comparison evaluation and ADR reports.

---

[3]There are some technical problems with comparing empirical data from a filing sample and a termination sample, but the consistency of the interview information with the empirical information is encouraging. For a discussion of the statistical issue, see Kakalik (1996a), Appendix D.

OVERVIEW OF CJRA PROGRAM IN THE DISTRICT OF ARIZONA

OVERVIEW OF IMPLEMENTED CJRA PLAN

This is a comparison district, not a pilot district, so a CJRA plan must be implemented by December 1, 1993, and it need not contain the six pilot program principles. This district's plan was effective December 1, 1993.

The CJRA advisory group's report[1] did not recommend a "global assault" now on the problems of litigation in the district, since experiments are already being conducted in Arizona state court on discovery reforms and ADR. The group felt that the results of the state court programs should be assessed before global new procedures in those areas are established in federal court. Furthermore, demands of the criminal docket will likely consume all available resources and vitiate any benefits from civil justice reform, if they are left unchecked. Therefore, the demand of the criminal process must be curbed.

In the civil area, the advisory group proposed that judges become more involved at an earlier stage and made several recommendations for improving pretrial case processing: adopting a calendaring system that would allow for dedicated judge time for civil case trials; implementing a differentiated case management system with tracks and early setting of trial dates; considering automatic disclosure as a part of the discovery plan in appropriate individual cases; making greater use of magistrate judges; adopting a court-annexed Alternative Dispute Resolution program, and adopting written rules of civility and conduct.

The CJRA plan[2] indicates that the court can make contributions to reducing cost and delay by implementing differentiated case management with tracks, and early ongoing judicial control of the pretrial process with firm schedules and Rule 16 case management conferences before a judicial officer for standard and complex track cases. The December 1993 amendments to Federal Rule of Civil Procedure 26(a)(1) con-

---

[1] Segal et al. (1993) (hereinafter referred to as the advisory group report). The 20-member committee conducted interviews with all the district judges and magistrate judges, the Clerk of Court, courtroom deputies, and law clerks; reviewed plans from other districts; and reviewed relevant statistics. The Clerk of Court was a member of the advisory group. The group did not survey lawyers and litigants.

[2] United States District Court for the District of Arizona, *Civil Justice Expense and Delay Reduction Plan* (undated) (hereinafter referred to as the plan). Effective date of the plan was December 1, 1993.

cerning mandatory initial disclosure have been adopted in this district. The court is continuing its voluntary court-annexed arbitration program, and is evaluating other ADR mechanisms for possible implementation when available resources make it practical to do so. Full implementation of all provisions of the plan had not taken place as of late 1994. However, the court has not abandoned any of the provisions. The full-time staff position for DCM, ADR, and CJRA reporting was initially filled but was subsequently vacant because that person transferred to other duties.

The plan indicated that the growing federalization of crimes has had and will increasingly have an adverse effect on the civil docket; and that mandated criminal procedural requirements, including the Speedy Trial Act, the Sentencing Guidelines, and mandatory minimum sentences, are sources of civil delay. The plan stressed that proposed legislation should be carefully assessed for its potential impact on the Judiciary.

The CJRA annual report[3] indicates that model scheduling orders have been developed for each differential case management track, with the scheduling orders for expedited track cases generated at case opening by the clerk's office and for other tracks generated later by a judicial officer. Because of increases in the number of prisoner pro se cases, the district's efforts have been committed to those new cases rather than developing additional ADR programs. This change in priorities necessitated by the change in filings has delayed the plan's implementation schedule. Finally, the district is experimenting in one division with referring 25 percent of all civil cases to a magistrate judge to conduct pretrial proceedings.

CJRA POLICY 1: DIFFERENTIAL CASE MANAGEMENT

Policy Before CJRA Plan

No formal program of differential case management existed prior to CJRA. Differential management was determined on a discretionary basis by individual judges.

CJRA Plan Implementation

Approved Plan: The plan includes the following provisions.

1. Implementing a program of Differentiated Case Management (DCM) wherein the following five different tracks of cases will have distinct milestones, firm dates, discovery limits, and individualized types of case management techniques and hearings:

   a) *Expedited.* This track will usually be resolved on pleadings. Assignment to the track is based upon the nature of suit of the case. The track would include bankruptcy appeals, Social Security, student loan, veteran's benefits, other recovery, forfeiture and penalty, and other cases determined by the

---

[3]United States District Court for the District of Arizona (1995).

parties at filing or the judge at a preliminary scheduling conference. Disposition should be expected within 12 months of filing.

b) *Arbitration.* Cases would be assigned by the Clerk (Expedited cases are excluded). If a case is removed from arbitration, it will be reassigned to its other appropriate track. The advisory group report indicated that these cases comprise 1 percent of the civil docket (which is fewer than 50 cases), but should account for 5 percent when the program matures.

c) *Prisoner Pro Se.* Assignment will be based upon nature of suit, and would include general habeas corpus, motions to vacate sentence, mandamus petitions, §1983 petitions, and Bivens actions. Disposition is expected within 18 months of filing.

d) *Complex.* Designated by the judge, counsel, and parties. This track would include those cases requiring innovative and extensive management techniques.

e) *Standard.* This track consists of all cases not fitting the above criteria. Disposition is expected within 24 months of filing. In 1992, cases that would be either standard or complex under the new DCM tracks constituted about 50 percent of the civil docket.

2. Established a full-time Administrator for the DCM and ADR programs. This person would be responsible for administration of all case management activities (including enforcement, problem resolution, training, information, and refinement of the program). The Administrator would oversee compliance with defined case management requirements for Complex and Standard track cases.

3. The Expedited, Prisoner Pro Se, and Arbitration tracks are considered to be primarily administrative in nature, and central management by the Clerk's office is expected.

Differences Between Plan and Advisory Group Recommendations: There were some differences in the composition of the case types in the tracks. The plan went into greater detail about the assignment to tracks, but the plan and the advisory group report exhibit general concurrence about the need for and value of DCM.

Differences Between Plan and Implementation: The CJRA annual report indicates that model scheduling orders have been developed for each differential case management track, with the scheduling orders for expedited track cases generated at case opening by the Clerk's office and for other tracks generated later by a judicial officer. The volume of filings by track during 1994 was reported to be 175 expedited, 1604 prisoner pro se, 1882 standard, and 27 complex habeas corpus death penalty cases.[4]

---

[4]In addition to the death penalty cases, some unreported number of additional cases were also designated as complex.

CJRA POLICY 2: EARLY AND ONGOING CONTROL OF PRETRIAL BY JUDICIAL OFFICER

Policy Before CJRA Plan

The District has completed a pending civil case reduction program to reduce the number of pending civil cases. The program activated case management in cases that required additional attention and verified or corrected scheduling information in all cases. This reduced the number of pending cases, and led to the development of internal monitoring of performance against track disposition goals. It also improved internal case management/inventory reports, and clarified the responsibilities of case managers in the Clerk's office. A Local Rule governed pretrial, and according to the advisory group many of the judges use their law clerks for the creation of the initial schedule order and for the handling of the preliminary case management devices.

CJRA Plan Implementation

Approved Plan: The plan calls for:

1. Establishing distinct milestones, firm dates, discovery limits, and individualized types of case management techniques and hearings based upon a case's track designation.

2. Standard scheduling orders for all cases. These include pretrial order requirements.

3. No preliminary scheduling conference for Expedited cases.

4. Management of Arbitration cases pursuant to 28 U.S.C. § 651 et seq. and Local Rule.

5. The following specialized deadlines for Prisoner Pro Se cases that involve §1983 and Bivens actions:

   a) Maximum date to effect service is 60 days from filing of the service order or pursuant to F.R.Civ.P., whichever is later.

   b) Discovery cutoff is 150 days from maximum service date.

   c) Deadline for dispositive motions or proposed pretrial orders is 180 days from maximum service date.

6. Requiring the submission of a joint proposed scheduling order in Standard and Complex cases, and a subsequent scheduling conference before the judicial officer or his/her designee.

7. Holding the preliminary scheduling conference in standard cases within 180 days of filing. The Rule 16(b)(4) scheduling order issued from the conference would include dates for filing a joint proposed pretrial order and for conducting a pretrial conference.

8. In Standard cases, the trial date would be set at the pretrial conference (not at the pretrial scheduling conference). If the assigned judge is unable to try the case on the scheduled date, the case will be referred to the Chief Judge for reassignment to any available judge.

9. Complex cases would also have a Rule 16(b)(4) scheduling order issued at the preliminary scheduling conference. Attorneys should notify the Clerk and the judge if the matter involves multi-district litigation.

10. Provision is made for discovery and case management conferences for Standard and Complex cases.

11. Deadlines established by the court's scheduling order will be enforced.

12. Ensuring firm trial dates by providing for the use of Senior Judges to conduct trials.

13. Joint discovery/case management plans may be required at the discretion of the judge.

14. Repeal of Local Rule 42(c)[5] since pretrial conferences and orders can and should be achieved under Rule 16, as amended.

15. Judge may order at the scheduling conference, or at some later point, compliance with a pretrial order that includes some components of former Local Rule 42(c).

16. Discovery Limits:

    a)   Expedited Track: Presumptive limits include 15 single part interrogatories and one fact witness deposition per party.

    b)   Standard: Presumptive limits include 40 single part interrogatories and eight fact witness depositions per party.

17. Motion Practice:

    a)   Oral argument only by permission of the court.

    b)   Presumption of no oral argument on non-dispositive motions.

    c)   Motions or stipulations for extensions of time are required to reflect the number of previous requests.

Differences Between Plan and Advisory Group Recommendations: Some of the advisory group's recommendations regarding the setting of a trial date early in the litigation, and the use of some management devices pertaining to trial, were not adopted. Otherwise, the differences were minor.

Differences Between Plan and Implementation: None indicated.

---

[5]Local Rules were amended, reorganized and renumbered after adoption of the CJRA plan. The Local Rule numbers referred to in the description of the plan were those in effect at the time the plan was written.

CJRA POLICY 3: MORE INTENSIVE MANAGEMENT OF COMPLEX CASES

Policy Before CJRA Plan

Complex cases were managed on a discretionary basis, with judges determining the procedures to be followed on a case-by-case basis.

CJRA Plan Implementation

Approved Plan: Regarding Complex cases, the plan called for:

1. Discovery and case management conferences.
2. Submission of a joint proposed scheduling order and a subsequent scheduling conference.
3. A Rule 16(b)(4) scheduling order issued at the preliminary scheduling conference.
4. Notification to the Clerk and the judge by attorney if the matter involves multi-district litigation.
5. Repealing Local Rule 36 relating to complex civil cases.

Differences Between Plan and Advisory Group Recommendations: None.

Differences Between Plan and Implementation: None indicated.

CJRA POLICY 4: EXCHANGE OF DISCOVERY INFORMATION

Policy Before CJRA Plan

Pre-discovery disclosure of information was previously governed by Local Rule 42.A, which required attorneys in non-exempt types of cases to meet early in the case to discuss their respective contentions of material facts and applicable rules of law, to display exhibits tentatively intended to be offered into evidence at trial, and to exchange a list of witnesses together with a brief summary of their proposed testimony. Exempt cases were similar to those now in the expedited and prisoner pro se tracks.

CJRA Plan Implementation

Approved Plan: The court elected to defer discovery changes until there is more experience with the State's new discovery rules (similar to the then proposed December 1993 revised Federal rules) and until Congress has acted on the proposed changes to the Federal rules of civil procedure. Local Rule 42.A was repealed in its entirety. Therefore, until adoption of a mandatory Federal Rules of Civil Procedure policy, the plan indicates that the court will evaluate the need for voluntary disclosure case by case. After the plan was adopted, the court subsequently decided to follow the December 1993 revised F.R. Civ. P. 26.

Differences Between Plan and Advisory Group Recommendations: None.

Differences Between Plan and Implementation: The December 1993 amendments to Federal Rule of Civil Procedure 26(a)(1) concerning mandatory initial disclosure are in effect in this district.[6]

CJRA POLICY 5:   CERTIFY GOOD FAITH EFFORT BEFORE FILING DISCOVERY MOTION

Policy Before CJRA Plan

Local Rule prohibited consideration of, or decision upon, any discovery motion, unless the movant certifies that after personal consultation and sincere efforts to do so, the matter has not been satisfactorily resolved.

CJRA Plan Implementation

Approved Plan: No change to prior policy.

Differences Between Plan and Advisory Group Recommendations: None.

Differences Between Plan and Implementation: None reported.

CJRA POLICY 6: ALTERNATIVE DISPUTE RESOLUTION PROGRAMS

Policy Before CJRA Plan

The district reports having a voluntary court-annexed arbitration program since February 1, 1992. Local Rule provides for the voluntary, non-binding arbitration of civil cases if the relief sought consists only of money damages not in excess of $100,000. Several types of civil cases are exempted. Within 21 days after the case is at issue, the Clerk sends a Notice of Referral to all parties. At any time prior to the expiration of a 21-day period after the Notice, any party may file a Notice of Withdrawal from Arbitration, advising that the case is removed from arbitration. The advisory group report indicated that arbitration cases comprise about 1 percent of the civil docket, but should account for 5 percent when the program matures. The court's 1993 annual report indicated arbitrators were assigned for 48 cases, and 28 arbitration hearings were held.[7] In addition, settlement conferences are frequently conducted at the discretion of the judicial officer.

CJRA Plan Implementation

Approved Plan: The main elements of the court's plan are as follows:

1. ADR mechanisms are endorsed, and the voluntary arbitration program is continued. The Clerk of Court indicated that the volume of cases in voluntary

---

[6]Stienstra (1995).

[7]United States District Court for the District of Arizona *1993 Annual Report* (undated), p. 14.

arbitration in 1994 was 4 percent of civil filings.[8] In 1994, 271 cases were sent notices of referral to arbitration, of which 183 opted out and 71 had arbitrators appointed.

2. A staff position is established for the administration of ADR programs and DCM. The person would be responsible for research, development, and subsequent implementation of the ADR programs when available resources make it practical to do so.

3. Future consideration of a program of mediation (particularly suited for contract dispute cases), with the completion of research and development set for January 1994 and implementation targeted for July 1994.

4. Other mechanisms, including Early Neutral Evaluation, will be evaluated with the completion of research and development set for January 1995 and implementation targeted for July 1995.

5. The court will continue to use settlement conferences.

Differences Between Plan and Advisory Group Recommendations: The advisory group also mentioned summary jury trials and mini-trials as possible ADR mechanisms. It also proposed Local Rules that would allow the court to refer a case to ADR with agreement of the parties, require attorneys to discuss ADR with their clients, and require the Clerk to give each party in a case an ADR brochure.

Differences Between Plan and Implementation: The CJRA annual report indicates that because of increases in the number of prisoner pro se cases, the district's efforts have been committed to those new cases rather than to developing additional ADR programs. This change in priorities necessitated by the change in filings has delayed the plan's ADR implementation schedule.

OPTIONAL CJRA TECHNIQUES

The CJRA indicates that each court shall consider and may include the following five litigation management techniques:[9]

I.   **Requiring that counsel jointly present a discovery/case management plan at the initial pretrial conference:**

The plan indicated that such plans may be required at the discretion of the judge but did not set a time frame for presentation. A joint proposed scheduling order is required in Standard and Complex cases. The court subsequently decided to follow the December 1993 revised F.R.Civ.P. 26.

II.   **Requiring that each party be represented at each pretrial conference by an attorney with authority to bind that party:**

---

[8]Letter from Richard H. Weare to RAND, April 25, 1995.

[9]28 U.S.C. § 473(b).

The court approved and adopted this technique.

III.   **Requiring the signature of the attorney *and* the party for all requests for discovery extensions or postponements of trial:**

The court did not approve this technique but did indicate that amendments to Local Rules 11 and 39 mandate that a request for an extension of any deadline must indicate how many motions or stipulations for extension have been filed previously.

IV.   **Offering a Neutral Evaluation program:**

This technique is included in principle within the ADR implementation plan. Such a program will be studied and implementation may take place by July 1995 if the court so decides.

V.   **Requiring the attendance of party representatives with authority to bind to be present or available by telephone at settlement conferences:**

This would be used only when required by the court. At the discretion of the judge, parties would be allowed to appear telephonically.

OTHER POLICIES ADOPTED IN CJRA PLAN

Approved Plan:

1. Sequestration of judge time for civil litigation: The rotation of judges to concentrate on civil cases will be given consideration consistent with other docket demands. Load differences between the two divisions (Phoenix and Tucson locations) make a formalized program infeasible. Members of the court agree to try to informally implement the technique.

2. Adopts 7th Circ. Proposed Standards of Professional Conduct.

Differences Between Plan and Advisory Group Recommendations:

1. Sequestration of judge time for civil litigation: The advisory group had called for formal implementation of a program that would allow each judge to devote some time each year to civil trials.

2. Magistrate judges: The advisory group recommended seeking additional magistrate judges, and expanding their use in the preliminary administration of the pretrial management systems as well as ADR.

Differences Between Plan and Implementation: The CJRA annual report indicates that the district is experimenting in one division with referring 25 percent of all civil cases to magistrate judge to conduct pretrial proceedings.

OVERVIEW OF CJRA PROGRAM IN CALIFORNIA, CENTRAL DISTRICT

OVERVIEW OF IMPLEMENTED CJRA PLAN

This is a comparison district, not a pilot district, so a CJRA plan must be implemented by December 1, 1993, and it need not contain the six pilot program principles. This district's plan was adopted December 1, 1993.

The CJRA advisory group's report[1] indicated that the single most significant cause of delay and expense is the failure to fill judicial vacancies in a timely fashion. Resources are perceived as insufficient to process the ever-increasing criminal docket and still maintain the desired quality of justice in civil disputes. Congress should cooperate in filling vacancies promptly, and should assess the potential impact of any proposed legislation on the judicial system. Disposition times were on the whole satisfactory, but it was noted that increases in the pending civil caseload may herald future problems. In addition, it was asserted that since most judges in the district superimpose their own procedures on the Local Rules, significant and problematic inter-judge variation exists. This is seen as complicating federal practice for the bar, and probably increasing costs.

The advisory group recommended that the court should be divided into Civil and Criminal divisions, and that civil cases should be managed with a three-tier tracking system for pretrial purposes ("Simple," "Standard," and "Complex") with different procedures and discovery controls in the different tracks. Early firm trial dates were recommended, as well as an increased number of status conferences. It recommended the use of Early Neutral Evaluation for Standard cases, special masters for Complex cases, and mandatory settlement conferences before a judicial officer. Other types of ADR would also be encouraged but would not be mandatory. The group endorsed the Los Angeles County Bar Association guidelines for the conduct of litigation, and would have discovery disputes in Simple and Standard cases handled by magistrate judges, and in Complex cases by a special master.

---

[1]Smaltz et al. (1993) (hereinafter referred to as the advisory group report). The 25-member advisory group (mostly attorneys plus the Clerk of Court, one judge as an ex-officio member, and a reporter) examined the condition of the docket and sent out questionnaires to the district's judicial officers, practitioners, bar organizations, and to the lawyers and litigants in a group of 300 terminated cases.

The CJRA plan[2] adopted by the court agreed with the advisory group's observation that the district's efficiency in disposing civil cases compares favorably with other courts. However, it also concurred that the district is losing ground. The plan also cited a noticeable decline in civility and professionalism among lawyers practicing before the court. The court indicated that adoption of a civil justice plan will not fix certain problems because their causes are beyond the court's control. Such causes include: the persistent federalization of crimes by Congress; the mandatory minimum sentences and the sentencing guidelines; the resultant tendency to prosecute dual-jurisdiction crimes in the federal courts; Congressional failure to match increases in federal investigative and prosecutorial resources with proportional increases in federal judicial resources; and delay in filling judicial vacancies.

The plan indicated that the district already utilized many of the CJRA principles and operated according to many of the recommendations of the advisory group. Where this is the case, no change is needed. For example, the district already required the early exchange of certain information between the parties without a formal discovery request. The court declined to adopt many of the advisory group recommendations that were not already in place because it felt that the areas they address are best left to judicial discretion. Then, when necessary for an individual case, a judge can utilize such techniques as differential case management, limitations on discovery, referral of discovery motions to a magistrate judge, and special masters. But the judge is not obliged to use such approaches in cases for which they are inappropriate. The plan affirmed that it is already the policy of the court to make every reasonable effort to maintain firm civil trial dates and to encourage disposition of civil litigation by settlement when in the best interest of the parties. The court rejected splitting into criminal and civil divisions, rejected civil case management tracks, and rejected widespread use of early neutral evaluation (except as one option for meeting the court's new mandatory settlement conference requirement). Various other types of ADR are optional, but without a formal structured program. Several revisions were made in pretrial case processing rules and procedures. Judges are to refrain from adopting their own rules when these are inconsistent with the Local Rules or with F.R.Civ.P., and the court adopted the Ninth Circuit's *Civility and Professionalism Guidelines*.

As of January 1996, a CJRA Annual Report had not been issued by either the Court or the Advisory Group.

CJRA POLICY 1: DIFFERENTIAL CASE MANAGEMENT

Policy Before CJRA Plan

Local Rules did not directly call for differentiated case management in most types of cases. However, Local Rule 26 described procedures in habeas corpus petitions, and

---

[2]United States District Court for the Central District of California (1993) (hereinafter referred to as the plan).

various General Orders assigned certain types of cases to magistrate judges. Cases were managed on an individualized basis by judicial officers.

CJRA Plan Implementation

Approved Plan: The plan calls for:

1. Rejecting the concept of formalized differential case management tracks, as management is better left to the discretion of individual judges on a case-by-case basis.

2. In complex cases, seeking the assistance of the Chief Judge or a designated committee whenever a firm trial date cannot be maintained due to a conflict with a complex criminal case (see discussion below on **CJRA Policy 3**).

Differences Between the Plan and the Advisory Group Recommendations: The advisory group urged adoption of a three-tier tracking system for pretrial purposes ("Simple," "Standard," and "Complex"). The track would have defined the amount of discovery and procedures for handling it, set the number and scope of required personal appearances, established outer limits for trial dates, and determined which person would handle pretrial matters.

Differences Between Plan and Implementation: None reported.

CJRA POLICY 2: EARLY AND ONGOING CONTROL OF PRETRIAL BY JUDICIAL OFFICER

Policy Before CJRA Plan

No specific requirement existed for a case management plan or for a case management conference before a judicial officer. Local Rules did allow or require a number of CJRA-like features. Local Rule 6.1 required an "Early Meeting of Counsel" with the exchange of preliminary schedules of discovery. Local Rule 6.2 required a report to the court regarding that meeting. Local Rule 6.4 set out provisions for a status conference following the report. And Local Rule 9 set out the structure of pretrial conferences. Stipulations were recognized as binding only when made in open court, on the record at a deposition, or when formally filed. Written stipulations affecting the progress of the case were filed with the court but were not effective until approved by the judge. Telephonic conferences were not used. There was no requirement that a trial date be set within a specific period of time. The only limit on discovery, other than what judges might impose on a discretionary basis, was set out in Local Rule 8.2.1, which limits interrogatories to 30 except for good cause.

CJRA Plan Implementation

Approved Plan: The plan calls for the following:

1. Make every reasonable effort to maintain firm trial dates. In complex cases, judges are urged to seek the assistance of the Chief Judge or a designated committee of the court whenever a firm trial date cannot be maintained due to a conflict with a complex criminal case (see discussion on **CJRA Policy 3**).

2. Eliminate the requirement that the court approve certain stipulations. For example, Local Rule 3.11 no longer requires judge approval for written stipulations to a 30 day maximum extension for response to the *initial* complaint, or to extensions relating to discovery requests or depositions (provided that the extended date is not later than the discovery cutoff date or 30 days prior to date set for the Local Rule 9 pretrial).

3. Set no mandatory limits on discovery (other than the current limitation of 30 interrogatories by Local Rule 8.2.1).

4. No mandatory referral of discovery motions and disputes to magistrate judges.

5. Adopt Local Rule 27A to protect litigants from vexatious litigation. After opportunity to be heard, and based on a finding that the litigant has abused the court's process and would likely continue to do so, the court can require:

    i) A party to put up security to secure possible payment of costs, sanctions, and other awards against a vexatious litigant.

    ii) The Clerk not to accept further filings from a party without the party's paying normal filing fees and/or having a written authorization from a judicial officer.

6. Judges are urged to refrain from adopting idiosyncratic rules that are inconsistent with the Local Rules or with F.R.Civ.P.

Differences Between Plan and Advisory Group Recommendations: The advisory group made detailed recommendations concerning discovery, the number of required personal appearances, early and firm trial dates, and track-specific pretrial procedures. It would have made regular status conferences mandatory in all cases, and also would have eliminated mandatory personal appearances in Simple and Standard track cases in favor of allowing telephonic conferences. It would have created procedures for raising deposition disputes with a judicial officer during the course of the deposition, would have had discovery disputes initially handled by a magistrate judge in Simple and Standard cases and by the Special Master in Complex cases, and would have endorsed restrictions on F.R.Civ.P. provisions allowing the broadest sort of discovery. It would have required discussion of possible bifurcation or separate trial of specific dispositive issues in pretrial statements, would have required a cover sheet for all civil filings that set out the authority for the private right of action, the basis of plaintiff's standing, statute of limitation issues, and certain other information.

Differences Between Plan and Implementation: None reported.

CJRA POLICY 3: MORE INTENSIVE MANAGEMENT OF COMPLEX CASES

Policy Before CJRA Plan

The district's policy with respect to complex cases was discretionary management by judges. The judge of record would tailor the amount of management provided in any individual case to that judge's perception of the needs of the case. Thus, there was considerable inter-judge variation with respect to this issue because some judges in this court believe in intensive management and some do not.

CJRA Plan Implementation

Approved Plan: The plan called for the following provisions to be established:

1. Whenever a judge believes the goal of a firm trial date for complex civil cases will not be met because of a conflict with a complex criminal case, the judge can call upon the Chief Judge (or a designated committee) for assistance. The techniques to be employed include seeking the assistance of other judges, senior judges, or visiting judges to try the civil or the conflicting criminal case.

2. The use of Special Masters in complex cases will not be mandatory, but is allowed.

Differences Between Plan and Advisory Group Recommendations: The advisory group treated complex cases as a separate track, set out guidelines for determining whether a case is complex, and recommended special pretrial procedures, among which was the referral of all pretrial matters to a Special Master.

Differences Between Plan and ImplementationL None reported.

CJRA POLICY 4: EXCHANGE OF DISCOVERY INFORMATION

Policy Before CJRA Plan

Local Rules 6.1.1–6.1.4 call for mandatory exchange of certain documents and other evidence at the "Early Meeting of Counsel." That exchange is to include all documents then reasonably available to a party which are contemplated to be used in "support of the allegations of the pleading filed by the party," and a list of witnesses known to have knowledge of the facts "supporting the material allegations of the pleading filed by the party." Documents later shown to be reasonably available to a party and not exchanged may be subject to exclusion at the time of trial.

CJRA Plan Implementation

Approved Plan: No change to pre-CJRA policy.

Differences Between Plan and Advisory Group Recommendations: None.

Differences Between Plan and Implementation: None reported. Adoption of the December 1993 amendments to Federal Rule of Civil Procedure 26(a)(1) concerning mandatory initial disclosure was deferred in this district. However, 1995 proposed amendments to Local Rules 6 and 9 would put F.R.Civ.P 26(a)(1) into effect. [3]

CJRA POLICY 5: CERTIFY GOOD FAITH EFFORT BEFORE FILING DISCOVERY MOTION

Policy Before CJRA Plan

Consideration of discovery motions by the court would only take place if they were accompanied by a "meet and confer" stipulation concerning unresolved issues or a declaration of counsel of non-cooperation by the opposing party (Local Rule 7.15).

CJRA Plan Implementation

Approved Plan: No change to pre-CJRA policy.

Differences Between Plan and Advisory Group Recommendations: None.

Differences Between Plan and Implementation: None reported.

CJRA POLICY 6: ALTERNATIVE DISPUTE RESOLUTION PROGRAMS

Policy Before CJRA Plan

There was little use of ADR and no formal provision for doing so. Local Rules 6.1 and 6.1.5 required parties to meet to discuss settlement and other relevant issues. Local Rule 9.4.11 required parties to exhaust all possibilities of settlement prior to a Pretrial Conference. No other ADR provisions were set out in Local Rules.

CJRA Plan Implementation

Approved Plan: Mandatory Settlement Conferences are to be held in every civil case, unless excused or exempted by the court. However this provision does not preclude or replace any judicial officer's settlement practices.

New Local Rule 23 provides:

1. Relaxation of the Settlement Conference provision only when:

    a)   The case involves 28 U.S.C. §§ 2242, 2254, and 2255 type petitions.

    b)   The party is a pro se (only that party would be excluded).

    c)   Otherwise ordered by the court.

2. The judge can excuse counsel either on application of a party or sua sponte.

---

[3]Stienstra (1995).

3. Prior to 45 days before the final Local Rule 9 pretrial conference, the parties must participate in one of four approved settlement procedures, unless excused or exempted by the court.

4. The settlement procedure choices are:

a) *No. 1*: With the consent of all the parties and the court, the parties would appear before the assigned judge.

b) *No. 2*: With the consent of the court, the parties would appear before a judicial officer other than the assigned judge.

c) *No. 3*: The parties would appear before an attorney. If the parties are unable to agree on the attorney, the court will select one.

d) *No. 4*: The parties would appear before a retired judicial officer or other private or non-profit dispute resolution body for mediation-type settlement discussions.

5. The parties must jointly file a Notice of Settlement Procedure Selection 14 days before the date scheduled. The Notice shall include the name of the settlement officer and the type, date, time, and place of the procedure.

6. The parties must make timely selection of one of the approved settlement procedures or have the court choose one by default.

7. Each party shall submit, in camera, at least five days prior to the conference, a five page maximum letter setting forth settlement positions as well as past and anticipated offers and demands. The letter will not be filed and will be returned to the party.

8. Each party (or representative with full authority to settle) shall appear at the settlement conference (may be telephonically if outside the district).

9. The expected trial attorney for each party shall also be present (unless excused).

10. Each party shall make a thorough analysis of the case prior to the conference and be fully prepared to discuss all factors relevant to settlement.

11. Settlements are to be reported immediately to the courtroom clerk and promptly memorialized.

12. Proceedings will be confidential and statements are not admissible. There will be no reporting or recording without consent, except for recording of settlement.

Differences Between Plan and Advisory Group Recommendations: The advisory group had also recommended that the court encourage, but not require, ADR. It suggested an Early Neutral Evaluation program for "Standard" cases. It would also have had the Mandatory Settlement Conferences held by a judicial officer (no attorney or other non-court dispute resolution group would have been utilized).

Differences Between Plan and Implementation: None reported, but detailed information does not exist about implementation.

OPTIONAL CJRA TECHNIQUES

The CJRA indicates that each court shall consider and may include the following five litigation management techniques:[4]

I.   Requiring that counsel jointly present a discovery/case management plan at the initial pretrial conference:

The plan did not specially mention this technique but Local Rule 6.1 requires an "Early Meeting of Counsel" and Local Rule 6.2 requires a report to the court regarding that meeting. Local Rule 6.4.2 requires a Joint Status Report before any Status Conference that includes discovery schedules and cut-off dates, proposed pretrial and trial dates, and other management issues. Adoption of the December 1993 amendments to Federal Rule of Civil Procedure 26(f) was deferred in this district. However, 1995 proposed amendments to Local Rules 6 and 9 would put F.R.Civ.P. 26(f) into effect. [5]

II.   Requiring that each party be represented at each pretrial conference by an attorney with authority to bind that party:

There was no specific requirement mentioned.

III.   Requiring the signature of the attorney *and* the party for all requests for discovery extensions or postponements of trial:

There was no specific requirement mentioned.

IV.   Offering a Neutral Evaluation program:

Some aspects of Early Neutral Evaluation are incorporated, on a optional basis, into the plan's provisions for Mandatory Settlement Conferences (see discussion under **CJRA Policy 6**).

V.   Requiring the attendance of party representatives with authority to bind to be present or available by telephone at settlement conferences:

The requirement that party representatives with authority to bind to be present at settlement discussions is incorporated into the Mandatory Settlement Conference program (see discussion under **CJRA Policy 6**).

---

[4]28 U.S.C. § 473(b).

[5]Stienstra (1995).

OTHER POLICIES ADOPTED IN CJRA PLAN

Approved Plan:

1. Specifically rejected the concept of splitting the workload of the court into two separate civil and criminal divisions, "because a reallocation of the existing workload will not solve the problem."

2. Adopted Local Criminal Rule 13 which governs settlement conferences in complex criminal cases.

3. Adopted the Ninth Circuit's *Civility and Professionalism Guidelines.*

Differences Between Plan and Advisory Group Recommendations: The advisory group had recommended that the work of the court be split between criminal and civil divisions, and that a split calendar be used for law and motion matters so that all law and motion matters are not scheduled for the same time. Also the group's definition of what determines inappropriate conduct during depositions goes beyond rules described in the plan's *Civility and Professionalism Guidelines.* The group advocated that the court use the Los Angeles County Bar's version of litigation conduct guidelines. The group also wanted to establish procedures to ensure uniformity in Rule 11 applications.

Differences Between Plan and Implementation: None reported.

OVERVIEW OF PILOT PROGRAM IN CALIFORNIA, SOUTHERN DISTRICT

OVERVIEW OF IMPLEMENTED CJRA PLAN

The CJRA advisory group's report[1] found that the district had been plagued by underfunding, space problems, and judicial vacancies. An increase in median time to disposition had occurred in recent years due to increases in criminal filings, federalization of crimes, and judicial vacancies, and the ability of judges to hold civil trials was declining. There was clear need to expedite routine civil cases and to solve the difficulty of setting and keeping early trial dates and hearings for dispositive motions. There was also delay and abuse of discovery and pretrial by litigants. Case management recommendations included: making several changes in the criminal case area; setting prompt trial dates in certain types of civil cases with continuances only for good cause; authorizing magistrate judges to supervise pretrial discovery and management and to conduct Early Neutral Evaluation conferences and encourage settlement; having non-binding mini-trials, summary jury trials, or arbitration/mediation for certain types of cases; and making several refinements in pretrial procedures. Mandatory early exchange of information was not recommended, nor was a "track" system of differential case management.

The CJRA plan[2] repeated the advisory group's identification of the sources of cost and delay in the district (a growing criminal calendar, unfilled judicial vacancies, difficulty in setting and keeping early civil trial and motion dates, and civil litigants' abuse of the discovery process). The plan adopted by the court implemented the recommendations of the advisory group in principle, with relatively minor refinements.

The first annual report on the implementation of the CJRA plan[3] notes that the primary procedural changes made were the implementation of the Early Neutral Evaluation conference handled by a magistrate judge early in every civil case, and the

---

[1]Steiner et al. (1991) (hereinafter referred to as the advisory group report). The 24-person committee included lawyers in public and private practice, two former or current judicial officers, the Clerk of Court, and non-lawyers from the business community.

[2]United States District Court for the Southern District of California (1991) (hereinafter referred to as the plan).

[3]United States District Court for the Southern District of California (1994).

establishment of settlement conferences in criminal cases handled by district judges. The annual report notes many of the critical statistics have turned in the right direction or are stable, and that several provisions of the plan have not been fully implemented due to lack of full judicial staffing. The perceived success of the Early Neutral Evaluation approach has made the utilization of other ADR procedures authorized by the plan (e.g., summary trials, mini-trials, arbitration/mediation) less necessary. The consequence is that these other approaches are being used to a far lesser extent than the plan envisaged. In the arbitration/mediation area, for instance, only 13 cases were referred in 1992 and only 3 in 1993.

The second annual report of the implementation of the CJRA plan[4] indicates that the court has been successful in reducing the proportion of older civil cases on its docket, and in reducing the disposition time in criminal cases. It also shows a decline in the median civil case time to disposition, but indicates the workload of the judicial officers has been rising substantially. The Early Neutral Evaluation by Magistrate Judges continues to be a primary component of the CJRA program. The ENE is held about 2 months after answer, and the majority of lawyers surveyed felt this was about the right time. However, one-fourth of the respondents felt this was too soon, and suggested 90 days after answer would be better. Half the respondents felt that ENE reduced costs, most often discovery costs. The criminal settlement conference program was suspended, pending an appeal. Effective February 14, 1995, the program of mandatory referral of certain cases to non-binding mediation or arbitration was officially deleted and made voluntary (it had, in practice, never been fully implemented because of the preference given to the district's ENE program).

CJRA POLICY 1: DIFFERENTIAL CASE MANAGEMENT

Policy Before CJRA Plan

Judicial discretion was used to manage individual cases.

CJRA Plan Implementation

Approved Plan: The plan calls for:

1. Distinguishing certain types of cases for the purpose of setting early trial dates. Case type groups and their target dates are:

    a) *Social Security, judgment enforcement, prisoner petitions challenging conditions of confinement, and forfeiture and penalty cases*: Within 12 months of filing of complaint.

    b) *Federal Tort Claims Act*: Within 15 months of filing of FTCA complaint.

    c) *Twenty-five percent of all other cases not designated as "complex"*: Within 18 months of filing of complaint.

---

[4]United States District Court for the Southern District of California (1995).

2. Cases falling within the above categories would have the following: early trial dates firmly set; continuances granted only for good cause and the trial date extended only by written judicial order; magistrate judge trials encouraged; the resolution of cases tracked and monitored; and exemptions to the early trial date requirements allowed only if the case involves complex issues, new parties are added, or some other exceptional reason pertains.

3. Certain types of cases would undergo non-binding mini-trial, summary jury trial, or arbitration/mediation (see discussion below on **CJRA Policy 6**).

Differences Between Plan and Advisory Group Recommendations: The advisory group would have any changes in the promptly set trial date accommodate the calendar commitments of the lawyers. The plan makes no formal statement on this issue, although it clearly implies that judicial officers should permit such changes only under exceptional circumstances.

Differences Between Plan and Implementation: The plan in generally has been implemented as defined. However, because of the growth in the role of the magistrate judges with respect to Early Neutral Evaluation and resultant settlement efforts and case management during pretrial, there has not been a perceived need to fully utilize all of the detailed pretrial management and ADR provisions of the plan for all cases.

CJRA POLICY 2: EARLY AND ONGOING CONTROL OF PRETRIAL BY JUDICIAL OFFICER

Policy Before CJRA Plan

Local Rules required meetings between opposing counsel on pretrial matters. The number of interrogatories and requests for admission were limited to 25 each.

CJRA Plan Implementation

Approved Plan: The plan:

1. Sets a target early trial date in certain classes of cases (see the discussion of **CJRA Policy 1**).

2. Orders in such cases that:

   a) The early trial dates be firmly set.

   b) Continuances be granted only for good cause.

   c) Extensions of the trial date be made only by written judicial order.

   d) Magistrate judge trials be encouraged.

   e) The resolution of the cases be tracked and monitored.

    f) Exemptions to the early trial date requirements be granted only if the case involves complex issues, new parties are added, or some other exceptional reason pertains.

3. Orders the judicial officer managing pretrial discovery (usually the magistrate judge, but may be the district judge should s/he opt to manage pretrial discovery) to:

    a) Closely manage each case from the outset.

    b) Encourage settlement as early as possible.

    c) Supervise negotiations and motions to confirm settlements.

    d) Control the discovery process.

4. Establishes the following deadlines with respect to service:

    a) All complaints to be served within 120 days (extensions only for good cause).

    b) Ten days after either the 120 day period and/or any extensions, if proof of service has not been filed, the Clerk will prepare an order to show cause why the case should not be dismissed without prejudice for the assigned district judge to sign.

5. Establishes the following procedures for answers and motions to dismiss:

    a) Extensions of time shall be granted only by the judicial officer and then only upon a showing of good cause.

    b) Failure to file within the proper time period will result in the Clerk entering a default and serving notice to all parties. If the plaintiffs fail to thereafter move for default judgment within 30 days, the Clerk will prepare an order to dismiss without prejudice for the assigned district judge to sign.

    c) Allows displacement of summary judgment or other non-emergency motions in order to facilitate the hearing of a motion to dismiss within 60 days of its filing.

    d) Requires the Clerk to notify the assigned district judge when an answer has been filed.

6. Establishes the following procedures for Case Management Conferences:

    a) If no settlement is reached at the Early Neutral Evaluation conference (see discussion of **CJRA Policy 6**), the Case Management Conference would normally be set within 60 days thereafter (or 30 days thereafter if no arbitration/mediation is agreed upon or ordered or other ADR program is being contemplated). In practice, Case Management Conferences are usually held at the conclusion of the Early Neutral Evaluation conference rather than 30 to 60 days later.

    b) Conferences shall be attended by the parties who have responsibility over the litigation and the counsel who will try the case.

    c) Court may approve attendance of a party or counsel by conference call.

d) At a reasonable time before the conference:

    i)   Counsel will discuss discovery and endeavor to resolve disputes.

    ii)   Counsel will make a good faith, written specification of the essential details of their claims/their defenses and the identify of their principal witnesses. This is no longer mandatory (see "differences" section below).

    iii)   Counsel will provide the above written specifications to the judicial officer assigned to the case (judge or magistrate judge).

e) At the conference, counsel will discuss the written specifications in order to focus the issues.

f) At the conference, the judicial officer will:

    i)   Discuss the complexity of the case.

    ii)   Encourage a cooperative discovery schedule.

    iii)   Discuss the likelihood of further motions.

    iv)   Discuss the number of anticipated expert and other witnesses.

    v)   Evaluate the case and the need for early supervision of settlement discussions.

    vi)   Discuss the availability of ADR mechanisms.

    vii)   Discuss any other special factors applicable to the case.

g) A Case Management Order will be prepared by the judicial officer at the end of the conference that will:

    i)   Set out the issues in the case (judicial officer may direct the parties to prepare a stipulation of the issues). This is no longer mandatory (see "differences" section below).

    ii)   Include a discovery schedule.

    iii)   Set a date for:

        a) A further Case Management Conference if necessary.

        b) Identification of experts initially, in response, and in supplementation.

        c) The depositions of experts.

        d) A Mandatory Settlement Conference (unless determined that such a conference should be excused).

    iv)   Set a deadline for filing pretrial motions.

    v)   Set a firm pretrial conference date.

7. Additional settlement conferences may be ordered by the judicial officer (see discussion of **CJRA Policy 6**).

Differences Between Plan and Advisory Group Recommendations: The advisory group would have any changes in the promptly set trial date accommodate the calendar commitments of counsel. The plan makes no formal statement on this issue, although it clearly implies that judicial officers should permit such changes only under exceptional circumstances.

Differences Between Plan and Implementation: In practice, case management conferences are usually held at the conclusion of the Early Neutral Evaluation conference rather than 30 to 60 days later. General Order 394-C filed January 19, 1993 eliminated the mandatory requirement that counsel prepare and exchange statements of the claims, defenses, and witnesses. That same General Order eliminated the requirement that the Case Management Order contain a specification of the issues.[5]

CJRA POLICY 3: MORE INTENSIVE MANAGEMENT OF COMPLEX CASES

Policy Before CJRA Plan

Judicial Officers managed complex cases on a case-by-case basis.

CJRA Plan Implementation

Approved Plan: No discussion of management specific to complex cases, but, by inference, complex cases are not necessarily expected to come to trial within the 18 month guideline.

Differences Between Plan and Advisory Group Recommendations: None.

Differences Between Plan and Implementation: None reported.

CJRA POLICY 4: EXCHANGE OF DISCOVERY INFORMATION

Policy Before CJRA Plan

Discovery was managed by the judicial officer on a case-by-case basis.

CJRA Plan Implementation

Approved Plan: The plan has no specific discussion of automatic exchange but prior to the Case Management Conference, counsel for each side must make a good faith, written specification of the essential details of their claims/their defenses and the identity of their principal witnesses. Counsel will provide the above written specifications to the judicial officer assigned to the case (judge or magistrate judge) in advance of the Case Management Conference. This requirement was later eliminated (see below).

---

[5]Memorandum from the Honorable Barry Ted Moskowitz to the Honorable Judith N. Keep, transmitted to RAND May 4, 1995.

Differences Between Plan and Advisory Group Recommendations: None.

Differences Between Plan and Implementation : General Order 394-C filed January 19, 1993 eliminated the mandatory requirement that counsel prepare and exchange statements of the claims, defenses, and witnesses. The district opted out of the December 1993 revised F.R.Civ.P. 26(a)(1).[6]

CJRA POLICY 5:   CERTIFY GOOD FAITH EFFORT BEFORE FILING DISCOVERY MOTION

Policy Before CJRA Plan

Parties were required to certify that good faith efforts to resolve discovery disputes were made before filing a motion with the court.

CJRA Plan Implementation

Approved Plan: Counsel must "meet and confer" prior to filing any discovery motion and seek to resolve the matter informally. Meeting must be in person if in the same county, but a telephonic conference may be substituted otherwise. Written correspondence will not satisfy the meeting requirement regardless of residence.

Differences Between Plan and Advisory Group Recommendations: None.

Differences Between Plan and Implementation: None reported.

CJRA POLICY 6: ALTERNATIVE DISPUTE RESOLUTION PROGRAMS

Policy Before CJRA Plan

Settlement conferences were held in almost all civil cases, with the exception of Social Security cases. Other types of ADR were used on an occasional basis.

CJRA Plan Implementation

Approved Plan: Features of the plan's ADR program include:

1. The judicial officer managing pretrial discovery is to:

    a)   Encourage settlement as early as possible.

    b)   Supervise negotiations and motions to confirm settlements.

2. After a hearing, the judicial officer shall order a non-binding mini-trial or summary jury trial in any case where the potential judgment does not exceed $250,000 and the use of the procedure will probably resolve the case.

---

[6]Stienstra (1995).

3. The judicial officer will order to non-binding arbitration/mediation all even-numbered simple contract and tort (other than FTCA) cases where the potential judgment does not exceed $100,000, and all even-numbered trademark and copyright cases. Data from the non-binding arbitration/mediation program will be collected and analyzed. This requirement was deleted by General Order 394-B filed December 8, 1992. Non-binding arbitration/mediation is available in the discretion of the judicial officer in any case, but is not mandatory for any class of cases.

4. A committee would seek competent volunteer arbitrators/mediators (pro bono, expected commitment of one case and up to eight hours per year).

5. A program of Early Neutral Evaluation (ENE) conferences managed by a judicial officer (who is usually a magistrate judge in practice). Features of the program include:

   a) Within 45 days of the answer, counsel and the parties will appear before the judicial officer supervising discovery for an ENE conference.

   b) The appearance would be made with the authority to discuss and enter into settlement.

   c) The judicial officer and the parties shall discuss the claims and defenses and seek to settle the case.

   d) The conference would be informal, off the record, privileged, and confidential.

   e) Attendance will be excused only by written order and for good cause. Unexcused failure to attend may result in sanctions.

   f) While ENE procedures are under way, there is no stay in discovery unless specifically ordered for good cause.

   g) If no settlement is reached at the ENE conference, the judicial officer would set a Case Management Conference and do one of the following:

      i) Encourage the parties and counsel to confer for the next 45 days with the objective of reaching an agreement to pursue ADR (Case Management Conference 60 days after the ENE).

      ii) Refer to non-binding arbitration/mediation (to occur within 45 days) any case that met the criteria mentioned above (Case Management Conference 60 days after the ENE).

      iii) Send the case to the Case Management Conference 30 days after the ENE if no arbitration/mediation is agreed upon or ordered.

6. ADR mechanisms and need for early supervision of settlement discussions are to be discussed at the Case Management Conference. Local Rule 37 addresses supervision of settlement negotiations by magistrate judges.

7. Settlements:

   a) Date for a Mandatory Settlement Conference would be set at the Case Management Conference (unless determined that such a conference should be excused).

   b) Any time after the Mandatory Settlement Conference, the judicial officer can calendar additional settlement conferences even over the objection of parties or counsel.

   c) The judicial officer handling settlement should schedule as many follow-up settlement conferences as s/he finds to be appropriate.

   d) Regarding settlement conferences:

      i) The judicial officer handling settlement would be disqualified from trying the case unless parties agree.

      ii) The judicial officer handling settlement may receive in camera communications and can maintain such in confidence unless stipulation to the contrary.

      iii) Each party's representative at the settlement conference must have full authority to settle (unless waived for good cause).

Differences Between Plan and Advisory Group Recommendations: The advisory group recommended providing ADR materials to counsel, and encouraged dissemination of ADR information to general public.

Differences Between Plan and Implementation: The district has concentrated pretrial in the hands of the magistrate judges, and a concerted, court-wide implementation of the ENE procedures has resulted in their use in many civil cases (340 of the civil cases terminated in 1993).[7] The perceived success of this approach has made the utilization of other procedures authorized by the plan (e.g. summary trials, mini-trials, arbitration/mediation) less necessary. The consequence is that these other approaches are being used to a far lesser extent than the plan envisaged. In the arbitration/mediation area for instance, only 13 cases were referred in 1992 and only 3 in 1993.

The Early Neutral Evaluation by magistrate judges continued to be a primary component of the CJRA program in calendar 1994, with 1068 ENEs scheduled. Of all cases filed in 1994, the court reports that about 50 percent had ENEs scheduled. The ENE is held about 2 months after answer, and the majority of lawyers surveyed felt this was about the right time. However, one-fourth of the respondents felt this was too soon, and suggested 90 days after answer would be better. Half the respondents felt that ENE reduced costs, most often discovery costs. The criminal settlement conference program was suspended, pending an appeal. Effective February 14, 1995, the program of mandatory referral of certain cases to non-binding mediation or arbitration was deleted and made voluntary (in effect, giving preference to the

---

[7]United States District Court for the Southern District of California (1994), Chart B.

district's ENE program). The number of cases referred to arbitration, mediation, or summary/mini trials in 1994 were 9, 7, and 2 respectively.

OPTIONAL CJRA TECHNIQUES

The CJRA indicates that each court shall consider and may include the following five litigation management techniques:[8]

I.   **Requiring that counsel jointly present a discovery/case management plan at the initial pretrial conference:**

The Court required counsel to discuss discovery and endeavor to resolve any disputes prior to the Case Management Conference. At the conference, the judicial officer would encourage a cooperative discovery schedule. A Case Management Order would be generated after the conference and would include a discovery and management plan. The district opted out of the December 1993 revised Federal Rules[9] so there was no implementation of the new rule 26(f).

II.   **Requiring that each party be represented at each pretrial conference by an attorney with authority to bind that party:**

The plan discussed such a requirement only for the Early Neutral Evaluation conference and settlement conferences. The plan did require that parties who have responsibility over the litigation and the counsel who will try the case must appear at the Case Management Conference.

III. **Requiring the signature of the attorney *and* the party for all requests for discovery extensions or postponements of trial:**

No discussion regarding this technique.

IV.   **Offering a Neutral Evaluation program:**

The plan established a program using this technique in all cases (see discussion in **CJRA Policy 6**).

V.   **Requiring the attendance of party representatives with authority to bind to be present or available by telephone at settlement conferences:**

The plan discussed such a requirement for the Early Neutral Evaluation conference and settlement conferences. As a matter of policy, the district required before CJRA that party representatives with authority to bind be present or available by telephone at settlement conferences. With the CJRA plan, this policy was codified as a rule.

---

[8]28 U.S.C. § 473(b).

[9]Stienstra (1995).

OTHER POLICIES ADOPTED IN CJRA PLAN

Approved Plan:

1. Judges and the assignment systems.

   a) Sequestration of Judges: Each year, on a rotating basis, each judge would be excluded from the criminal draw in order to spend two full months of uninterrupted civil case management time.

2. Criminal cases:

   a) Authorized the Chief Judge to increase efforts to find visiting judges to preside over criminal trials.

   b) Authorized the Chief Judge to appoint a committee to recommend settlement procedures in criminal cases.

3. Reporting and analysis:

   a) The Clerk is to make regular monthly reports to the Chief Judge of all civil cases pending more than 18 months and all criminal cases pending more than 6 months.

   b) An administrator is to be employed to implement and supervise a statistical monitoring system as recommended in the advisory group report.

   c) At the conclusion of a case:

      i) Parties and counsel are issued a questionnaire by the judicial officer.

      ii) The judicial officer is to informally debrief parties and counsel to evaluate comments, criticisms, and suggestions.

      iii) The judicial officer is to prepare confidential report to the Chief Judge regarding the comments made at the debriefing (to be used as an internal tool to assess the new civil case management features).

Differences Between Plan and Advisory Group Recommendations: The advisory group had also called for promptly filling the two judicial vacancies and urged Congress to eliminate mandatory criminal sentences, sentencing guidelines, and continued federalization of crimes. The group also recommended a complete statistical analysis of 10 percent of non-complex cases, additional funds for a statistical monitoring system, and retaining an advisory group until 1995.

Differences Between Plan and Implementation: *Criminal cases*: The rotation of judges out of the criminal calendar for 2 months each year was deferred pending the filling of judicial vacancies by Congress. The settlement conference committee recommended criminal settlement conference procedures that were implemented in early 1992 by the judges. The court reported that the conferences contributed to a reduction in the average and median time from first appearance to guilty plea, and that in a study of cases filed in 1992, 40 percent of criminal defendants tracked settled at one of the settlement conferences. However, the criminal case settlement procedures are suspended pending an appeal.[10]

Civil Cases: Debriefing by a judicial officer upon civil case closure has also been deferred due to workload considerations. Although the advisory group recommended statistical analysis of 10 percent of the non-complex cases, internal court needs required more extensive reviews and the CJRA analyst has been analyzing the court's entire caseload. Methods were developed to export ICMS data into spreadsheets, thereby enabling the reporting of more complete data than a 10 percent sample would have provided. These data have been helpful not only in reporting on the progress of CJRA programs, but in informing judicial officers and the Clerk's office of the court's case management needs.

---

[10]Roberta Westdal, Clerk of Court, United States District Court for the Southern District of California, letter to RAND, April 14, 1995.

OVERVIEW OF PILOT PROGRAM IN THE DISTRICT OF DELAWARE

OVERVIEW OF IMPLEMENTED CJRA PLAN

The CJRA advisory group's report[1] concluded that problems of excessive cost and delay in the district are limited; however, cost and delay could be further controlled without adversely affecting the administration of justice. The Court has managed its dockets effectively in the view of the group. Judicial vacancies need to be filled in a timely fashion. Criminal filings have increased dramatically in recent years, whereas civil filings have been stable. There is a high proportion of complex cases in the District and there has been an increase in the number of civil cases pending. This has been accompanied by a slight increase in the median time to termination in civil cases. While case management practices among the judges vary, they are generally seen as effective in achieving prompt disposition in civil cases. Typical case processing and discovery methods in the high volume of pro se prisoner § 1983 cases contribute to excessive cost and delay.

The advisory group made several recommendations for refining case management procedures and increasing uniformity among judges in case processing. The group recommended different procedures for case management of expedited, standard and complex cases. They also recommended early mandatory disclosure of certain information in personal injury and medical malpractice cases only, and proposed the required filing of a medical authorization form. For ADR, they recommended that lawyers certify that settlement discussions had been held, and that the possibility of mediation and arbitration be considered in the Rule 16 conference.

The CJRA plan[2] adopted by the Court effective December 23, 1991 included nearly all of the advisory group's recommendations without significant change, with the following relatively minor exceptions: The advisory group would have made quarterly reports and additional conferences for complex cases a requirement rather than an

---

[1] Herndon et al. (1991) (hereinafter referred to as the advisory group report). The 17-member advisory group (plus the district's judicial officers and the Clerk of Court as ex officio members, a reporter, and a special consultant) collected empirical data and performed statistical analysis on the dockets, conducted a survey of attorneys in over 200 cases, interviewed the district's judicial officers, reviewed existing rules and procedures as well as litigant and attorney practices, analyzed particular types of litigation, and assessed the impact of new legislation.

[2] United States District Court for the District of Delaware (undated) (hereinafter referred to as the plan). Effective date of the plan was December 23, 1991.

option. The plan requires early mandatory disclosure of certain information for personal injury, medical malpractice, employment discrimination, and RICO cases, rather than just for personal injury and medical malpractice cases.

The first annual report on the plan indicated that "it is clear that cases are being processed more rapidly than they were in the pre-CJRA period. In part this is the consequence of the court being at full strength, but it is also clear that the procedures implemented under the plan have produced a more prompt resolution of civil cases."[3]

CJRA POLICY 1: DIFFERENTIAL CASE MANAGEMENT

Policy Before CJRA Plan

Case management prior to CJRA had been a matter of judicial discretion. Some inter-judge variations existed, but the small number of judges made this only a minor problem for the bar.

CJRA Plan Implementation

Approved Plan: The plan calls for:

1. Creating a Rule with variations in Rule 16 scheduling procedures for Expedited, Standard, and Complex cases.

2. Providing the following guidelines for designating complex cases:

   a) Parties seeking determination of complexity must file a Notice of Intent with the complaint or answer and a short supporting statement.

   b) All other parties must file a short response thereafter within 15 days or with a responsive pleading.

   c) The court will make the determination of complexity at the time of the Rule 16 scheduling conference. The judge may consider a variety of factors:

      i)   type of action.

      ii)   number of parties and their capacities.

      iii) legal and factual issues.

      iv)   technical complexity of the factual issues.

      v)   retroactivity of circumstances giving rise to the claims and defenses.

      vi)   volume and nature of the documents subject to discovery.

      vii) amount of necessary third-party and foreign discovery.

      viii) number of depositions, witnesses, and locations.

---

[3]Herndon et al. (1994), p. 5.

ix)   need for expert testimony.

x)   nature of the issues to be determined during pretrial.

3. Employing particular case management techniques in cases that are determined to be complex (see discussion in section on **CJRA Policy 3**).

4. Requiring certain initial disclosures in personal injury, medial malpractice, employment discrimination, and RICO cases (see discussion in section on **CJRA Policy 4**).

5. Adopting a master scheduling order for the processing of prisoner § 1983 cases and habeas corpus petitions (see discussion in section on **CJRA Policy 2**).

6. Modify the current practices regarding magistrate judge referrals in prisoner § 1983 cases, Social Security cases, and habeas corpus petitions (see discussion in section on **CJRA Policy 2**).

Differences Between Plan and Advisory Group Recommendations: The advisory report and the plan are very similar. One difference is that the advisory report would have had the determination of case complexity made at a hearing held within 15 days of the response to the Notice of Intent, not at the Rule 16 conference.

Differences Between Plan and Implementation: None reported, except that, in practice, the complex case designation has been granted sparingly.

CJRA POLICY 2: EARLY AND ONGOING CONTROL OF PRETRIAL BY JUDICIAL OFFICER

Policy Before CJRA Plan

Some inter-judge variation existed before the plan. For example, one judge might fix a firm trial date at the Rule 16 conference while another might not do so until the final pretrial conference. Judges did not use the same scheduling procedures or the same form of scheduling order. Some judges sent out a proposed Rule 16 order for the parties to accept or modify by agreement, other judges had telephonic conferences, and others required counsel to attend a Rule 16 conference in person. Generally, judges set and enforced deadlines for completion of discovery. The usual limits on discovery were 50 interrogatories and 25 requests for admissions. All motions, unless made at a hearing or a trial, had to be written, and supporting briefs were normally filed within 10 days of the motion. Opening and answering briefs had a maximum size of 50 pages and reply briefs had a maximum of 25 pages. The following types of cases were exempt from the Rule 16 requirement: pro se prisoner; review of government administrative decisions on the record; prize proceedings; forfeitures; condemnations; foreclosures; bankruptcy; citizenship; arbitration; certain proceedings to compel testimony or document production; and educational loan recovery.

CJRA Plan Implementation

Approved Plan: The plan contains the following elements.

1. Scheduling Conferences and Orders:

   a) Adopt a Local Rule describing Rule 16 scheduling procedures with variations in Rule 16 scheduling procedures for Expedited, Standard, and Complex cases. The nature of the variations are not described in the plan, but an amended Local Rule 16.1(b)(3) indicates that for complex cases the following may be considered: use of magistrate judge or special master; staged resolution of issues; limiting or sequencing discovery; managing expert discovery; and limiting experts or trial time.

   b) Require counsel to certify that they have discussed settlement prior to the Rule 16 conference.

   c) Identify the topics to be discussed at the Rule 16 conference, including:

      i) The possibility of settlement.

      ii) Voluntary mediation or binding arbitration.

      iii) Briefing practices to be employed (length, topics).

      iv) Trial date, which under revised Local Rule 16.2(c) is to be within 12 months after filing the complaint, if practicable, and no later than 18 months unless the court certifies a reason for needing longer.

   d) Issue Rule 16 scheduling orders with the following standard dates set (exceptions if circumstances so warrant):

      i) Termination of discovery.

      ii) Various motions (including joinder, amended pleadings, and case dispositive motions).

      iii) Pretrial conference (if appropriate).

      iv) Trial (if appropriate).

   e) In prisoner § 1983 cases and habeas corpus petitions, adopt a master scheduling order that include provisions to:

      i) Require defendants to file a responsive pleading (if necessary) within 45 days of the service of the complaint.[4]

      ii) Require defendants to accompany their responsive pleadings with a production of all relevant documents (along with an affidavit of thorough search and production).

      iii) Require affidavits of fact (if appropriate) and briefs in the support of any motion.

      iv) Require notice that any dispositive motion may be considered a summary judgment motion if reference is made to any matter outside the pleadings.

---

[4]For §1983 cases, this was changed to 60 days in light of the waiver of service provision of F.R.Civ.P Rule 4.

2. Requests for Extensions of Deadlines: The plan also called for a Rule to require, in connection with a request for extension of any deadline set in any order or by statute, the following:

   a) That the applicant identify each prior request for extension in the case.

   b) That the applicant identify the reasons for the request.

   c) That any other information or certification requested by the judge be provided.

   d) That the request be signed by counsel and supported by a client's affidavit or accompanied by a certification that the counsel has sent a copy of the request to the client.

3. Motions Practice:

   a) Amend Local Rule 3.1.C to require parties to file briefs in support of motions at the time the motion is filed.

4. Magistrate judge assignments:

   a) In prisoner § 1983 cases and habeas corpus petitions, return case management to the assigned judge if the magistrate judge does not recommend granting a dispositive motion, or if the judge does not accept the magistrate judge's decision to grant.

   b) Retain the judge's responsibility for all habeas corpus petitions and social security cases. If the court cannot do this, divide some of the prisoner § 1983 cases and habeas corpus petitions among judges and magistrate judges.

5. Management by the Clerk's Office: Courtroom clerks should be trained to participate in case management including the duty to provide routine notices at least for the following:

   a) Local Rule 5.2 (inactivity for three months).

   b) Discovery.

   c) Briefs late by more than 5 days.

   d) Show Cause orders for failure to serve process.

   e) Requests for default or stipulations for extensions of time to answer.

   f) Rule 16 conferences.

6. Other Issues: Allow certain additional case management techniques to be employed in cases that are determined to be complex (see discussion in section on **CJRA Policy 3**).

Differences Between Plan and Advisory Group Recommendations: The advisory report's recommendation regarding deadline extensions requests would have only applied to dates set in a pretrial scheduling order whereas the plan is much more general and applies to deadlines set by any order or rule or statute. On August 1, 1992, Local Rule 16.5 was adopted, essentially implementing the plan's requirement for requests for extension of deadlines. On December 31, 1994, Local Rule 16.5 was modified to apply only to extensions of discovery and trial dates.

Differences Between Plan and Implementation: None reported, except the plan did not explicitly mention trial date within 12 or 18 months (with exceptions) as recommended by the advisory group, but the subsequently revised Local Rule 16.2(c) that implements the plan includes those dates.

CJRA POLICY 3: MORE INTENSIVE MANAGEMENT OF COMPLEX CASES

Policy Before CJRA Plan

Case management prior to the plan was a matter of judicial discretion and differential approaches were taken on a case-by-case basis.

CJRA Plan Implementation

Approved Plan: Regarding complex cases, the plan called for:

1. Adopting guidelines for determination if a case is complex (see discussion of **CJRA Policy 1**).

2. Giving the court the option to:

   a) Order separate trials of certain issues, or arrange for staged resolution of issues.

   b) Set an early date for joinder of parties and amendment of the pleadings.

   c) Make use of a magistrate judge or special master to monitor discovery and resolve disputes.

   d) Limit discovery without court order.

   e) Set a schedule of expert discovery.

   f) Limit or restrict the use of expert testimony.

   g) In trials, limit the time for presentation of evidence or the number of witnesses or documents and use a state-of-the-art courtroom.

   h) Require the parties to file reports concerning the status of discovery and any motions or procedural matters.

   i) Hold conferences as appropriate to discuss the issues in contention, monitor the progress of discovery, determine or schedule pending matters, and explore settlement.

Differences Between Plan and Advisory Group Recommendations: The advisory group would have made the reports and additional conferences a requirement rather than an option for the judge and would have scheduled the reports quarterly and the conferences biannually. As of August 1, 1992, Local Rule 16.1(b)(1) requires the filing of quarterly reports.

Differences Between Plan and Implementation: None reported.

CJRA POLICY 4: EXCHANGE OF DISCOVERY INFORMATION

Policy Before CJRA Plan

Judges generally encouraged such disclosure without requiring it. In practice, therefore, the matter was usually up to the attorneys.

CJRA Plan Implementation

Approved Plan: Provisions of the plan included:

1. In personal injury, medical malpractice, employment discrimination, and RICO cases, a party must include in its initial pleading:

   a) Names, addresses, and telephone numbers of each person:

      i)   with knowledge of the facts relating to the litigation.

      ii) interviewed in connection with the litigation.

      iii) who conducted any interviews.

   b) A general description of documents in the possession, custody, or control of the party, "which are reasonably likely to bear significantly on the claims or defenses asserted."

   c) Identification of all experts presently or expected to be retained by the party (with the dates of any written opinions).

   d) A brief description of any applicable insurance coverage.

2. In prisoner § 1983 cases and habeas corpus petitions, defendants who are required to file initial responsive pleadings would have to accompany those pleadings with a production of all relevant documents (along with an affidavit of thorough search and production).

Differences Between Plan and Advisory Group Recommendations: The advisory group recommended that the initial test of the automatic disclosure provisions be used in personal injury and medical malpractice cases only, and proposed the required filing of a medical authorization form.

Differences Between Plan and Implementation: The Local Rule 26.2 adopted to implement this part of the plan did not require the names of persons interviewed or who conducted the interviews, but did make provision for withholding of privileged or work product documents. The December 1993 amendments to Federal Rule of Civil Procedure 26(a)(1) concerning mandatory initial disclosure initially were *not* adopted in this district. However, as of January 1995 the district is following the December 1993 amendments to F.R.Civ.P. 26. [5]

CJRA POLICY 5: CERTIFY GOOD FAITH EFFORT BEFORE FILING DISCOVERY MOTION

Policy Before CJRA Plan

Local Rule 3.1.D required a party filing any non-dispositive motion to accompany the motion with a certificate setting forth the dates, time spent, and methods used to attempt to resolve the dispute with opposing counsel.

CJRA Plan Implementation

Approved Plan: No change in policy.

Differences Between Plan and Advisory Group Recommendations: None.

Differences Between Plan and Implementation: None reported.

CJRA POLICY 6: ALTERNATIVE DISPUTE RESOLUTION PROGRAMS

Policy Before CJRA Plan

The court encouraged settlement discussions but had no mandatory ADR program. Settlement conferences with judicial officers were held for less than a third of the cases according to the advisory group survey. Also, forms of ADR other than settlement discussions were seldom used.

CJRA Plan Implementation

Approved Plan: Revised Local Rule 16.2(b) mentions that one of the matters for discussion at the scheduling conference is "whether the matter could be resolved by voluntary mediation or binding arbitration." The advisory group recommended that counsel be required to certify to the Court that they have conferred prior to the Rule 16 conference to discuss settlement and that this "provides a program of alternative dispute resolution." The Court's plan requires such a certification that settlement has been discussed.

Differences Between Plan and Advisory Group Recommendations: None.

Differences Between Plan and Implementation: In 1994, the court reported increased use of a Magistrate Judge for purposes of voluntary case mediation[6] (what might be called a settlement conference in other districts).

---

[5]Stienstra (1995).

[6]United States District Court for the District of Delaware (1995).

OPTIONAL CJRA TECHNIQUES

The CJRA indicates that each court shall consider and may include the following five litigation management techniques:[7]

I.   Requiring that counsel jointly present a discovery/case management plan at the initial pretrial conference:

There was no specific discussion regarding this technique. Initially this district did opt out, but later decided not to opt out of the December 1993 revised Federal Rule 26(f) [8] so there was implementation of that portion of the new Rule 26.

II.   Requiring that each party be represented at each pretrial conference by an attorney with authority to bind that party:

There was no specific discussion regarding this technique.

III.   Requiring the signature of the attorney *and* the party for all requests for discovery extensions or postponements of trial:

The plan did not specifically call for the adoption of this technique, but did require, in connection with request for extension of any deadline set in any order or by statute,[9] that the request be signed by counsel and supported by a client's affidavit or accompanied by a certification that the counsel has sent a copy of the request to the client.

IV.   Offering a Neutral Evaluation program:

There was no specific discussion regarding this technique.

V.   Requiring the attendance of party representatives with authority to bind to be present or available by telephone at settlement conferences:

There was no specific discussion regarding this technique.

OTHER POLICIES ADOPTED IN CJRA PLAN

Approved Plan:

1. Encouraging Congress to:

   a) Specify if a private remedy is intended with the enactment of regulatory legislation.

   b) Evaluate the impact on the Judicial Branch of new or amended legislation.

---

[7]28 U.S.C. § 473(b).

[8]Stienstra (1995).

[9]As of December 31, 1994, Local Rule 16.5 was modified to apply only to extensions of discovery and trial dates.

   c) Identify the courts whose caseload would be increased by such legislation and provide additional resources to such courts.

2. Developing and adopting model jury instructions for standard charges such as burden of proof.

3. Conducting further study of an electronic courtroom.

4. Developing legal education programs for the Bar that address the Court's practices and procedures, including CJRA.

5. Seek authorization for:

   a) A third law clerk for the Chief Judge.

   b) An additional floater secretary.

   c) An additional law clerk for pro se prisoner § 1983 petitions.

6. Establish a panel of lawyers to be appointed counsel for in forma pauperis petitions in prisoner § 1983 and habeas corpus proceedings.

Differences Between Plan and Advisory Group Recommendations: The advisory report recommended adoption of an Internal Procedures Manual, recommended efforts to ensure timely filling of vacant judgeships, and urged the State Department of Corrections to facilitate the resolution of prisoner complaints and to provide additional paralegal assistance to petitioners.

Differences Between Plan and Implementation: None reported.

OVERVIEW OF CJRA PROGRAM IN FLORIDA, NORTHERN DISTRICT

OVERVIEW OF IMPLEMENTED CJRA PLAN

This is a comparison district, not a pilot district, so a CJRA plan must be adopted by December 1, 1993, and it need not contain the six pilot program principles. This district's plan was adopted November 19, 1993, and was effective on January 1, 1994.

The CJRA advisory group's report[1] indicated that the criminal docket significantly affects the pace of civil litigation and that the Court should take a more active role in the case management process early in the life of the case. It concluded that systematic differential case management for categories of cases is not warranted (except for prisoner and certain administrative cases such as Social Security appeals), made several detailed recommendations for improving pretrial case management procedures (including increased use of pretrial conferences), rejected early mandatory disclosure of core information prior to formal discovery, and recommended an expanded ADR program including both mediation and early neutral evaluation with a program administrator. The advisory group also recommended an expanded role for magistrate judges on civil cases.

The CJRA plan[2] adopted by the Court indicated that demands placed upon the court by the district's heavy criminal docket, and other factors, may realistically prohibit the full implementation of the plan. The plan commits the district judges to take a more active role in case management early in the life of the case, and sets out several specific detailed procedures for doing this. The court retained its individual case management policy rather than establishing systematic tracks. The December 1993 revisions to F.R.Civ.P. 26 are being followed, including the requirement for early disclosure of certain core information. The mediation program is refined, but the court declined to adopt a more formally administered program and declined to adopt a neutral evaluation program. The role of magistrate judges in civil matters was not increased due to the pressing demands of their criminal work. As of January 18, 1996, no CJRA annual report had been prepared by the CJRA advisory group or the Court.

---

[1]Goldstein et al. (1993) (hereinafter referred to as the advisory group report). The 19-member committee reviewed statistics regarding past case filings, filing trends, and the use of court resources; and considered the results of a survey of members of the district's bar.

[2]United States District Court for the Northern District of Florida (1993) (hereinafter referred to as the plan). Effective date of the plan was January 1, 1994.

As of April 1, 1995, the court indicates that Local Rules have been rewritten and take precedence over any contrary provision contained in the CJRA. The motivations for the Local Rule revisions included conformity with the CJRA Plan and the 1993 F.R.Civ. P. revisions, plus standardization of practice in the district. The court has also been authorized an additional magistrate judge, subject to upcoming funding, and as a consequence is undertaking a complete overhaul of the magistrate judge utilization policy. It is expected that the magistrate judges will be given very broad civil caseload responsibility, although the particulars are not yet defined.[3]

CJRA POLICY 1: DIFFERENTIAL CASE MANAGEMENT

Policy Before CJRA Plan

Only prisoner cases and certain administrative cases such as Social Security appeals were in a distinctly different management category from other cases. The remainder of the cases are managed individually. Judicial officers and/or the attorneys tailored each case's discovery schedule to its individual needs.

CJRA Plan Implementation

Approved Plan: The plan calls for no change in current practices.

Differences Between Plan and Advisory Group Recommendations: None.

Differences Between Plan and Implementation: None reported.

CJRA POLICY 2: EARLY AND ONGOING CONTROL OF PRETRIAL BY JUDICIAL OFFICER

Policy Before CJRA Plan

All judges utilized a uniform scheduling order. The scheduling order dealt with discovery, time deadlines, specific procedures for handling discovery disputes, summary judgment motions, time records, and similar case management matters. The uniform scheduling order also required disclosure of expert witness and their opinions, and required the losing party in a discovery dispute to pay fees and expenses. The order was entered and sent to attorneys as soon as the case was at issue.

The number of interrogatories and requests for admissions was limited to 50 by Local Rule and the uniform scheduling order.

CJRA Plan Implementation

Approved Plan: The plan does the following:

---

[3]Chief Judge Maurice M. Paul, United States District Court for the Northern District of Florida, letter to RAND, April 13, 1995.

1. Affirms that intermediate or additional case management conferences prior to the final pretrial conference can be beneficial, and that the Court should be involved in monitoring of cases and discovery schedules.

2. Specifies procedures for scheduling orders and the initial pretrial conference:

    a) The standard scheduling orders should be retained with only minor changes but will be entered immediately after the first defense appearance.

    b) Except for certain classes of cases, attorneys shall be required to meet within 30 days after the entry of the scheduling order and shall:

        i)   Discuss the nature and basis of their claims and defenses, and in good faith try to identify the principal factual and legal issues in dispute.

        ii)   Discuss the possibilities for prompt settlement or resolution of the matter and whether mediation or other ADR process might be helpful and at what stage of the proceedings these would be warranted.

        iii) Discuss proposed timetables and cutoff dates and whether the initial scheduling order should be revised.

        iv)   Discuss their respective discovery requirements in the cases and, if they choose, develop their own plan specifically addressing time and form of discovery, phased discovery, any limits, and changes to the procedures and deadlines found in the initial scheduling order, Local Rules, or F.R.Civ.P.

        v)   Make a good faith estimate when they will be ready for trial with a written explanation if the estimated date is not within 18 months of filing.

        vi)   Address any other appropriate issues.

        vii) Unless otherwise stipulated, provide (or make arrangements to promptly provide) certain types of information without having to make a specific discovery request. Those types of information are very similar to those required by the December 1993 amendment to the F.R.Civ.P. 26, which this district is now following.

    c) A joint report shall be filed within 14 days after the post-initial scheduling order meeting of the parties' attorneys. The report would address each of the items required to be discussed and set out each party's position if they are unable to agree.

    d) The Court will promptly consider the filed report and within 14 days after filing will do one or more of the following:

        i)   Modify the initial scheduling order as necessary.

        ii)   Adopt the parties' submissions by separate order.

        iii) Set the matter for a pretrial conference (either in person or by telephone).

        iv)   Take no action and the original order would continue in full force and effect.

e) The Court will allow changes to the time periods in the scheduling orders only for good cause and in the interests of justice.

3. Specifies procedures for setting trial date: the parties' estimated trial date will be the presumptive time when the case will be set for final pretrial conference and trial, unless revised by the court. The actual trial date will ordinarily be set after discussions with the attorneys at the final pretrial conference.

4. Specifies discovery limits:

   a) The current 50 interrogatory/requests for admission limit shall be continued.

   b) No action is taken regarding the deposition limitation of F.R.Civ.P. 30(a)(2)(4).

5. Specifies procedures for discovery disputes:

   a) The Court will utilize magistrate judges only if this is a realistic and practical alternative.

   b) The Court approved of the advisory group's recommendation to make greater use of sanctions in discovery disputes, and to have judges consistently apply them as a deterrent to involving the court in such matters. It is recognized that awarding and calculating attorney's fees sometimes increases litigation.

6. Specifies procedures for motions:

   a) After the opposing party's response has been filed and the motion is ripe, the court should rule within 60 days for non-dispositive motions and within 120 days for dispositive motions. If oral argument has been held, rulings should be made within the 30 days after oral argument or the time limits noted above whichever is greater.

   b) The Clerk of Court should continue the current practice of monitoring the progress of pending motions, and should notify judges of their status at least monthly.

   c) Pretrial progress should be monitored to insure that deadlines for filing motions and the time for their disposition would be well understood by the parties.

7. Specifies procedures for attorney's fees:

   a) Approved of the advisory group's recommendation to make greater use of sanctions in discovery disputes and to have the judges consistently apply them as a deterrent to involving the court in such matters (while nevertheless recognizing that awarding and calculating attorney's fees may increase litigation).

   b) Continues to require monthly summaries of time spent on a case, when attorneys are seeking award of fees.

   c) Is in favor of Rule 54 regarding bifurcation of motions for attorney fees (first determine liability then calculate fees).

   d) Intends to modify the standard scheduling order to minimize need for evidentiary hearings involving attorney's fees. Procedures will be developed as quickly as possible but may include presumptive fees for routine matters and Rule 68-type procedures in fee disputes.

e) Requires that, absent a statutory provision or court order, any motion seeking fees or to tax costs must be filed within 30 days.

Differences Between Plan and Advisory Group Recommendations: Differences in management are not so much on principle as on details of sequencing and implementation. For example, the advisory group suggested the lawyers confer, file a report, and have a pretrial conference with the court before a scheduling order is issued. The court's plan is to issue a scheduling order, after which the lawyers are to meet, file a report, and then have a pretrial conference with the court if the court requires it prior to deciding whether to amend the scheduling order. Both methods embrace the principle of the court becoming more involved in case management early in the litigation.

However, there was a substantial difference regarding the use of magistrate judges:

a) Specific rejection of the advisory group's recommendation to refer more pretrial civil motions to the magistrate judges, primarily due to the burden of criminal matters on magistrate judges.

b) Specific rejection of the advisory group's recommendation for greater utilization of magistrate judges to resolve discovery disputes. The Court will utilize them only if it is realistic and practical to do so, but again noted the burden of criminal matters.

c) The Court felt that while it may be appropriate for magistrate judges to conduct the pretrial conferences in some cases, there were drawbacks in that the judge would then not be educated about the nuances of the case.

d) The Court indicated that the district needs one, or preferably two, more full-time magistrate judges. The advisory group agrees.

Differences Between Plan and Implementation: On July 26, 1994, the court refined its policy on the use of magistrate judges by issuing an order assigning to them all pretrial discovery disputes and Rule 16(b) scheduling conferences.

CJRA POLICY 3: MORE INTENSIVE MANAGEMENT OF COMPLEX CASES

Policy Before CJRA Plan

Complex case management is a matter of judicial discretion.

CJRA Plan Implementation

Approved Plan: There is no specific discussion regarding complex cases.

Differences Between Plan and Advisory Group Recommendations: None.

Differences Between Plan and Implementation: None reported.

CJRA POLICY 4: EXCHANGE OF DISCOVERY INFORMATION

Policy Before CJRA Plan

Disclosure of expert witness and their opinions was required in the uniform scheduling order as well as Local Rules and the F.R.Civ.P.

CJRA Plan Implementation

Approved Plan: The Court believed that certain automatic disclosures are very cost-effective and efficient. The plan stated that the court:

1. Will not opt out of proposed Rule 26(a)(1) as recommended by the advisory group.

2. Will implement proposed Rules 26(a)(2), (3), and (4) .

3. Will require attorneys to meet within 30 days after the entry of the initial standard scheduling order except for certain classes of cases and to provide (or make arrangements to promptly provide) certain types of information without having to make a specific discovery request. Those types of information are very similar to those required by the December 1993 amendment to the F.R.Civ.P. 26(a)(1), which this district is now following.

Differences Between Plan and Advisory Group Recommendations: The primary difference is that the advisory group recommended that the district opt out of the core information disclosure procedure in the F.R.Civ.P. 26(a)(1).

Differences Between Plan and Implementation: None reported. The December 1993 amendments to Federal Rule of Civil Procedure 26(a)(1) concerning mandatory initial disclosure are in effect in this district.[4]

CJRA POLICY 5: CERTIFY GOOD FAITH EFFORT BEFORE FILING DISCOVERY MOTION

Policy Before CJRA Plan

The district has had a long-standing requirement for certification of consultation regarding motions filed.

CJRA Plan Implementation

Approved Plan: No change to prior policy.

Differences Between Plan and Advisory Group Recommendations: None.

Differences Between Plan and Implementation: None reported.

---

[4]Stienstra (1995).

CJRA POLICY 6: ALTERNATIVE DISPUTE RESOLUTION PROGRAMS

Policy Before CJRA Plan

The court indicates that good results have been experienced from referring cases to mediation as an ADR procedure over the past few years. They do not keep a tally of the number of cases referred to mediation, but docket analysis of RAND's sample of cases indicates mediation referrals are about 4 percent of annual civil filings. The mediator's fees are paid by the litigants. Cases may be referred to mediation at:

1. The completion of discovery, when attorneys are directed to prepare for the final pretrial conference. Participation is voluntary and parties are advised by order that they may elect to mediate in lieu of filing the extensive pretrial stipulations and attachments.

2. The time of the pretrial conference. At this point, the referral may be mandatory after the court has discussed the matter with the attorneys and analyzed the differences between the sides.

3. Any time the parties voluntarily make the request.

4. Any time the court decides the case is appropriate for mediation. Referral may be mandatory.

CJRA Plan Implementation

Approved Plan: The plan continues the existing mediation program, with some refinements:

1. Requiring the parties to consider mediation at the earliest practical time. The joint report will allow the court to determine whether the best time is early in the litigation, after the opportunity to conduct some basic discovery, or after the case is ready for trial.

2. The Court should utilize mediation whenever there is a reasonable likelihood that it will be successful.

3. The Court will continue to monitor results of the program.

Differences Between Plan and Advisory Group Recommendations: Early Neutral Evaluation: The Court declined to adopt any such program, considering that the results may not offset the disadvantages, and it may be difficult to initiate, administer, and mandate such a program.

ADR Administrator: The Court declined to establish a more formalized ADR program as recommended by the advisory group, and declined to establish an administrator of ADR programs in the district.

Differences Between Plan and Implementation: None reported.

OPTIONAL CJRA TECHNIQUES

The CJRA indicates that each court shall consider and may include the following five litigation management techniques:[5]

I.   **Requiring that counsel jointly present a discovery/case management plan at the initial pretrial conference:**

See the discussion regarding the joint report to be filed by counsel after the issuance of the standard scheduling order in the above section on **CJRA Policy 2.** The court decided to follow the December 1993 revised F.R.Civ.P. 26.

II. **Requiring that each party be represented at each pretrial conference by an attorney with authority to bind that party:**

The Court required that each party must be represented by an attorney or representative with an authority to bind in all matters including settlement at all pretrial, settlement, and mediation conferences.

III. **Requiring the signature of the attorney *and* the party for all requests for discovery extensions or postponements of trial:**

The Court specifically rejected such a requirement.

IV. **Offering a Neutral Evaluation program:**

The Court specifically declined to implement a program; it felt that the costs and delays associated with neutral evaluation would not be offset by the results. It opted instead to refine the current mediation program.

V.   **Requiring the attendance of party representatives with authority to bind to be present or available by telephone at settlement conferences:**

The Court adopted this technique.

OTHER POLICIES ADOPTED IN CJRA PLAN

Approved Plan: No additional policies were adopted.

Differences Between Plan and Advisory Group Recommendations

1. Experts:
   a) The Court established no requirements for submission of the entire direct testimony of expert witnesses.
   b) The Court did not encourage parties to use video depositions of experts in lieu of live testimony.

---

[5]28 U.S.C. § 473(b).

2. Attorney's Fees: The advisory group would have made significant changes in procedures involving their award and determination.

3. The advisory group recommended establishing a Prisoner Pro Bono Committee and finding ways of non-judicial resolution of minor criminal offenses.

Differences Between Plan and Implementation: None reported.

OVERVIEW OF PILOT PROGRAM IN GEORGIA, NORTHERN DISTRICT

OVERVIEW OF IMPLEMENTED CJRA PLAN

The CJRA advisory group indicated that "the principal problem in this district is, as elsewhere, the costs associated with discovery."[1] The advisory group indicated no necessity for additional categories or tracks for case management, but recommended requiring plaintiffs to indicate on the civil cover sheet whether the case is complex. Some detailed recommendations were made for improving pretrial rules and procedures. The recommendations included requiring both sides to complete standardized mandatory interrogatories that include naming witnesses and describing or producing each document in the party's custody or control or of which they have knowledge which they contend supports their claims or defenses; and requiring that the parties indicate on the Preliminary Statement and Scheduling Order the reasons why additional time would be needed to complete discovery beyond the standard four-month period. The group recommended adding a provision into the Scheduling Order that includes the presumption that the case will be ready for trial within 18 months of the filing date. For ADR, it recommended creating a mandatory court-annexed arbitration program using magistrate judges, and authorizing the parties in complex litigation to agree jointly on a Special Master.

The CJRA plan[2] adopted by the Court included most of the recommendations of the advisory group, but made significant revisions that are noted below. The effective date of the plan was December 31, 1991, and the effective date for the Local Rules adopted or amended to implement the part of the plan was July 1, 1992. The plan included differential case management in tracks determined by the nature of the suit, and created three separate tracks with different allowable times for discovery (zero, four, and eight months). Several changes in pretrial rules and procedures were

---

[1]Vickery et al. (1991) (hereinafter referred to as the advisory group report). The 18-person committee was chaired by a lawyer, and included the Clerk of Court, the United States Attorney for the District, various attorneys, and officers and executives of major litigants in the district. The advisory group met monthly as a whole and four subcommittees were created (Impact of Recent Legislation, Assessment of the Court's Docket, Alternative Dispute Resolution, and Analysis of Court Procedures), which met more frequently. The group also conducted a survey of attorneys in 90 closed cases.

[2]United States District Court for the Northern District of Georgia (1991) (hereinafter referred to as the plan).

made. Mandatory interrogatories must be answered by all parties. The plan approved a mandatory court-annexed arbitration program using private attorneys and former judges as arbitrators (rather than magistrate judges) and a program for the voluntary use of Special Masters in complex cases. However, the court has postponed implementation of the two ADR programs until additional funds become available, and until statutory authority for this district to have arbitration becomes available.

The annual report provided a statistical update to the plan through September 30, 1992, and did not recommend any changes in it. [3]

CJRA POLICY 1: DIFFERENTIAL CASE MANAGEMENT

Policy Before CJRA Plan

Local Rules of Practice, especially Local Rule 235, already provided for the individualized management of civil cases and standardized pretrial procedures. The standard Preliminary Statement (to be filed within 40 days of the issue being joined) and Scheduling Order contained provisions that applied to almost all civil cases (with the judge incorporating individualized case management directives based upon information provided by the parties).

Though there were no formalized tracks, there were standard ways of managing different types of cases (i.e., habeas corpus cases were screened by a staff law clerk; certain Title VII cases were to be heard by a magistrate judge or Special Master; no settlement conference requirements or joint preliminary statements were required for administrative appeals and pro se cases; and reports and recommendations by magistrate judges were authorized for truth-in-lending cases, IRS proceedings, and Social Security actions).

CJRA Plan Implementation

Approved Plan: The plan calls for:

1. Modifying F.R.Civ.P. 8 and 12 to require the defendant to file an answer at the time of filing a Rule 12 motion. The objective is to accelerate the case management by accelerating the joinder of issue, which triggers the Preliminary Statement and Scheduling Order.

2. Revising the Local Rules to accelerate the case management timetable as much as possible.

3. Adopting the recommendation of the advisory group which would require a written explanation of why any party needs additional time to complete discovery beyond that allowed for the assigned discovery track. This would make counsel

---

[3]Bowden and Vickery (1993).

work together in planning discovery, and facilitate control of excessive or unguided discovery.

4. Adopting three tracks for all cases, and defining for each the length of the discovery period and the requirements for management. The tracks include:

   a) Zero-months discovery period. Cases in this track are not subject to the settlement conference requirements of Local Rule 235-2 and it is not necessary to file a Preliminary Statement under Local Rule 235-3 or a Pretrial Order under Local Rule 235-4. A total of 14 case types are in this track, including Recovery and Overpayment cases, Prisoner Petitions, Bankruptcy, and Social Security.[4]

   b) Eight-month discovery period. These cases have required settlement conferences, Preliminary Statements, and Pretrial Orders. A total of 3 case types are included: Antitrust, Securities/Commodities, and Patent.[5]

   c) Four-month discovery period. These cases are also subject to standard settlement conference, Preliminary Statement, and Pretrial Order requirements. A total of 68 case type categories—all types not mentioned in the other two tracks—are incorporated.

Differences Between Plan and Advisory Group Recommendations:

1. The advisory group did not recommend adoption of case tracking other than the tracks implicit in the Local Rules (there were standard ways of managing different types of cases such as habeas corpus, certain Title VII cases, administrative appeals, pro se cases, truth-in-lending cases, IRS proceedings, and Social Security actions).

2. The plan added language regarding tracks to the Preliminary Statement and required explanation if parties felt discovery could not be completed in the allotted time.

Differences Between Plan and Implementation: None reported.

CJRA POLICY 2: EARLY AND ONGOING CONTROL OF PRETRIAL BY JUDICIAL OFFICER

Policy Before CJRA Plan

The district conducted case management largely through a combination of Local Rules and judicial discretion (for example, using the Preliminary Statement and Scheduling Orders; requiring attorneys to report to the Court the results of one settlement conference held 30 days after the issue is joined and also of one held 10 days after close of discovery). For cases not terminated within 30 days after the close of discovery, Local Rule 235-4(b) set forth detailed instructions for the preparation of

---

[4]Nature of Suit codes: 150, 151, 152, 510, 530, 540, 422, 423, 861–865.

[5]Nature of Suit codes: 410, 830, 850.

a consolidated pretrial order and prohibition of further motions. It also required each party to file a separate witness and exhibit list, and to designate the portions of depositions which would be introduced at trial. Existing rules also required each judge to use the same form of pretrial order, with the objective of creating predictability and avoiding duplication in the event that cases had to be transferred to another judge.

Local Rule 235-3 and its corresponding form required that motions (other than those with a specific filing time set by the F.R.Civ.P. or other Local Rules, especially Local Rule 220) be filed within 100 days of filing the complaint. This provision and the filing times set forth in Local Rule 200 assured compliance with the principle of having guidelines for motion filing and disposition. Also, the consolidated Pretrial Order required that parties list any pending motions and prohibited further motions to compel discovery.

Existing rules also provided for time limits on discovery. Local Rule 225-1, for example, imposed a four-month discovery period and permitted extension only by Court order (although such orders were common according to the advisory group), limited the number of interrogatories to 40 and the length of depositions to 6 hours, promoted timely compliance with discovery requests by requiring early initiation of discovery, assisted the Court in the monitoring of discovery by requiring the filing of certificates of service, and required early consideration of settlement.

There was no requirement in Local Rules or practice that the Court set a fixed trial date nor any requirement that trials should be held within 18 months of filing.

CJRA Plan Implementation

Approved Plan: The plan calls for:

1. Amending Local Rule 235-2(a)(1) to incorporate into the Preliminary Statement the settlement certificate which reports the results of the initial settlement conference (held either in person or telephonically). This would consolidate two required filings and give the judge an early opportunity to assess settlement likelihood.

2. Advancing the date for filing consolidated Preliminary Statement to 30 days after the issue is joined.

3. Amending Local Rule 235-2(b) to require that a person with authority to bind parties be present at the post-discovery settlement conference.

4. Adopting Recommendation 4 of the advisory group insofar as it amended the Scheduling Order in Local Rule 235-3(10) to allow the judge to set a trial date for a specific month, or otherwise to set trial within 18 months of filing, or to indicate that the criminal calendar prevents scheduling a trial date.

5. Encouraging each judge to adopt individual procedures setting a more specific trial date after the Pretrial Order is filed, or to enter an order stating that trial within 18 months of filing is not possible (for CJRA-recognized reasons).

6. Revising the Preliminary Statement to allow the parties to indicate their willingness to have the case tried by a magistrate judge.

7. Amending Local Rule 235-3(12) to provide for the issuance of a Scheduling Order that would also address settlement initiatives and the possible referral of the case to trial before a magistrate judge.

8. Amending Local Rule 225-1(b) to allow the court to shorten the time for discovery and to require that motions requesting extensions must be made prior to the expiration of the existing period. Such requests should be granted only in those cases when the exigent circumstances were different from, and could not be anticipated at, the time the Preliminary Statement was filed.

Differences Between Plan and Advisory Group Recommendations: The plan added language regarding criminal calendar demands to the advisory group's Recommendation 4. The advisory group said that if 16 months after the complaint was filed, no pretrial order had been entered, the trial judge, to satisfy the time period mandated by § 473(a)(2), should then step in and either order a closure of pretrial proceedings and set a trial date or order that a fixed trial date could not be set for CJRA-specified reasons. It also added the requirement that the circumstances underlying a motion for discovery extension must be different from the original circumstance or at least must have been unanticipated.

Differences Between Plan and Implementation: None reported.

CJRA POLICY 3: MORE INTENSIVE MANAGEMENT OF COMPLEX CASES

Policy Before CJRA Plan

There are no formal case management approaches to complex cases, other than discretionary tailoring of pretrial orders to specialized case needs.

CJRA Plan Implementation

Approved Plan: The plan called for:

1. Adopting Recommendation 1 of the advisory group that would modify the JS44 to allow the plaintiff to indicate that the matter is a complex case. This would alert the judge that special oversight and management may be needed, or that a Special Master might be advisable. Features that make a case complex include:

   a) An unusually large number of parties.

   b) An unusually large number of claims or defenses.

   c) Factual issues that are exceedingly complex.

   d) A greater-than-normal volume of evidence.

   e) Extended discovery needs.

   f) Problems locating or preserving evidence.

g) Pending parallel investigations or action by the government.

h) Multiple use of experts.

i) The need for foreign discovery.

j) The existence of highly technical issues and proof.

2. Specifying the basis of the assertion that the case is complex (from the check-off on the JS44) in the Preliminary Statement.

Differences Between Plan and Advisory Group Recommendations: None except that the reason why the case was considered complex was also added to the JS44.

Differences Between Plan and Implementation: None reported.

CJRA POLICY 4: EXCHANGE OF DISCOVERY INFORMATION

Policy Before CJRA Plan

There was no formal policy of standard, mandatory exchange.

CJRA Plan Implementation

Approved Plan: The Court adopted Recommendation 2 of the advisory group which proposed a new Local Rule requiring all parties to answer mandatory, Court developed, interrogatories, with the answers being filed with the court and served on other parties.

The interrogatories included a statement of the cause of action and an outline of the factual and legal issues; listing of current and previous related cases; identification of lay and expert witnesses with some summary information of their testimony; outline of discovery to be pursued; information concerning parties; insurance; and names of persons or entities with a subrogation interest. Plaintiffs claiming injury or damages are to provide information on the damages claimed and produce or describe "each document in your custody or control or of which you have knowledge which you contend supports your claims . . . ." Defendants are to provide a detailed factual basis for the defenses asserted and describe or produce "each document in your custody or control or of which you have knowledge which you contend supports your defense or defenses . . . ."

Differences Between Plan and Advisory Group Recommendations: The plan modified the advisory group report in three respects: 1) all defendant responses are to be filed within 15 days of the filing of the answer (rather than 45); 2) the four-month standard discovery period is changed to 0, 4, or 8, according to the case's particular track; and 3) the interrogatory regarding election of trial by jury or judge is deleted since the parties already indicate their desires in the Pretrial Order.

Differences Between Plan and Implementation: None reported. The December 1993 amendments to F.R.Civ.P. 26(a)(1) concerning mandatory initial disclosure were *not* in effect in this district[6] before February 1, 1996. Those disclosures were adopted in the February 1996 Local Rules amendments (although the Court does not follow the federal rule's timing provisions).

CJRA POLICY 5: CERTIFY GOOD FAITH EFFORT BEFORE FILING DISCOVERY MOTION

Policy Before CJRA Plan

Local Rule 225-4(a) already imposed the duty to make a good faith effort to resolve any dispute which arise in the course of discovery. A certificate stating that counsel attempted to resolve the controversy must have been signed by the moving party and attached to the motion to compel.

CJRA Plan Implementation

Approved Plan: No change to prior policy.

Differences Between Plan and Advisory Group Recommendations: None.

Differences Between Plan and Implementation: None reported.

CJRA POLICY 6: ALTERNATIVE DISPUTE RESOLUTION PROGRAMS

Policy Before CJRA Plan

No routine offering of alternatives to trial or established ADR programs or procedures existed. The district did have a settlement conference provision in Local Rule 235-2 but no participation by a designated neutral was required. Special Masters were used for some Title VII cases.

CJRA Plan Implementation

Approved Plan: The court adopted, with some modifications, the advisory group recommendation to create a mandatory court-annexed, non-binding arbitration program. However, it was concluded on advice of the general counsel of the Administrative Office of the U.S. Courts that the arbitration statutes (28 U.S.C. § 651 et seq.), when read together with the F.R.Civ.P. and the CJRA, prevented the district from implementing such a program without further authorization because the district is not one that was approved by statute to use arbitration. The Court indicated preference for mediation over other non-arbitration ADR techniques mentioned in the CJRA, but concluded that experience with arbitration is needed first. Features of the proposed arbitration program included:

---

[6]Stienstra (1995).

1. A request would be made for allocation of funds by the United States government to compensate private attorneys who serve as arbitrators (the Court is not willing to pass the cost of the program on to litigants).

2. Other features found in the advisory group's recommendation that would be adopted without modification include:

   a) An optimal size of 250–300 civil cases per year.

   b) Choice of a sample from all cases except agency appeals, prisoner petitions for habeas corpus, 28 U.S.C. § 1343, and actions involving pro se parties.

   c) Random selection from each civil assignment wheel.

   d) Statistical monitoring of the test program's progress and the creation of a data collection and evaluation program.

   e) Mandatory court-annexed arbitration unless the assigned judge sua sponte, or upon motion filed within 30 days of selection, found that the intended objectives of arbitration would not be met.

   f) Inclusion of cases not already assigned if all parties consent.

   g) The assigned judge would still oversee the case, and parties could still file pre-trial motions.

   h) The arbitration hearing would normally be a one-time summary proceeding of not more than four to six hours. Documentary evidence would be allowed upon proper notice to other parties and evidence would be presented primarily by attorneys rather than witnesses.

   i) The presence of parties would be encouraged but not required.

   j) The arbitrator's award would be advisory and non-binding. The assigned judge would not be informed of the decision and a trial-de-novo would be allowed if the award was rejected.

   k) The arbitrator must have been practicing in Georgia for not less than 10 years, with 50 percent or more time in litigation over not less than five years (or be a former judge), and must have completed approved arbitration training.

   l) The administration of the program would be by the Clerk's Office.

Additionally, the Court adopted a broadened version of an advisory group recommendation to authorize the parties in complex litigation to agree jointly on a Special Master. The Special Master would be authorized under an Order of Reference to manage discovery, conduct a trial, enter Findings of Fact and Conclusions of Law, and render a binding decision on the parties. Such a decision could be reversed by the Court only if clearly erroneous.

New Local Rules implementing these two ADR programs would be prepared when the Court receives the funding for the two programs and the authority for arbitration start-up. But, for the time being, they have not been implemented.

Differences Between Plan and Advisory Group Recommendations: The arbitration program would be implemented district-wide (not just in the Atlanta Division) and attorneys meeting the eligibility standards would serve as arbitrators (not the district's magistrate judges). Other differences include: no requirement for arbitrator to practice before this district court; rejection of hiring of an administrator; and, on consent of all parties, the arbitration case may instead be referred to a mediator.

Special Master's authority would be acknowledged in compliance with provisions of F.R.Civ.P. 53. Also, a list of persons qualified to be Special Masters would be developed and any Special Master selected from this list would be paid out of government funds allocated for the program (Special Masters chosen outside the list would be paid by the parties pursuant to their agreement).

Differences Between Plan and Implementation: The provisions of the plan have not been implemented due to lack of funding and authority, as discussed above.

OPTIONAL CJRA TECHNIQUES

The CJRA indicates that each court shall consider and may include the following five litigation management techniques:[7]

I. **Requiring that counsel jointly present a discovery/case management plan at the initial pretrial conference:**

The plan indicated that the proposed amendment to the Preliminary Statement "provides counsel an opportunity to set forth a specific discovery/case management plan for the case, if needed." The proposed preclusion against attempts to restructure discovery later in the life of the case—amended Local Rule 225-1(b)—was also seen as contributing to the implementation of this first technique. The district opted out of the December 1993 revised Federal Rules[8] so there was no implementation of the new Rule 26(f) before February 1996, after which date Local Rule 235-2(a) requires an in-person early planning conference at which discovery and other management issues must be discussed. After February 1996, the court renamed its "Preliminary statement" to "Preliminary planning report and Scheduling Order" (Local Rule 235-3).

II. **Requiring that each party be represented at each pretrial conference by an attorney with authority to bind that party:**

The Court felt that Local Rule 235(2)(3)(4) already required the participation of lead counsel in two required settlement conferences and also required counsel to sign the joint Preliminary Statement/Scheduling Order, and the Pretrial Order (required in all cases except those in the new zero-month discovery track). Although there generally

---

[7]28 U.S.C. § 473(b).
[8]Stienstra (1995).

is not any conference with a judge prior to filing of these two documents, the Pretrial Order could be used to request a conference if it was believed to be useful.

III. Requiring the signature of the attorney *and* the party for all requests for discovery extensions or postponements of trial:

The Court felt that this would not be the best procedure to curb delays (the advisory group suggested simple certification by the attorney and would have made the misrepresentation of a client's approval to seek extension or postponement grounds for disbarment). The Court would defer implementation of this third technique until the success of the other new amendments to the Local Rules has been assessed.

IV. Offering a Neutral Evaluation program:

The Court felt that the Local Rules already prompted an early settlement evaluation. Local Rule 235-2(a)(1) required lead counsels to confer in a good faith effort to settle the case prior to filing the Preliminary Statement (the advisory group would have required this 30 days after issue is joined). Additionally, the Court felt that the district should first concentrate on the proposed arbitration and special master ADR programs.

V. Requiring the attendance of party representatives with authority to bind to be present or available by telephone at settlement conferences:

This technique would be implemented by the proposed amendment to Local Rule 235-2(b) (see discussion under **CJRA Policy 2**).

OTHER POLICIES ADOPTED IN CJRA PLAN

Approved Plan:

1. Recommends that the jurisdictional amount in diversity cases be raised to $75,000.

2. Recommends that F.R.Civ.P. 8 and F.R.Civ.P. 12 be amended to eliminate the provision providing for tolling the time for answering a complaint, when a motion to dismiss is filed instead.

3. Extends authorization to the appropriate official to seek funding for additional staff positions needed to implement the plan's new programs and procedures.

4. Requests that CJRA funds be made available to provide for funding of the arbitrators, mediators, and Special Masters under the proposed ADR programs.

Differences Between Plan and Advisory Group Recommendations: The court did not adopt the advisory group recommendation that diversity jurisdiction for resident plaintiffs be abolished.

Differences Between Plan and Implementation: None reported.

OVERVIEW OF CJRA PROGRAM IN ILLINOIS, NORTHERN DISTRICT

OVERVIEW OF IMPLEMENTED CJRA PLAN

This is a comparison district, not a pilot district, so a CJRA plan must be implemented by December 1, 1993, and it need not contain the six pilot program principles. This district's plan was adopted November 15, 1993 and the plan was implemented through Local Rule and *Standing Order* changes. That implementation process was completed in early 1995. Three groups have also been appointed to develop an ADR pamphlet, develop guidelines for the conduct of depositions, and propose standards for fee petitions and guidelines for their review.

The CJRA Advisory Group notes that this court generally manages its docket well, "is the fastest in the country in the median time within which its civil cases terminate," and that this court "should exercise due care in changing its rules and practices."[1] It was supportive of active judicial case management and offered a number of recommendations for refinement of how it is done in this district. It also indicated the court is already doing differentiated case management, and that automatic prediscovery disclosure should not be required. While generally being supportive of settlement conferences and encouraging judges to employ ADR on a voluntary basis when appropriate, it suggested that the court study the results of the ongoing evaluation of ADR in CJRA pilot and other districts before establishing any court-wide mandatory programs.

The court's CJRA plan concurs with the Advisory Group report in most respects, such as retaining the current differentiated case management system rather than incorporating tracks, opting out of the automatic prediscovery provisions of the December 1993 revised Rule 26, and deferring a decision on adoption of any court-wide mandatory ADR programs until after ongoing evaluations in other districts are finished. The court accepted and adopted most of the refinements in existing case management procedures that were recommended by the Advisory Group. The plan also notes: "The success of the court in managing its calendar procedures suggests that a certain amount of caution is called for in any movement to modify the procedures used by

---

[1]McGarr et al. (1993), pp. v, vii. The 18-member committee was chaired by a lawyer and former Chief Judge, had a lawyer as reporter, met as a whole about monthly beginning in April 1991, and also worked in subcommittees. Three judges, a magistrate judge, and the Clerk of Court were ex-officio members. The Advisory Group interviewed judicial officers, surveyed over 2000 lawyers and held a public hearing.

the court. After all, since the median disposition time in this district is already half that of the national average, there is not a little danger that any change may result in an *increase* in delay, regardless of the intended effect."[2]

The Advisory Group's annual report for the year 1994[3] noted that a number of the provisions of the CJRA plan "have been incorporated into the local rules only in the last several weeks [March 9, 1995] and thus cannot be said to have had an impact on litigation management." However, "for the first time in decades, the Northern District has a full complement of active sitting judges and, in addition, a number of senior judges who are continuing to accept a substantial number of case assignments. This is a great boon to the district."

CJRA POLICY 1: DIFFERENTIAL CASE MANAGEMENT

Policy Before CJRA Plan

Pursuant to F.R.Civ.P. 16, the court has a Local Rule that requires the court to adopt a *Standing Order Establishing Pretrial Procedure* together with model pretrial order forms. In addition, the rule specifically exempts 11 classes of cases from the pretrial procedures set forth in the *Standing Order*, unless ordered by the assigned judge. The following types of cases are exempt: Recovery of overpayments and student loan cases; mortgage foreclosure cases; prisoner petitions; U.S. forfeiture/penalty cases; bankruptcy; deportation; Selective Service; Social Security reviews; tax suits and IRS third party; customer challenges (12 U.S.C. §3410); and cases concerning various Acts (Agricultural Acts, Economic Stabilization Act, Environmental Matters, Energy Allocation Act, Freedom of Information Act, Appeal of Fee Determination Under Equal Access to Justice Act, NARA Title II). All other types of cases are subject to the *Standing Order*, have a Rule 16 scheduling conference and are managed individually.

CJRA Plan Implementation

Approved Plan: Same. The Advisory Group indicated that "[t]he court's current system of exempting specific classes of cases from the pretrial provisions of F.R.Civ.P. 16, of having specific procedures for prisoner litigation, and of treating other cases individually, constitutes differentiated case management within the meaning of CJRA."[4]

Differences Between Plan and Advisory Group Recommendations: None.

Differences Between Plan and Implementation: None reported.

---

[2]United States District Court for the Northern District of Illinois (1993), p. 5.

[3]McGarr et al. (1995), p. 1.

[4]McGarr et al. (1993), p. 90.

CJRA POLICY 2: EARLY AND ONGOING CONTROL OF PRETRIAL BY JUDICIAL OFFICER

Policy Before CJRA Plan

Initial and final pretrial conferences are held, with at least one settlement conference with a judicial officer. In addition, nearly all judges hold status conferences, which are usually short, every couple of months for all cases not exempt from a Rule 16 conference. The *Standing Order* noted above covers pretrial procedures and requires the judge to begin supervision of the case within 120 days after filing. The limit is 20 interrogatories by local rule. The court has programs to help judges with unusually long criminal trials or unusual workloads, including: providing for skips in criminal case assignments for judges with unusually long criminal trials; transfer of civil cases awaiting trial (if the estimated trial length is no more than 5 days) to a short civil trial calendar for trial by visiting judges or judges with free time as a result of a last-minute settlement; and provision for disposition of pending motions by a judge other than the assigned judge.

CJRA Plan Implementation

Approved Plan: Same, with some refinements and clarifications: (1) Proposes amendment of the *Standing Order* to begin supervision of the case 60 days after defendant appearance and within 90 days after service on a defendant; (2) urges judges to set firm trial dates as early in the proceedings as practicable; (3) agrees with the concept that a trial should start within 18 months of filing; (4) clarifies that, although the *Standing Order* provides for the use of standard pretrial order forms, judges in individual cases may have varying requirements for final pretrial order forms as well as for motions, and provides that such variances be available from the minute clerk and the Clerk of Court, respectively; (5) endorses the recommendation that costs be taken into account in the discovery process; (6) forms a committee to develop guidelines on the conduct of depositions; (7) proposes a rule amendment establishing a procedure for parties to anonymously obtain information on the status of an undecided motion or bench trial;[5] (8) encourages oral rulings on motions and bench trials when possible; (9) proposes amendment of the *Standing Order* to explicitly authorize the judge to require that representatives of the parties with authority to bind them in settlement discussions be present or available by telephone during any settlement discussions; (10) proposes amendment of the *Standing Order* to eliminate the reference to a "face to face" meeting and permit telephonic meetings by counsel in preparation of the proposed pretrial order when the case is nearing readiness for trial; and (11) allows parties to consent to a magistrate judge ruling on dispositive motions. The court will continue to require the filing of a joint written discovery plan only when directed by the court, not for all cases.

---

[5] The court adopted General Rule 12Q in April 1994. It allows a party to request a report on the status of any motion pending for 7 months or longer, or fully briefed for 6 months or longer. Such requests are made to the Clerk of Court. The clerk reviews the docket and if a motion meets the Rule's criteria, then the judge is notified that a request for a status report has been received. The judge has the option of commenting or not. During calendar year 1995, 9 requests were received.

Differences Between Plan and Advisory Group Recommendations: Same, except: (1) the Advisory Group recommended that a judge presented with a motion should give the parties a time frame within which the judge expects to rule; (2) the court agrees that the standard pretrial order form should be uniformly used, but that the judge in the individual case is in the best position to determine the extent to which to depart from the standard forms and procedures in the *Standing Order*; (3) the court supports the suggestion that staff law clerks be used to hold settlement conferences via telephone in appropriate prisoner cases, but does not have sufficient law clerk staff to conduct this experiment now; and (4) the court supports the suggestion that a handbook be developed to help counsel appointed to represent pro se plaintiffs in Title VII cases, but has not yet been able to interest any organization in preparing such a handbook.

Differences Between Plan and Implementation: None reported.

CJRA POLICY 3: MORE INTENSIVE MANAGEMENT OF COMPLEX CASES

Policy Before CJRA Plan

Individualized case management, generally with more intensive management for more complex cases.

CJRA Plan Implementation

Approved Plan: Same, with some refinements: (1) proposes amendment to *Standing Order* indicating that the judge may use phased discovery in complex cases; may use *the Manual on Complex Litigation 2d*; and may establish timetables for filing motions; and (2) proposes amendment to *Standing Order* indicating that if a joint discovery/case management plan is required for a case and the lawyers cannot agree, then they can submit multiple plans and court will resolve the impasse.

Differences Between Plan and Advisory Group Recommendations: Similar, except Advisory Group recommended phased discovery for all cases with discovery.

Differences Between Plan and Implementation: None reported.

CJRA POLICY 4: EXCHANGE OF DISCOVERY INFORMATION

Policy Before CJRA Plan

No formal policy.

CJRA Plan Implementation

Approved Plan: The court encourages the voluntary exchange of materials and other cooperative discovery devices, and proposes amending the local rules to opt out of the F.R.Civ.P 26(a)(1) which would have required mandatory prediscovery exchanges. The recent amendments to Federal Rule of Civil Procedure 26(a) concerning mandatory initial disclosure thus are partially in effect in this district. Rule 26(a)(2) & (3), concerning disclosure of experts and pretrial disclosure about evidence that may be presented at trial, are in effect. Rule 26(a)(1), concerning initial disclosure without awaiting a discovery request, is not in effect although judges are permitted to apply it case by case.[6]

Differences Between Plan and Advisory Group Recommendations: None. The Advisory Group noted that since this court has the fastest median time to disposition in the country, mandatory prediscovery disclosure "could easily slow down our faster cases, without improving the speed of our more difficult cases."[7]

Differences Between Plan and Implementation: None, except in the process of amending the Local Rules to implement the opting out of F.R.Civ.P 26(a)(1), it was noted that it was the only rule permitting court-required exchange of insurance information. So language in new General Rule 5.00H provides that any party may inspect for copying any relevant insurance agreement, while not making all provisions of 26(a)(1) mandatory for all cases.

CJRA POLICY 5: CERTIFY GOOD FAITH EFFORT BEFORE FILING DISCOVERY MOTION

Policy Before CJRA Plan

Local Rule indicates the court will refuse to hear any motion for discovery or production of documents that is not accompanied by a statement indicating that after personal consultation and sincere attempts to resolve differences, counsel are unable to reach an accord, or counsel's attempts to engage in such personal consultation were unsuccessful due to no fault of counsel's. Specifics about any meeting, or if no meeting why none took place, are required.

CJRA Plan Implementation

Approved Plan: Same. Minor nonsubstantive clarifications are to be made in the Local Rule wording.

Differences Between Plan and Advisory Group Recommendations: None.

Differences Between Plan and Implementation: None reported.

CJRA POLICY 6: ALTERNATIVE DISPUTE RESOLUTION PROGRAMS

Policy Before CJRA Plan

A settlement conference is usually held with a judicial officer. The court encourages the use of ADR in appropriate circumstances. No formal court-wide ADR program is

---

[6]Stienstra (1995).

[7]McGarr et al. (1993), p. 65.

in place, and our interviews indicate that the number of cases that go through an ADR process (other than a settlement conference) is less than 100 per year.

CJRA Plan Implementation

Approved Plan: Same, and proposes changes to the *Standing Order* to provide explicit reference to two settlement techniques that have been used with some frequency by most members of the court: (1) the court may offer sua sponte to preside over settlement talks; and (2) the preferred method of having the court preside over settlement talks if there is to be a bench trial is to arrange for another judge or magistrate judge to conduct the settlement talks. The Advisory Group recommended that before adopting a court-wide formal ADR program, the court should await the analysis of the experience of those courts that are experimenting with particular ADR methods under CJRA; the court agrees. In addition the court established a panel that developed a pamphlet listing the various ADR methods available and giving a general description of available private ADR options; this pamphlet is provided to everyone filing a civil case.

Differences Between Plan and Advisory Group Recommendations: None.

Differences Between Plan and Implementation: None reported.

OPTIONAL CJRA TECHNIQUES

The CJRA indicates that each court shall consider and may include the following five litigation management techniques:[8]

I. **Requiring that counsel jointly present a discovery/case management plan at the initial pretrial conference:**

The *Standing Order* allows this to be required for individual cases, but the CJRA Plan rejects making it a requirement for all cases. Such a provision was thought to increase costs, and in cases other than the more complex, the additional cost would not usually be offset by any savings or reduction in delay. Refer to the section on **CJRA Policy 3** for more information. The district did not opt out of the December 1993 revised Federal Rule 26(f) [9] so there was implementation of that portion of the new Rule 26.

II. **Requiring that each party be represented at each pretrial conference by an attorney with authority to bind that party:**

The *Standing Order* already requires this. Refer to the section on **CJRA Policy 2** for more information.

---

[8] 28 U.S.C. § 473(b).
[9] Stienstra (1995).

III.   Requiring the signature of the attorney *and* the party for all requests for discovery extensions or postponements of trial:

The Advisory Group recommended against this, and the court concurred. The Advisory Group observed that it did not think the prevailing practice among lawyers is to seek repeated or substantial extensions that they then hide from their client, and that lawyers cannot afford to alienate a client by dragging out a case that the client wants to see resolved.

IV.   Offering a Neutral Evaluation program:

The court encourages the use of a neutral evaluation program, but concurs with the Advisory Group that they should wait for the results of ongoing evaluations in other courts and not adopt a formal program at this time.

V.   Requiring party representatives with authority to bind to be present or available by telephone at settlement conferences:

 An amendment to the *Standing Order* explicitly authorizes judges to require this. Refer to the section on **CJRA Policy 2** for more information.

OTHER POLICIES ADOPTED IN CJRA PLAN

Approved Plan: The court will request two additional magistrate judges, is taking steps to provide a larger facility for the Western Division, and recommends that the Judicial Conference urge Congress to consider the impact of its legislation on the rate of civil and criminal case filings.

Differences Between Plan and Advisory Group Recommendations: The Advisory Group recommended three new district judgeships. The court indicated the current guidelines on the number of district judgeships do not support the recommendation. The court does not believe that the demands on judicial time required in handling mortgage foreclosures and employer contributions to employee benefit plans cases are such as to warrant their special handling as suggested by the Advisory Group.

Differences Between Plan and Implementation: None reported.

OVERVIEW OF CJRA PROGRAM IN INDIANA, NORTHERN DISTRICT

OVERVIEW OF IMPLEMENTED CJRA PLAN

This is a comparison district, not a pilot district, so a CJRA plan must be implemented by December 1, 1993, and it need not contain the six pilot program principles. This district's plan was effective December 31, 1991.

The CJRA Advisory Group made recommendations concerning the critical need for uniformity among judges, the timely disposition of motions, and better use of ADR. Two recommendations are at the heart of the report: (1) early mandatory disclosure of basic evidence and early firm trial dates; and (2) more Magistrate Judges and law clerks to handle pro se and Social Security cases.[1]

The plan indicates that some of the judges will experiment with different types of early mandatory disclosure and then determine whether a court-wide standardized mandatory early disclosure order should be adopted. The plan subsequently was revised so that the court now follows the December 1993 revised F.R.Civ.P. 26. Individualized case management will be used, rather than "tracks." The court will continue to engage in "early, ongoing, and active" judicial control of civil cases, will set trial dates at the initial pretrial conference, and intends to set trial dates that are within 16 months of the conference. One judge previously used and continues to use early neutral evaluation for about 100 cases per year, and two additional judges are experimenting with neutral evaluation on fewer than 10 cases each. The court concurred with the requirement for additional personnel. The Advisory Group recommended the following, which were not adopted: abolishing the trailing calendar system; adopting a uniform and simple Order Controlling Trial and a uniform initial pretrial order; and adopting an internal presumption that all motions will be ruled on within 30 days of the close of the briefing schedule.[2]

---

[1]United States District Court for the Northern District of Indiana (1991a). The 13-member committee had a law professor as reporter who functioned as unofficial chairperson, and met as a whole several times. Two judges, one magistrate judge, and the clerk of court served as ex-officio members. The Advisory Group interviewed judicial officers. Surveys and public hearings were not conducted.

[2]United States District Court for the Northern District of Indiana (1991b).

The annual report on the implementation of CJRA[3] noted a substantial growth in both civil and criminal filings since the plan was adopted. The early mandatory disclosure requirements of the plan were repealed when the court decided to follow the December 1993 revised F.R.Civ.P. 26(a)(1). As of December 1994, no conclusions had been reached regarding court-wide adoption of an early neutral evaluation program. Amendments were adopted to refine the Local Rules concerning the following: stipulated initial extensions of time to respond to a pleading or discovery order; materials to accompany summary judgment motions; and procedures for handling Social Security appeals.

CJRA POLICY 1: DIFFERENTIAL CASE MANAGEMENT

Policy Before CJRA Plan

The following types of cases are exempt from an initial Rule 16 scheduling conference by Local Rule: Social Security appeals, habeas corpus, motions to vacate sentence, forfeiture proceedings, IRS summons and summary proceedings, bankruptcy appeals, land condemnation, naturalization proceedings, interpleader cases, prisoner pro se, VA overpayment, student loan, out-of-district subpoena cases, HUD overpayment, and others at judicial discretion. All other types of cases are managed individually.

CJRA Plan Implementation

Approved Plan: The same types of cases are exempt from an initial Rule 16 scheduling conference, except prisoner civil rights cases are no longer exempt and a telephone conference will be held. In late 1994, the plan was amended to drop the requirement for the telephone conference for prisoner civil rights cases. The court declined to adopt a program that would place cases on "tracks" with presumptive scheduling deadlines at filing (other than the types of cases exempt from a Rule 16 conference). The court strongly favors individualized case management but feels tracks are not appropriate for this small district and feels that tracking would ignore recommendations of those most familiar with the case.

Differences Between Plan and Advisory Group Recommendations: None. The Advisory Group favors individualized differential cases management rather than systematic tracks (calling tracks "arbitrary compartmentalization of cases and the use of inflexible deadlines to accomplish the task of case management"[4]), and recommends not exempting prisoner civil rights cases from the initial pretrial conference requirement.

Differences Between Plan and Implementation: None reported.

---

[3]United States District Court for the Northern District of Indiana (1994).

[4]United States District Court for the Northern District of Indiana (1991a), p. 65.

CJRA POLICY 2: EARLY AND ONGOING CONTROL OF PRETRIAL BY JUDICIAL OFFICER

Policy Before CJRA Plan

Initial and final pretrial conferences are held, usually with one attempt to settle the case. Some judges set a trial date at the initial conference; others wait until later. Limit is 30 interrogatories and 30 requests for admission by local rule.

CJRA Plan Implementation

Approved Plan: Similar to prior practices. The judges will continue to engage in "early, ongoing, and active" judicial control of civil cases. With respect to setting deadlines, the plan indicates that, unless it would increase expense, judges will establish and enforce deadlines for pleading amendments, discovery completion, and filing dispositive motions. In all cases in which it is feasible to do so and the case is not too complex or otherwise inappropriate, the judges will set trial dates at the initial pretrial conference, and set trial dates that are within 16 months of the conference. Given existing docket conditions, the court declines to abolish the use of "trailing calendars" in trial settings. Deadlines will be set only after inviting counsels' views, and will be memorialized in a written order. Deadlines will not be changed except for good cause shown. Attorneys participating in conferences are required to have authority to bind the parties on various specified matters. The judges will continue to be available for settlement conferences, and to order them when deemed appropriate. The court declined to adopt any formal deadline for ruling on motions but will attempt to resolve them within 30 days after completion of briefing or hearing, whichever is later. The court declines to adopt a uniform district-wide order regarding trial. The court will seek a rule change to eliminate some items that have been required to accompany summary judgment motions. The process for handling Social Security cases is streamlined.

Differences Between Plan and Advisory Group Recommendations: The Advisory Group recommended the following, which were not adopted: abolishing the trailing calendar system; adoption of a uniform and simple Order Controlling Trial and a uniform initial pretrial order; and adopting an internal presumption that all motions will be ruled on within 30 days of the close of the briefing schedule.

Differences Between Plan and Implementation: None reported.

CJRA POLICY 3: MORE INTENSIVE MANAGEMENT OF COMPLEX CASES

Policy Before CJRA Plan

Individualized case management, generally with more intensive management for more complex cases.

CJRA Plan Implementation

Approved Plan: Same.

Differences Between Plan and Advisory Group Recommendations: None.

Differences Between Plan and Implementation: None reported.

CJRA POLICY 4: EXCHANGE OF DISCOVERY INFORMATION

Policy Before CJRA Plan

Each judge encouraged voluntary exchange of information and cooperative discovery. Two judges required disclosure of witnesses and damage calculations prior to the initial pretrial conference.

CJRA Plan Implementation

The court will continue to encourage the voluntary exchange of information and cooperative discovery. In addition, some of the judges will experiment with various types of early, court-mandated, standardized disclosure. If discovery disputes arise, the court will consider the proportionality of requested discovery to the issues and stakes involved and exercise authority to assess costs when disputes show breakdown of cooperative discovery.

Three different standardized mandatory disclosure experiments will be conducted by different judges for types of cases not exempt from a Rule 16 conference. (1) One experiment involves a case-by-case determination at the initial pretrial conference of what is to be disclosed, but disclosure will usually include names and summary of information of all witnesses, including experts, each cause of action and defense and the facts and authority supporting them, specifying damages/relief sought and giving names of people with information and calculations of damages, and all documents and things that support parties' claims/defenses. (2) A second experiment requires the following information to be disclosed: name and address of all persons with information, production or description by category, with location, of all documents or things that "are likely to bear significantly on any claim or defense" (of both sides of the case), computation of damages plus evidence supporting computation, and insurance contracts), and later disclosure of experts and summary of their testimony. (3) A third experiment expands on two judges' pre-CJRA requirements (witnesses and damage calculation before initial pretrial conference) by adding disclosure of insurance, medical and employment and special damages records, and experts and their opinions. The magistrate judge in the same division will also experiment for cases assigned to him by parties' consent. By May 1993, the court will review the experiments and determine whether a court-wide standardized mandatory early disclosure rule or order should be adopted. In 1994, the court decided to amend its CJRA plan and follow the December 1993 revised F.R.Civ.P. 26.

Differences Between Plan and Advisory Group Recommendations: None. The Advisory Group recommended an experimental program with court required disclosure of basic factual information early in the life of a case. They did not recommend its "wholesale adoption in the district. Rather, the plan should be discretionary with each judge."

Differences Between Plan and Implementation: None reported. The recent amendments to Federal Rule of Civil Procedure 26(a)(1) concerning mandatory initial disclosure are in effect in this district.[5]

CJRA POLICY 5: CERTIFY GOOD FAITH EFFORT BEFORE FILING DISCOVERY MOTION

Policy Before CJRA Plan

By Local Rule, discovery motions must be accompanied by certificate of good-faith effort to reach agreement.

CJRA Plan Implementation

Approved Plan: Same.

Differences Between Plan and Advisory Group Recommendations: None.

Differences Between Plan and Implementation: None reported.

CJRA POLICY 6: ALTERNATIVE DISPUTE RESOLUTION PROGRAMS

Policy Before CJRA Plan

A settlement conference was usually held with a judicial officer. In addition, one judge in one division has used early neutral evaluation by a pro bono neutral lawyer since 1990 (the judge calls it a Mediation Evaluation Conference, and the plan refers to it as Early Neutral Evaluation). That judge's formally structured program has a panel of several dozen neutral evaluators and had about 100 cases volunteer in 1992, which is a majority of those for which a Rule 16 conference was held.

CJRA Plan Implementation

Approved Plan: The court will expand the range of court-assisted settlement programs, but continues to view private negotiations as the most cost-effective approach to settlement. Settlement conferences with judicial officers will continue to be held for most cases. Cautious use will be made of voluntary mini-trials and summary jury trials in cases in which the actual trial would be unusually expensive. The one judge with the preexisting early neutral evaluation program will continue it, except in mid-1992 the program will convert from pro bono to paid neutral evaluators (with the parties sharing the costs). In addition, two other judges will experiment

---

[5]Interviews with district court personnel, December 12, 1994. Stienstra (1995).

with early neutral evaluation and report to the court and the Advisory Group concerning their experience with the program by January 1, 1993. As of December 1994, the two judges experimenting with early neutral evaluation had had fewer than 10 cases volunteer, the experiments were not yet concluded, and no decision had been made on court-wide adoption of an early neutral evaluation program.

Differences Between Plan and Advisory Group Recommendations: The Advisory Group recommended that ADR methods such as early neutral evaluation and magistrate-led mediation should be expanded, and that summary jury trial should be used sparingly. Summary jury trials are rarely used, and the early neutral evaluation expansion recommended has occurred, but fewer than 10 additional cases volunteered in 1992 in the two judges' experimental programs. Magistrate-led mediation expansion was not part of the CJRA plan.

Differences Between Plan and Implementation: None, except the neutral evaluation experimentation is progressing slowly and a decision on more widespread adoption had not been made as of December 1994.

OPTIONAL CJRA TECHNIQUES

The CJRA indicates that each court shall consider and may include the following five litigation management techniques:[6]

I.   **Requiring that counsel jointly present a discovery/case management plan at the initial pretrial conference:**

Plan does not prohibit individual judges from requiring written submissions in preparation for the initial pretrial conference. There is no district-wide requirement, though Plan agrees that submission of a joint plan is a useful tool in appropriate cases. In 1994, the court decided to amend its CJRA plan and follow the December 1993 revised F.R.Civ.P. 26. The Advisory Group Report had recommended that all written preliminary pretrial reports be abandoned. However, a comment to the Plan encourages counsel to meet and discuss matters to be addressed at the pretrial conference.

II.   **Requiring that each party be represented at each pretrial conference by an attorney with authority to bind that party:**

Plan requires such authority to bind regarding a wide range of topics at an initial pretrial conference. Comment to the Plan suggests that this requirement also exists in other pretrial conferences as well.

III.   **Requiring the signature of the attorney *and* the party for all requests for discovery extensions or postponements of trial:**

Plan declines to adopt this technique but allows its requirement in appropriate cases.

---

[6]28 U.S.C. § 473(b).

IV.   Offering a Neutral Evaluation program:

Plan expands, on an experimental basis, the early neutral evaluation process that was being used in Fort Wayne. See **CJRA Policy 6** discussion above. Advisory Group Report felt that neutral evaluation was one of the two primary ADR techniques to be considered by the court and that evaluation should not be required just before a trial date.

V.   **Requiring party representatives with authority to bind to be present or available by telephone at settlement conferences:**

Plan gives the judge conducting the settlement conference the option of requiring attendance of persons with settlement authority.

OTHER POLICIES ADOPTED IN CJRA PLAN

Approved Plan: The court will seek two additional magistrate judges, full staffing of the clerk's office, and one additional law clerk.

Differences Between Plan and Advisory Group Recommendations: None.

Differences Between Plan and Implementation: None reported.

OVERVIEW OF CJRA PROGRAM IN KENTUCKY, EASTERN DISTRICT

OVERVIEW OF IMPLEMENTED CJRA PLAN

This is a comparison district, not a pilot district, so a CJRA plan must be implemented by December 1, 1993, and it need not contain the six pilot program principles. This district's plan was adopted October 21, 1993, and is to be implemented, in part, through Joint Local Rules changes.

The CJRA Advisory Committee notes the "the condition of the court's civil docket is satisfactory, considering the fact that there has been a judicial vacancy in the district since 1991."[1] The Committee did not recommend mandatory tracks for differential case management. The Committee did recommend continuation and refinement of Joint Local Rules that have provided for standardization and uniformity between the Eastern and Western Districts of Kentucky, a voluntary mediation program, a mandatory status conference early in the litigation, an early meeting of lawyers before the status conference and exchange of information (essentially the same as the requirements of the December 1993 revised F.R.Civ.P. 26), and increased staffing and facilities.

The Court ordered adoption of the Advisory Committee's report as the Court's CJRA plan with minor refinements: (1) incorporation of the Local Rules into the Plan; (2) a change in one recommendation; and (3) the notation that the Court endorsed the recommendations that it did not have the power to implement. The one recommendation changed was in the use of Magistrate Judges. The Advisory Committee indicated that any civil motion referred to a Magistrate Judge for report and recommendation should automatically revert back to the District Judge if not ruled on within 90 days of referral. The court's plan excludes "criminal cases, prisoner cases such as habeas corpus, extraordinary writs, and U.S. cases such as student loans and forfeitures," and indicates that the 90 days will run from the date of submission (after all briefs are filed and hearings and oral arguments held) rather than from the date of referral to the Magistrate Judge. The voluntary mediation program is being experi-

---

[1]Savage et al. (1993), p. 17. The 25-member committee was chaired by a lawyer, had a law professor as reporter, met as a whole several times beginning in October 1991, and also worked in subcommittees. The Clerk of Court was a member, as was one lawyer who became a Judge in this district after the Committee's report was submitted. Two Magistrate Judges attended some meetings. The Advisory Group interviewed judicial officers and surveyed 500 lawyers and litigants.

mented with by one judge, before consideration of court-wide adoption, and no decision had been made as of late 1995.[2]

The first CJRA annual report indicates that "overall, the civil docket is doing well. Actual civil trials appear to be down from 1993 and the life span of a civil case has been reduced."[3] The second annual report concludes that "the docket management of the Court has been improved and is more efficient."[4] ADR continues to be ad hoc and voluntary in this district. The report notes that prisoner cases are likely to rise in this district, and recommend increasing the size of and restructuring the pro se law clerk's office.

CJRA POLICY 1: DIFFERENTIAL CASE MANAGEMENT

Policy Before CJRA Plan

The following types of cases were exempt from F.R.Civ.P. 16(b) by Local Rule: habeas corpus, pro se prisoner civil rights, Social Security, and civil penalty. All other cases were subject to Rule 16 and were individually managed by judicial officers.

CJRA Plan Implementation

Approved Plan: Same. The Advisory Committee recommended against mandatory tracks.

Differences Between Plan and Advisory Group Recommendations: None.

Differences Between Plan and Implementation: None reported.

CJRA POLICY 2: EARLY AND ONGOING CONTROL OF PRETRIAL BY JUDICIAL OFFICER

Policy Before CJRA Plan

Initial pretrial conferences are held by some, but not all judges. Most judges request inputs from lawyers by mail before establishing a pretrial schedule, rather than holding an initial pretrial conference in person. Most cases have a settlement conference with a judicial officer as part of the final pretrial preparations. Local Rule limits interrogatories and requests for admissions to 30 each.

CJRA Plan Implementation

Approved Plan: The court should continue to refine and implement those measures that have provided for standardization and uniformity through the Joint Local Rules.

---

[2]United States District Court for the Eastern District of Kentucky (1993), p. 1.

[3]Savage et al. (1994), p. 14.

[4]Hawse et al. (1995), p. 15.

This recommendation is an endorsement of the concept of continuing to have Joint Local Rules the same for both Eastern and Western Kentucky District Courts, but does not contain any suggestions for changing those rules.

The court should have a mandatory status conference early in the litigation (except criminal cases, prisoner cases such as habeas corpus, extraordinary writs, U. S. cases such as student loans and forfeitures), at which time the court should address case management techniques which should include: limiting interrogatories to 25 and depositions to no more than 10, limiting expert witnesses where appropriate, setting deadlines for discovery and dispositive motions, identification of trial witnesses and experts, identification of documents and exhibits to be used at trial, and setting of a final pretrial conference and firm trial dates. The Advisory Committee was unanimous in agreement as to a mandatory status conference early in the litigation, indicating that it should be in person.

For most types of cases, any civil motion referred to a Magistrate Judge shall revert to the Judge if not reported on within 90 days after all briefs have been filed and all hearings on the motion have been held.

Differences Between Plan and Advisory Group Recommendations: The Advisory Committee indicated that any civil motion referred to a Magistrate Judge for report and recommendation should automatically revert back to the District Judge if not ruled on within 90 days of referral. The court's plan excludes "criminal cases, prisoner cases such as habeas corpus, extraordinary writs, and U.S. cases such as student loans and forfeitures," and indicates the 90 days will run from the date of submission rather than from the date of referral to the Magistrate Judge.

Differences Between Plan and Implementation: None reported.

CJRA POLICY 3: MORE INTENSIVE MANAGEMENT OF COMPLEX CASES

Policy Before CJRA Plan

Individualized case management, generally with more intensive management for more complex cases.

CJRA Plan Implementation

Approved Plan: Same (no mention of special management of complex cases in the plan).

Differences Between Plan and Advisory Group Recommendations: None.

Differences Between Plan and Implementation: None reported.

CJRA POLICY 4: EXCHANGE OF DISCOVERY INFORMATION

Policy Before CJRA Plan

No formal policy. One judge experimented with early mandatory disclosure.

CJRA Plan Implementation

Approved Plan: Intent was to be the same as the F.R.Civ.P. 26 proposed amendments that were effective in December 1993.

Differences Between Plan and Advisory Group Recommendations: None.

Differences Between Plan and Implementation: None reported. December 1993 amendments to Federal Rule of Civil Procedure 26(a)(1) concerning mandatory initial disclosure are in effect in this district.[5]

CJRA POLICY 5: CERTIFY GOOD FAITH EFFORT BEFORE FILING DISCOVERY MOTION

Policy Before CJRA Plan

Local Rule indicates that the moving party shall attach to the discovery motion a certification of counsel that counsel have conferred and that they have been unable to resolve their differences. The certification shall detail the attempts of counsel to resolve the dispute.

CJRA Plan Implementation

Approved Plan: Same.

Differences Between Plan and Advisory Group Recommendations: None.

Differences Between Plan and Implementation: None reported.

CJRA POLICY 6: ALTERNATIVE DISPUTE RESOLUTION PROGRAMS

Policy Before CJRA Plan

A settlement conference is usually held with a judicial officer. By Local Rule, a judge may set any civil case for summary jury trial or other alternative method of dispute resolution. No formal court-wide ADR program is in place, and the number of cases that go through an ADR process (other than a settlement conference) is less than 50.

---

[5]Stienstra (1995).

CJRA Plan Implementation

Approved Plan: The court should adopt and implement a voluntary mediation program. The court encourages the use of any private ADR procedure. The specific detailed plan for voluntary mediation is to be jointly developed by the Eastern and Western Districts of Kentucky, and implemented in the Joint Local Rules.

Differences Between Plan and Advisory Group Recommendations: None.

Differences Between Plan and Implementation: One judge is experimenting with mediation, and all judges will consider revisions in the Local Rule to implement it court-wide after the experiment is completed. As of late 1994, this was still under consideration.

OPTIONAL CJRA TECHNIQUES

The CJRA indicates that each court shall consider and may include the following five litigation management techniques:[6]

I. **Requiring that counsel jointly present a discovery/case management plan at the initial pretrial conference:**

Discovery/case management plan would be formulated at a mandatory settlement conference early in the litigation; however, no discussion of a joint presentation by counsel. The court subsequently decided to follow the December 1993 revised F.R.Civ.P. 26.

II. **Requiring that each party be represented at each pretrial conference by an attorney with authority to bind that party:**

No discussion.

III. **Requiring the signature of the attorney *and* the party for all requests for discovery extensions or postponements of trial:**

No discussion.

IV. **Offering a Neutral Evaluation program:**

Voluntary mediation was the only ADR program explicitly under experimentation.

V. **Requiring party representatives with authority to bind to be present or available by telephone at settlement conferences:**

No discussion.

---

[6] 28 U.S.C. § 473(b).

OTHER POLICIES ADOPTED IN CJRA PLAN

Approved Plan: Other aspects of the Plan called for the following:

Endorsed Advisory Committee recommendations that judicial vacancies be filled, that each judge should have a full-time magistrate judge assigned, that each magistrate judge should have an additional law clerk, that additional pro se clerk staff be added, that the clerk's office should be fully staffed, and that facilities should be expanded.

Differences Between Plan and Advisory Group Recommendations: None.

Differences Between Plan and Implementation: None reported.

OVERVIEW OF CJRA PROGRAM IN KENTUCKY, WESTERN DISTRICT

OVERVIEW OF IMPLEMENTED CJRA PLAN

This is a comparison district, not a pilot district, so a CJRA plan must be implemented by December 1, 1993, and it need not contain the six pilot program principles. This district's plan was adopted November 30, 1993, and was effective December 1, 1993.

The CJRA Advisory Committee concludes that civil litigation in this district is "generally well managed" but indicates there are some ways in which pretrial management can be improved. The Committee indicated four areas that contribute to some unnecessary cost and delay: "(1) a reluctance to adhere to pretrial deadlines; (2) delays associated with pretrial motions; (3) inefficiencies in discovery practice; and (4) underuse of alternatives to litigation."[1] The Committee did not recommend mandatory tracks for differential case management. The Committee did recommend: (1) a Local Rule requiring that trials normally be commenced within 18 months of filing; (2) measures to address the issue of delay in rulings on pretrial motions, including scheduling and prioritizing, and a Local Rule requiring parties to immediately notify the court of any reasonably anticipated settlement of a case where there is a pending motion; (3) a Local Rule requiring development of a case management plan before the scheduling conference is held; (4) a Local Rule concerning the conduct of depositions, timing of disclosure of experts, and procedures governing a claim of privilege; (5) a Local Rule regarding the availability of Magistrate Judges to resolve discovery disputes telephonically; and (6) a Local Rule establishing mediation and early neutral evaluation programs.

The court's plan indicated that the most significant reason for delay in the civil docket has been the lack of full judicial resources for the past several years.[2] The court generally indicated its agreement with the intent of the Advisory Group's report, but felt that revision of Local Rules was not necessary and that further study was required in some areas such as ADR, where one judge is experimenting with

---

[1]Westberry et al. (1993), pp. 26, 27. The 45-member committee was chaired by a lawyer, had a law professor as reporter, met as a whole several times and also worked through a steering committee. The Clerk of Court was an ex-officio member, as was the reporter. The Advisory Group surveyed judicial officers, and surveyed lawyers and litigants on 100 cases.

[2]United States District Court for the Western District of Kentucky (1993).

mediation prior to the court's considering adopting it on a more widespread basis in 1995. The court continued its present practice of exempting certain case categories from F.R.Civ.P. 16 conferences but did not adopt any more formalized system of tracks (although as of late 1994, a system of management tracks was being considered). The court further indicated it would not develop separate local requirements for mandatory disclosure, and is following the new F.R.Civ.P 26. Note that this district has Joint Local Rules with the Eastern District of Kentucky, and any revision of those Joint Local Rules would require the concurrence of both districts.

As of January 1996, a CJRA Annual Report had not been issued by either the Court or the Advisory Group.

CJRA POLICY 1: DIFFERENTIAL CASE MANAGEMENT

Policy Before CJRA Plan

The following types of cases were exempt from F.R.Civ.P. 16(b) by Local Rule: habeas corpus, pro se prisoner civil rights, Social Security, and civil penalty. The court also exempted government collection, foreclosure, and forfeiture cases. All other cases were subject to Rule 16 and were individually managed by judicial officers.

CJRA Plan Implementation

Approved Plan: Same. The Advisory Committee recommended against a formal system of tracks (other than for the above), indicating they would not aid efficiency.

Differences Between Plan and Advisory Group Recommendations: None.

Differences Between Plan and Implementation: None reported. However, as of late 1994 the court was considering using a formal system of management tracks (Fast, Standard, and Complex, perhaps defined by nature of suit and grouped by expected length of time to disposition). It also hired a consultant provide some judicial training in this area.

CJRA POLICY 2: EARLY AND ONGOING CONTROL OF PRETRIAL BY JUDICIAL OFFICER

Policy Before CJRA Plan

An initial pretrial conference is held for most, but not all, cases that are not exempt from Rule 16(a). If a conference is not held, then a scheduling order is still issued. A trial date usually is not set at the initial pretrial conference. Most cases have a settlement conference with a judicial officer as part of the final pretrial preparations. Local Rule limits interrogatories and requests for admissions to 30 each.

CJRA Plan Implementation

Approved Plan: The court indicates it already takes an active role very early in the pretrial process, indicates general concurrence with the intent of the Advisory Group's recommendations in the area of pretrial management, but feels that Local Rule changes are either inappropriate or unnecessary.

Differences Between Plan and Advisory Group Recommendations: The Advisory Group recommended a Local Rule requiring that trials normally be commenced within 18 months of filing of the complaint, unless the complexity of the case or the demand of the court's docket indicate that trial cannot reasonably be held within such time. The court is committed to this laudable goal, but feels a Local Rule change codifying this is not appropriate.

The Advisory Group also recommended some specific measures for addressing the issue of delays in rulings on pretrial motions, such as additional staff, ways to deal with motions in the scheduling order, prioritizing work on motions, and a Local Rule change requiring parties to immediately notify the court of any reasonably anticipated settlement of a case where there is a pending motion. The court's plan agreed with the substance of the recommendations, said Local Rules should not be altered to require notice of anticipated settlement, and did not discuss other specific implementation measures.

The Advisory Group also recommended a Local Rule change to require counsel to confer, prepare and file a case management plan, after which the court would set a scheduling conference and issue a scheduling order. The content of the case management plan is specifically detailed, and the rule change indicates that deadlines shall not be altered except by agreement of the parties and the court, or for good cause shown. The court enthusiastically endorsed the concept of a case management plan, and indicated that any changes in individual judge's practices will be implemented with all deliberate speed. The court did not recommend a Local Rule change in its plan.

The Advisory Group also recommended a Local Rule concerning the conduct of depositions, the timing of disclosure of experts, and the procedures governing a claim of privilege. The court believes these issues are more appropriately handled as part of a case management plan and that a Local Rule is not necessary.

The Advisory Group also recommended a Local Rule to publicize the willingness of Magistrate Judges to resolve discovery disputes telephonically. Noting that Judges are also available for this, the court does not believe this is appropriate for codification in the Local Rules.

Differences Between Plan and Implementation: None reported.

CJRA POLICY 3: MORE INTENSIVE MANAGEMENT OF COMPLEX CASES

Policy Before CJRA Plan

Individualized case management, generally with more intensive management for more complex cases.

CJRA Plan Implementation

Approved Plan: Same. When the court approved the plan in 1993, it saw no need to have a more formal procedure than that already employed by the individual judges. As of late 1994, that decision was being reconsidered.

Differences Between Plan and Advisory Group Recommendations: None.

Differences Between Plan and Implementation: None reported.

CJRA POLICY 4: EXCHANGE OF DISCOVERY INFORMATION

Policy Before CJRA Plan

No formal policy.

CJRA Plan Implementation

Approved Plan: F.R.Civ.P. 26(a) revisions were pending when the plan was adopted, and the court indicated it would not develop separate local requirements for mandatory disclosure of certain standardized information early in the life of the case. Cooperative, accelerated disclosures are to be considered as part of the case management plan. The December 1993 amendments to Federal Rule of Civil Procedure 26(a) concerning mandatory initial disclosure are in effect in this district.[3]

Differences Between Plan and Advisory Group Recommendations: The Advisory Group expressed serious reservations about several of the Rule 26(a) changes, and urged cooperative, accelerated disclosure as an item to be considered in the preparation of a case management plan.

Differences Between Plan and Implementation: None reported.

CJRA POLICY 5: CERTIFY GOOD FAITH EFFORT BEFORE FILING DISCOVERY MOTION

Policy Before CJRA Plan

Local Rule indicates that the moving party shall attach to the discovery motion a certification of counsel that counsel have conferred and that they have been unable

---

[3]Stienstra (1995).

to resolve their differences. The certification shall detail the attempts of counsel to resolve the dispute.

CJRA Plan Implementation

Approved Plan: Same.

Differences Between Plan and Advisory Group Recommendations: None regarding discovery. However, the Advisory Group recommended a similar requirement for other types of motions such as for attorney's fees, sanctions, or attorney's disqualification; the court referred this recommendation back to the Advisory Group for clarification, indicating it was not specifically drawn.

Differences Between Plan and Implementation: None reported.

CJRA POLICY 6: ALTERNATIVE DISPUTE RESOLUTION PROGRAMS

Policy Before CJRA Plan

A settlement conference is usually held with a judicial officer. By Local Rule, a judge may set any civil case for summary jury trial or other alternative method of dispute resolution. No formal court-wide ADR program is in place, and the annual number of cases that go through an ADR process (other than a settlement conference) is less than 50.

CJRA Plan Implementation

Approved Plan: The court agrees with the concept of and need for ADR programs, and feels that they must be voluntary to be effective. The court will investigate whether or not to establish a central referral system or operate chamber by chamber. The plan notes that one judge is experimenting with mediation and considers that a test program for the district. The court designated June 1994 as the goal date for further development of a district-wide ADR program. Note that this district has Joint Local Rules with the Eastern District of Kentucky, and both districts have one judge experimenting with mediation.

Differences Between Plan and Advisory Group Recommendations: The Advisory Group recommended amending the Local Rules to adopt a voluntary mediation program with neutral mediators paid by the parties. They also recommended a pro bono early neutral evaluation program that would be mandatory for a particular case at judicial discretion. These would be formally structured programs with an ADR administrator and lists of qualified ADR providers.

Differences Between Plan and Implementation: One judge is experimenting with mediation, and all judges will consider revisions in the Local Rule to implement it court-wide after the experiment is completed. As of late 1994, the court was considering implementing a mediation program district-wide in mid-1995, after a state court mediation program is operational (so that they can design a federal program that is compatible with the state program).

OPTIONAL CJRA TECHNIQUES

The CJRA indicates that each court shall consider and may include the following five litigation management techniques:[4]

I. **Requiring that counsel jointly present a discovery/case management plan at the initial pretrial conference:**

Plan leaves discretion up to individual judges as to whether the parties would be required to prepare a written case management plan to be filed prior to the scheduling conference (or alternatively, require only consideration and consultation). Advisory Report recommended that counsel be required to confer, prepare, and file a case management plan prior to the scheduling conference in all cases not exempted from F.R.Civ.P. 16(b) by current Local Rule 22. The court subsequently decided to follow the December 1993 revised F.R.Civ.P. 26.

II. **Requiring that each party be represented at each pretrial conference by an attorney with authority to bind that party:**

Court Plan did not modify its existing practice of requiring counsel attending pretrial conferences to have the authority, or access thereto, to bind the parties on matters set for discussion at that conference.

III. **Requiring the signature of the attorney *and* the party for all requests for discovery extensions or postponements of trial:**

Court Plan referred this technique to the Advisory Committee for further consideration. It was not adopted in the plan.

IV. **Offering a Neutral Evaluation program:**

No immediate adoption of any ADR program, including neutral evaluation. Plan did set a goal of full district implementation of a voluntary ADR program. Neutral evaluation program was looked upon favorably as important in reducing costs to litigants. Advisory Report would have required counsel to consider ADR, including neutral evaluation, as part of a Case Management Plan. Early Neutral Evaluation was to be ordered in appropriate cases after the initial pretrial conference.

V. **Requiring party representatives with authority to bind to be present or available by telephone at settlement conferences:**

Court Plan did not alter current practices of requiring persons with authority to bind to be in attendance at settlement conferences.

---

[4]28 U.S.C. § 473(b).

OTHER POLICIES ADOPTED IN CJRA PLAN

Approved Plan: Endorses Advisory Committee recommendations that the one half time Judge position (a full time position shared with the Eastern District of Kentucky) be converted to a full time position for the Western District of Kentucky, that another full time Magistrate Judge be added, that the Judicial Conference approve a career classification of pro se Law Clerk; and that Congress appropriate sufficient funds for the Clerk's office.

Differences Between Plan and Advisory Group Recommendations: None.

Differences Between Plan and Implementation: None reported.

OVERVIEW OF CJRA PROGRAM IN THE DISTRICT OF MARYLAND

OVERVIEW OF IMPLEMENTED CJRA PLAN

This is a comparison district, not a pilot district, so a CJRA plan must be implemented by December 1, 1993, and it need not contain the six pilot program principles. This district's plan was implemented December 1, 1993.

The CJRA Advisory Group concluded[1] that the docket is reasonably current but expressed concerns about the near future. These concerns included the following: an anticipated increase in the criminal and bankruptcy court dockets; the reliance upon senior judges; the retirement of two active judges; delays in appointing judges to fill three judicial vacancies; a new federal prison expected to bring an increase in prisoner petitions; and the creation of a new southern division. The Group considered that the Court managed the docket well and that delay in adjudication occurs in isolated instances only. Therefore, a fine tuning of current management systems, rather than a major overhaul, is all that is needed. The principal cause of unnecessary litigation expense was believed to be "overlawyering." Though some discovery problems were expected to be addressed by amendments to the Federal Rules of Civil Procedure (in proposal form at the time of the report), the Group recommended that the Court adopt additional measures for more efficient and effective judicial control. Included were limits on deposition length; adoption of rules of conduct during discovery; improved access to judicial officers for discovery disputes; changing judicial attitudes towards discovery disputes; assuring that reasonable and realistic trial dates be set and held firm; greater use of magistrate judges and other existing resources; and making effective case management a common objective for all judicial officers.

Advisory Group recommendations included: Retaining the individual judge assignment system with greater centralized management to assure that all judges' dockets remain current; differential case management without formal case management tracks; some specific scheduling recommendations for different categories of cases;

---

[1] Beall et al. (1993) (hereinafter referred to as the advisory group report). The 18-person committee consisted primarily of lawyers representing a cross-section of the District's bar, one representative of the business community, and , as ex officio members, a district judge, a magistrate judge, and the Clerk of Court. The Advisory Group met in regular monthly sessions and also interviewed each of the district's judges and magistrate judges privately.

adoption of discovery guidelines and a "Code of Conduct" plus improved procedures for resolving discovery disputes; firm trial dates usually within 12 months after answer for routine cases and within 24 months after answer for complex cases; increased availability of settlement conferences; and voluntary paid mediation and voluntary mini-trials for ADR. The Advisory Group did not recommend early mandatory disclosure of certain information prior to formal discovery.

The CJRA plan[2] adopted by the Court included the following provisions: Retaining individualized differential treatment of civil cases but doing so within the informal framework of three categories of cases (*cases where discovery need not be taken, cases of an essentially routine nature,*[3] *and cases identified by the judge as complex)*; using uniform scheduling orders based on specified examples; some specific scheduling procedures similar to those recommended by the Advisory Group; refinements in procedures for handling discovery disputes; encouragement of prompt rulings on motions; encouragement of firm trial dates within specified time goals; refinements in settlement conference procedures; and upon request making available mini-trials or mediation by non-judicial officers. The plan did not include early mandatory disclosure of certain information prior to formal discovery, and the December 1993 amendments to Federal Rule of Civil Procedure 26(a)(1) concerning mandatory initial disclosure are not in effect in this district except for a limited number of case types.

As of January 1996, a CJRA annual report had not been prepared by either the Advisory Group or the Court.

CJRA POLICY 1: DIFFERENTIAL CASE MANAGEMENT

Policy Before CJRA Plan

Prior to the CJRA, there was no formalized system of case management tracks. However, there was an informal de facto assignment by the judicial officer of cases into categories of relatively non-complex, routine, and complex. Non-complex cases included Social Security appeals, student loans, prisoner litigation, and other cases requiring little discovery and a few days of trial time. These were managed on an expedited time schedule and trial was usually set within six months of filing. Routine cases were usually set for trial within one year of filing and were expected to consume four to nine trial days. Complex cases (e.g., antitrust, major disasters, malpractice, etc.) were given special management and were usually set for trial 18 months after filing.

---

[2]United States District Court for the District of Maryland (1993) (hereinafter referred to as the plan).

[3]Court officials indicate that cases of an essentially routine nature have two subcategories: cases of a type frequently resolved by summary judgment and cases of a type ordinarily not resolved by summary judgment. The distinction in case management between the two subcategories is that judges are encouraged to set trial dates in their initial scheduling orders in cases of a type ordinarily not resolved by summary judgment motions. The reason for the distinction is that it will result in more realistic trial schedules if cases likely to have summary judgment motions are not scheduled for trial in the initial scheduling order.

CJRA Plan Implementation

Approved Plan: The plan calls for:

1. Retaining the individual assignment system under which the court has operated for many years.

2. Retaining the responsibility of the judges to provide systematic, differential treatment of civil cases and to tailor judicial management to each case commensurate with the case's nature and complexity.

3. Encouraging judges to monitor and review cases personally (rather than assigning tasks to law or docket clerks) before deciding which case management treatment (see Item 3 following) to place them on.

4. Encouraging judges to implement the following differentiated treatments:

   a) *Cases where discovery need not be taken* (e.g., habeas corpus petitions, motions filed under 28 U.S.C. § 2255, Social Security appeals, petitions to review arbitration awards, and mortgage foreclosure actions): Enter into an immediate briefing schedule for deciding dispositive motions. Judges are encouraged to use uniform scheduling orders and to *not* set a trial date in the initial scheduling order.

   b) *Cases of an essentially routine nature:* Enter a scheduling order as soon as all critical defendants have answered and all preliminary jurisdictional and venue motions have been decided, or if the case is a state court removal or if some other reason exists for immediate review. Judges are encouraged to use uniform scheduling orders. Cases of an essentially routine nature have two subcategories:[4] cases of a type frequently resolved by summary judgment and cases of a type ordinarily not resolved by summary judgment (e.g., motor vehicle torts, FELA cases and actions under 42 U.S.C. § 1983 for the use of excessive force). The distinction in case management between the two subcategories is that judges are encouraged to set trial dates in their initial scheduling orders in cases of a type ordinarily not resolved by summary judgment motions. The reason for the distinction is that it will result in more realistic trial schedules if cases likely to have summary judgment motions are not scheduled for trial in the initial scheduling order. Interviews suggest that trial dates are not set in cases where a likelihood of a continuance exists.

   c) *Cases identified by the judge as complex* (e.g., antitrust, patent, RICO, and security fraud cases where all parties are represented by counsel): Hold a scheduling conference as soon as practicable in order to address matters set forth in 28 U.S.C. § 473(a)(3). The magistrate judge should be asked to attend the scheduling conference if the judge intends to refer discovery disputes to him or her. Judges are encouraged to set trial dates in the initial scheduling order for a date 12 to 18 months after the order is entered. Interviews suggest that trial dates are not set in cases where a likelihood of a continuance exists.

---

[4]Letter from Chief Judge J. Frederick Motz to RAND, August 2, 1996.

Differences Between Plan and Advisory Group Recommendations: The court's plan is more detailed than the advisory report and the plan sets up three informal differentiated case management "treatments."

Differences Between Plan and Implementation: None reported.

CJRA POLICY 2: EARLY AND ONGOING CONTROL OF PRETRIAL BY JUDICIAL OFFICER

Policy Before CJRA Plan

Local Rules already limited the number of interrogatories, requests for production, and requests for admission. They also: mandated the suspension of discovery during pendency of any motion regarding jurisdiction; specified a format for responses to interrogatories and requests for production; and established procedures for dispute resolution prior to requesting judicial resolution. Judges already had a practice of setting time limits for discovery in every civil case. Rule 16 was already used for management of most cases, establishing deadlines for joinder, amendment, motions, and discovery. In addition, counsel ordinarily could provide input into the terms of the scheduling order. Not all judges set trial dates at the beginning of a case, and not all cases had settlement conferences with a judicial officer.

CJRA Plan Implementation

Approved Plan: The plan contained the following provisions.

1. The Chief Judge or a designee will provide training to all newly appointed judges in case management techniques.

2. In non-complex cases, the use of uniform initial scheduling orders based upon three examples in the plan is urged.

   a) Sample provisions in initial scheduling orders for cases in which no party is appearing pro se included:

   i)   Creating a two-week window for the anticipated trial date. See discussion in section on **CJRA Policy 1** for the types of cases to which this applies.

   ii) Setting a date by which depositions and all other discovery (including that of experts) must be completed.

   iii) Indicating that no extension of the discovery deadline will be made for interrogatories or requests for production filed too close to the deadline to respond within the allotted time, nor will it be extended for motions to compel or for a protective order.

   iv) Motions to compel answers and for further answers must be filed in accordance with Local Rule 104.8.

   v)   Requiring that even if disputes arise over some aspects, discovery must proceed on other, non-disputed issues.

vi) Requiring that parties designate expert witnesses and make the disclosures required by F.R.Civ.P. 26(a)(2) at least 45 days prior to the discovery deadline.

vii) Requiring that counsel meet with one another and report to the court by a certain date regarding the number of hours needed for depositions or else have the limits set by default.

viii) Requiring that requests for admission be filed prior to or within 7 days after the discovery deadline.

ix) Setting a date by which joinder of additional parties must be completed.

x) Setting a date by which any motions to amend pleadings must be made.

xi) Setting a date by which all motions for summary judgment must be filed.

xii) Setting a date by which the parties must file a Status Report.

xiii) Indicating that the Status Report must include:

    a) Whether discovery has been completed.

    b) Whether motions are pending.

    c) Whether any party intends to file motions.

    d) Whether the case is to be tried by a jury or the bench, and the anticipated length of trial.

    e) A certification that the parties have met to conduct serious settlement negotiations. The certification would also include the date, time, place, and names of the persons in attendance in each meeting.

    f) Any other matters needed to be brought to the judge's attention.

xiv) Setting a Scheduling Conference after the Status Report is filed if it does not indicate that motions are anticipated. If there is an indication of future motions, the Scheduling Conference will not be set until the Court determines whether a motions hearing is needed. At the Scheduling Conference, a Pretrial Conference date and a trial date will be set.

xv) Indicating that no changes in the schedules would be permitted unless for good cause and in compliance with local rules.

b) The provisions in the sample initial scheduling order for cases in which any party was appearing pro se included:

i) Setting the discovery deadline

ii) Setting the summary judgment motion deadline.

iii) Requiring that if no summary judgment motion is filed, parties shall file status reports.

iv) Requiring that the status reports indicate the expected duration of the trial and other information pertinent to the scheduling of the trial.

3. In complex cases, holding a scheduling conference as soon as practicable in order to address matters set forth in 28 U.S.C. § 473(a)(3). No examples of uniform scheduling orders were suggested. A magistrate judge would attend the scheduling conference if the judge intended to refer discovery disputes to him or her.

4. Where parties are represented by counsel, another scheduling conference is to be held immediately after discovery is closed or after summary judgments have been decided. A supplemental scheduling order would then be entered.

5. The use of a uniform supplemental scheduling order is promoted, based upon one example in the plan. The provisions in the sample supplemental scheduling order included:

   a) Setting a date by which the parties shall advise the Court regarding consent to trial before a magistrate judge.

   b) Setting a date by which the pretrial order, motions in limine, proposed voir dire questions, proposed instructions, and proposed special verdict forms are due.

   c) Setting the date for the Pretrial Conference.

   d) Indicating whether the trial is to be tried before a jury or a judge.

   e) Indicating the expected length of the trial.

   f) Indicating the two-week window for the commencement of the trial.

6. Handling emergency discovery disputes:

   a) Judges are encouraged to make themselves available to hear such disputes telephonically.

   b) In the alternative, judges are encouraged to have a standing order to refer such disputes to a magistrate judge. Each week a magistrate judge will be assigned to handle discovery emergencies. This provision will be deferred until seven full-time magistrate judges have been appointed.

   c) All judicial officers are encouraged to render decisions on these disputes immediately by oral opinion.

7. Handling other discovery disputes:

   a) Judicial Officers are encouraged to issue decisions within 7 days of the filing of the motion papers under Local Rule 104.8.

   b) Written decisions may be in the form of letter opinions simply setting forth the ruling on each dispute and a synopsis of the reason for the ruling.

8. Motion practice:

   a) Judges are encouraged to decide all motions to dismiss or for summary judgment within 60 days of the filing of the last responsive memorandum.

   b) Judges are encouraged to state at the outset of a motions hearing their tentative conclusions (inviting counsel to address the issues thus framed).

9. Assignment of judges: The plan retains the current system of individual judge assignment. The Chief Judge will monitor all judges' dockets and will take appropriate steps to reduce overly crowded dockets by transferring cases to other judges.

Differences Between Plan and Advisory Group Recommendations: Significant differences between the plan and the Advisory Group report included:

1. The Advisory Group proffered no formal, inflexible rule for setting trial dates, but argued that after defendants have answered then trial should take place within one year in routine cases and within two years in all others. The plan was more specific.

2. The Advisory Group recommends establishing firm trial dates, and continuing the current practice whereby judges volunteer to take trials in calendar conflicts and encourage counsel in appropriate cases to consent to trial before a magistrate judge. The plan does not formalize this, but interviews with judges confirm that they intend to continue this practice.

3. The Advisory Group also suggested that the scheduling order set a deadline for designating experts and filing cross-, counter-, and third-party claims. Additionally, they would have held the supplemental scheduling conference in all cases rather than only in cases where all parties are represented by counsel.

Differences Between Plan and Implementation: None reported.

CJRA POLICY 3: MORE INTENSIVE MANAGEMENT OF COMPLEX CASES

Policy Before CJRA Plan

Judges reported that special management was already given to complex cases.

CJRA Plan Implementation

Approved Plan: The plan's provisions regarding cases identified by the judge as complex (e.g., antitrust, patent, RICO, and security fraud cases where all parties are represented by counsel) included:

1. Holding a scheduling conference as soon as practicable in order to address matters set forth in 28 U.S.C. § 473(a)(3).

2. Asking the magistrate judge to attend the scheduling conference if the judge intended to refer discovery disputes to him or her.

3. Encouraging judges to set trial dates in the initial scheduling order for a date 12 to 18 months after the order is entered.

Differences Between Plan and Advisory Group Recommendations: Advisory report did not have a specific time to trial for complex cases but set a outside limit for non-routine cases of 2 years.

Differences Between Plan and Implementation: None reported.

CJRA POLICY 4: EXCHANGE OF DISCOVERY INFORMATION

Policy Before CJRA Plan

The general practice in this district was for judges to individually govern the exchange of discovery information on a case-by-case basis. Interviews with judges indicate that this was a relatively common procedure.

CJRA Plan Implementation

Approved Plan: There is no discussion in the plan regarding automatic exchange of discovery information other than proposed scheduling orders requiring that parties designate expert witnesses and make the disclosures required by F.R.Civ.P. 26(a)(2) at least 45 days prior to the discovery deadline.

Differences Between Plan and Advisory Group Recommendations: No significant differences.

Differences Between Plan and Implementation: There is little reported difference between the plan and its implementation. However, the recent amendments to Federal Rule of Civil Procedure 26(a)(1) concerning mandatory initial disclosure are not in effect in this district except for a limited number of case types.[5]

CJRA POLICY 5: CERTIFY GOOD FAITH EFFORT BEFORE FILING DISCOVERY MOTION

Policy Before CJRA Plan

Existing Local Rule 104.7 already required counsel to confer concerning discovery disputes and make sincere attempts to resolve the differences between them before filing any discovery motion.

CJRA Plan Implementation

Approved Plan: No change to the prior policy embodied in Local Rule 104.7.

Differences Between Plan and Advisory Group Recommendations: Advisory report suggested incorporating into the Local Rules and/or scheduling orders a set of discovery guidelines (similar to those used in Maryland state courts) and a code of discovery conduct. Subsequently, discovery guidelines and a code of discovery conduct have been adopted, incorporated into the Local Rules, and referred to in the uniform scheduling orders.

---

[5]Stienstra (1995).

Differences Between Plan and Implementation: None reported.

CJRA POLICY 6: ALTERNATIVE DISPUTE RESOLUTION PROGRAMS

Policy Before CJRA Plan

The most widely accepted ADR practice in the district was settlement conferences. Magistrate judges and willing senior judges held settlement conferences at the request of the parties. Ordinarily, the judicial officer would require the attendance of representatives of all parties with authority to make settlement decisions. The judges were not unanimous regarding the issue of raising, at pretrial conferences, judicial involvement in settlement discussions. However, few judges appear to press attorneys to settle civil cases. An earlier experiment with a "settlement court" was not considered successful. There had been sparing use of summary jury trials.

CJRA Plan Implementation

Approved Plan: The plan's provisions included:

1. Settlement conference certification: Counsel are required to certify at the close of discovery that they have met to conduct serious settlement negotiations (see discussion regarding sample standard scheduling orders in **CJRA Policy 2** section).

2. Settlement Conference with Judicial Officer:

   a) Magistrate judges and senior judges will serve as before in regards to voluntary settlement conferences.

   b) Judges will be encouraged to affirmatively raise, at scheduling and pretrial conferences, the question of whether counsel believe a settlement conference would be helpful.

   c) The advisory group's recommendation that settlement conferences be routinely scheduled two to four weeks before trial was rejected (due to heavy demands on magistrate judges and senior judges).

3. Mediation:

   a) No mandatory court-annexed mediation.

   b) Upon request, the court will offer mediation by non-judicial officers.

   c) Mediators will be compensated as agreed by the parties, subject to court approval.

4. Mini-trials: Will consider holding mini-trials upon the request of the parties.

Differences Between Plan and Advisory Group Recommendations:

1. Settlement certification: The Advisory Group would have required counsel to certify good faith efforts to settle cases at various stages of the litigation process, rather than only at the close of discovery.

2. Settlement Conferences: The Advisory Group recommended an experimental pilot program of *mandatory* settlement conferences routinely scheduled two to four weeks before trial.

Differences Between Plan and Implementation: None reported.

OPTIONAL CJRA TECHNIQUES

The CJRA indicates that each court shall consider and may include the following five litigation management techniques:[6]

I.   **Requiring that counsel jointly present a discovery/case management plan at the initial pretrial conference:**

The plan made no mention of this requirement. However, a version of a discovery and case management plan is to be generated at the initial scheduling conference.

II.   **Requiring that each party be represented at each pretrial conference by an attorney with authority to bind that party:**

This was required by Local Rule 106.6 before CJRA, and has been retained.

III.   **Requiring the signature of the attorney *and* the party for all requests for discovery extensions or postponements of trial:**

No specific mention of this technique.

IV.   **Offering a Neutral Evaluation program:**

No specific mention of this technique.

V.   **Requiring the attendance of party representatives with authority to bind to be present or available by telephone at settlement conferences:**

The plan indicated that the judicial officer holding a settlement conference would ordinarily require the attendance of representatives of all parties with authority to make settlement decisions.

OTHER POLICIES ADOPTED IN CJRA PLAN

Approved Plan: None.

---

[6]28 U.S.C. § 473(b).

Differences Between Plan and Advisory Group Recommendations: The Advisory Group made a recommendation regarding the Office of the Clerk of the Court: It urged the District to continue to take full advantage of improvements in computer technologies and also to create one or two positions for individuals who could respond to public inquiries. The plan did not embrace this suggestion, but the court is engaged in a major automation improvement program.

The Advisory Group also urged the President and Congress to act promptly in filling vacancies and to consider the impact on courts of new legislation. Similarly, Appellate Courts should consider the impact of decisions on the litigation process. Lawyers must meet their ethical duty to act in the best interest of clients (not themselves) and should seek just resolution in the most expeditious and least costly manner.

Differences Between Plan and Implementation: None reported.

OVERVIEW OF CJRA PROGRAM IN NEW YORK, EASTERN DISTRICT

OVERVIEW OF IMPLEMENTED CJRA PLAN

This is a comparison district, not a pilot district, so a CJRA plan had to be implemented by December 1, 1993, and it did not have to contain the six pilot program principles. However, in many respects this district has operated like a pilot district. This district's plan was adopted December 17, 1991 and implemented on February 1, 1992. The plan included an expanded ADR program, which became operational on July 1, 1992.

The CJRA advisory group's report[1] identified three principal causes of unnecessary expense and delay: (1) a large criminal docket that had grown faster than the national average and had been accompanied by a dramatic increase in non-trial criminal proceedings, coupled with increases in civil filings; (2) space shortages in the present facilities; and (3) the failure to promptly fill vacant judgeships. These conclusions regarding causes of cost and delay were supported by what the advisory group learned during its investigations and by statistical analysis. Given these institutional impediments, none of which is addressed by the CJRA, the advisory group concluded that its recommendations for improving the conduct of litigation within the district would "produce at best peripheral improvements because of the failure to commit adequate resources to the civil justice system in the district . . . ." The advisory group was also of the view that within the institutional limitations it faced, the court was operating efficiently.

The advisory group pointed out that many of the procedures proposed by the CJRA had already been implemented in this district prior to the enactment of the CJRA, especially citing Local Civil Rule 49, Standing Orders on pretrial management.[2]

---

[1]Wesely et al. (1991) (hereinafter referred to as the advisory group report). The 27-person committee also had five ex officio members including the district's Chief Judge and Clerk of Court. Professor Edward D. Cavanagh was the reporter. Members included attorneys from practices of varying sizes and locales, corporate general counsel, attorneys from the government and community law officers, the federal defender's office, law school faculty, and lay persons. The group met as a body and in working subgroups. Members conducted interviews with each of the judicial officers of the district. A survey of 2,200 attorneys was made (437 responses). The Interim Report was disseminated to practitioners, academics, the public, and bar associations in the metropolitan area, and a public hearing was held prior to submission of the final report to the court.

[2]Letter from Edwin Wesely, Chair, Committee on Civil Litigation, E.D.N.Y., to RAND, August 19, 1996.

The advisory group made three major proposals aimed at expediting civil litigation. First, it endorsed, on an experimental basis and subject to limited exception, the adoption of mandatory automatic disclosure prior to discovery in all cases (including disclosure of information concerning all documents in the custody and control of the parties bearing significantly on claims and defenses). Second, it endorsed presumptive limitations on the number of interrogatories and depositions, but only where the parties cannot agree and the court does not impose limitations. Third, it endorsed an expanded ADR program, which not only would include the current mandatory court-annexed arbitration program for cases involving less than $100,000, but also would add a court-annexed mediation program and procedures for early neutral evaluation. The advisory group was of the view that the pretrial phase of civil cases ran smoothly due largely to the Standing Orders on Discovery and the practice among each of the district judges of referring all non-dispositive pretrial matters to magistrate judges. The advisory group did not endorse changing the current differential case management system to incorporate more-formal tracks.

The CJRA plan[3] adopted by the court accepted the recommendations of the advisory group. After the advisory group report was submitted, the court requested that the advisory group also draft a proposed plan. The Board of Judges promulgated the plan as proposed by the advisory group without change, but did make one addition, empowering a judge to suspend operation of any or all of the provisions of the plan for cause shown.

The annual assessments[4] indicate that since the plan was implemented, the advisory group has met periodically with the court and with the bar to evaluate its efficacy. The advisory group found that during the first year of the plan both bench and bar were slow to integrate the plan provisions into their practices. In particular, there was widespread ignorance of mandatory automatic disclosure and underutilization of court-annexed mediation and ENE. In the second year of the plan, ADR referrals increased significantly, particularly referrals for ENE. The effect of mandatory automatic disclosure on litigation is less clear. The advisory group conducted two surveys of practitioners regarding mandatory automatic disclosure, the first in January 1993 and the second in October 1994. The results of the 1993 survey demonstrated a widespread lack of awareness of mandatory automatic disclosure among the district's practitioners. The results of the 1994 survey demonstrate a greater familiarity among attorneys with the concept of mandatory automatic disclosure, and provide some insights as to attitudes regarding this practice.

A second source of information on the efficacy of mandatory automatic disclosure is the magistrate judges. The magistrate judges believe that mandatory automatic disclosure has had a beneficial impact on the pretrial process. While recognizing that some litigants opt out of mandatory disclosure by stipulation, the magistrate judges believe that mandatory automatic disclosure, where used, has had the positive effect

---

[3]United States District Court for the Eastern District of New York (1991) (hereinafter referred to as the plan).

[4]Cavanagh (1992), and letter from Edwin Wesely, Chair, Committee on Civil Litigation, E.D.N.Y., to RAND, May 18, 1995.

of jump-starting discovery and settlement discussions. The advisory group has undertaken to meet with magistrate judges individually to ascertain further their views on the efficacy of mandatory automatic disclosure.

The advisory group has continued to monitor the impact of the plan and to consider possible changes in the plan. In the fall of 1994, the advisory group impaneled a subgroup to explore whether the plan should be amended to conform to the 1993 Amendments to the Federal Rules of Civil Procedure. The advisory group agreed with the subgroup that while, in general, conformity is desirable, no changes should be made in the plan at the present time. The advisory group recognized that the implementation of the plan had created much uncertainty among practitioners but concluded that changes now—relatively early in the life of the plan—would only exacerbate the problem of uncertainty.

CJRA POLICY 1: DIFFERENTIAL CASE MANAGEMENT

Policy Before CJRA Plan

This district had no formal policy of differential case management. However, there was an informal policy calling for special treatment of habeas corpus and Social Security cases, mandatory court-annexed arbitration of cases involving $100,000 or less, and special treatment of complex cases by the assigned judge according to particular case needs. Pretrial management was conducted by magistrate judges.

CJRA Plan Implementation

Approved Plan: The plan embraced existing practices. The stated basis for this decision was that modification might lead to delay and inefficiencies. The district will, however, continue to evaluate formalized tracking systems and remains open to this concept.

Differences Between Plan and Advisory Group Recommendations: None.

Differences Between Plan and Implementation: None reported.

CJRA POLICY 2: EARLY AND ONGOING CONTROL OF PRETRIAL BY JUDICIAL OFFICER

Policy Before CJRA Plan

The general practice among judges in this district is to refer all civil cases, except some complex cases, to magistrate judges for all non-dispositive pretrial purposes. Magistrate judges are routinely assigned to cases at the same time a district judge is assigned, and the magistrate judges are responsible for all phases of pretrial management. Scheduling Orders pursuant to Fed.R.Civ.P 16(b) are routinely issued setting forth the dates of discovery cutoff, by which additional parties are to be added or pleadings amended, and by which substantive motions are to be filed. With respect to dispositive motions, the practice varies among the judges. All judges have their own individual rules regarding motion practice before them, including the necessity of a pre-motion conference, briefing schedules, page limitations on briefs and the desirability of oral arguments.

CJRA Plan Implementation

Approved Plan: The plan included a number of refinements in pretrial procedure:

1. Discovery Limits.

   a) For civil cases filed on or after February 1, 1992, a presumptive limit of 15 interrogatories is established but only if the parties do not otherwise agree or the court does not otherwise direct. The limit does not apply in actions under 28 U.S.C. § 3101, 18 U.S.C. § 981, or 21 U.S.C. § 881.

   b) For civil cases filed on or after February 1, 1992, a presumptive limit of 10 depositions per side is established, but only if the parties do not otherwise agree and the court does not otherwise direct. Plaintiffs and defendants are each considered one side, and all other parties are another "side."

2. Motion Practice.

   a) Judges are requested to keep motion hearings scheduled for any given day to a reasonable number.

   b) Motions should be decided in a reasonable time. The Clerk's Office will ascertain the status of all motions pending for more than six months after final submission; these reports are publicly available, but are not automatically sent to all parties.

   c) The court may convene a pre-motion conference on dispositive motions.

   d) The provisions of Standing Order 4 regarding discovery motions are extended to permit the use of letter submissions in procedural motions.

   e) Since the plan has been adopted, Standing Order 4 was broadened to provide that all non-dispositive pretrial matters shall be routinely referred to magistrate judges.

3. Pretrial Conferences.

   a) Counsel should confer on a possible Scheduling Order prior to any scheduling conferences (current Standing Order 3(b)).

   b) An Initial Pretrial Conference shall be held face-to-face with the judicial officer unless impracticable. All cases will have a final Pretrial Conference. Other conferences will be held at the discretion of the court.

   c) The initial Pretrial Conference agenda would include issues set forth in Fed.R.Civ.P. 16, plus:

      i)   Identification, definition, and clarification of issues of fact and law in dispute.

ii)   Stipulations of agreed facts and law.

iii) Scheduling of cutoff dates for discovery, and amendment of pleadings.

iv)   Scheduling of dates for filing and hearing motions, future conferences, and trial.

v)   Management of discovery (including control, scheduling, and orders affecting disclosure and discovery pursuant to Fed.R.Civ.P. 26 and 29–37), and motion practice where appropriate.

vi)   Bifurcation of trials and an order for separate trials under Fed.R.Civ.P. 42(b) regarding any claim or issue of fact.

vii) Procedures for management of expert witnesses.

viii) Feasibility of settlement, the use of ADR (including settlement judges, early neutral evaluation, and mediation), or reference of the case or certain matters to a magistrate judge or Special Master.

ix)   Having all requests for discovery or trial continuances signed by counsel and communicated to the parties.

x)   Use of testimony under Fed. Rules of Evidence 702.

xi)   Appropriateness of Fed.R.Civ.P. 56 summary judgment.

xii) Orders for early trial presentation of evidence that could be used as a basis for a judgment.

xiii) Establishing reasonable limits on the length of time for presentation of evidence and on the number of witness or documents presented.

xiv) Consideration and resolution of any other matters.

4. Trial date settings. The plan does not require trial within 18 months of filing of complaint. The advisory group was of the view that the time to trial be dictated by the needs of the case and that a flat 18-month deadline could actually increase costs in some cases. The plan does, however, create a mechanism of the reassignment of trial-ready cases when the assigned judge cannot reach the case within a reasonable time (but in no event more than six months).

Differences Between Plan and Advisory Group Recommendations: None.

Differences Between Plan and Implementation: None reported.

CJRA POLICY 3: MORE INTENSIVE MANAGEMENT OF COMPLEX CASES

Policy Before CJRA Plan

Management was left to the individual judicial officer's discretion. The general practice among judges in this district is to refer all civil cases, except some complex cases, to magistrate judges for all non-dispositive pretrial purposes. Magistrate judges are routinely assigned to cases at the same time a district judge is assigned, and the magistrate judges are responsible for all phases of pretrial management.

CJRA Plan Implementation

Approved Plan: It is acknowledged in the plan that complex cases need greater-than-normal hands-on control. To facilitate fulfillment of this need the plan indicates:

1. Conferences are to be held at least every six months for motion and discovery discussions.

2. Periodic settlement conferences are also to be scheduled.

3. Clients are to attend conferences if deemed useful by the court.

4. Staged, tiered, or milestone discovery is to be considered (e.g., discovery might initially be limited to matters that deal with jurisdictional or liability issues and then be subsequently extended).

5. The court may designate lead counsel for each side when there are multiple parties.

The CJRA plan suggests that judges may wish to exercise greater hands-on control in complex cases than in other cases. However, the degree of participation of the magistrate judge is left up to the district judge in each case.

Differences Between Plan and Advisory Group Recommendations: None.

Differences Between Plan and Implementation: None reported.

CJRA POLICY 4: EXCHANGE OF DISCOVERY INFORMATION

Policy Before CJRA Plan

No early automatic exchange required.

CJRA Plan Implementation

Approved Plan: *Early Automatic Disclosure.* The plan accepts a program of mandatory automatic disclosure prior to discovery. Features of the program include:

1. For 18 months, in every civil case filed after February 1, 1992[5] (excluding social security, habeas corpus, pro se, and civil rights cases with an immunity defense), parties must disclose or provide:

   a) The identity of all persons with pertinent information respecting claims, defenses, and damages.

_____

[5]The period has subsequently been extended by the Court, and is set to expire on July 31, 1997.

b) A general description of all documents bearing significantly on claims and defenses that are within a party's custody and control.

c) An authorization to obtain medical, hospital, no-fault, and worker's compensation records.

d) The documents relied on by the parties in preparing the pleadings or expect to use to support allegations.

e) The contents of any insurance agreement.

2. Requiring plaintiffs and the defendants to disclose the information listed under item 1 above within 30 days after service of the answer, and, for any party that has appeared, within 30 days after written demand (which includes the demanding party's disclosures).

3. Failure to disclose shall not be excused because investigations are not completed, or because the other party's disclosures are not sufficient or have not been made.

4. The court may impose Fed.R.Civ.P. 37(b) sanctions upon failure to disclose.

5. Nine months after the plan's effective date, the advisory group is requested to begin a study of the operation of the automatic disclosure procedures and report to the court.

Expert Evidence Disclosure. The plan requires that every party should disclose all experts and expert evidence to be presented at trial. This disclosure should be at least 30 days before the ready-for-trial date or as the court orders, or, if used solely to contradict, within 30 days after disclosure of the evidence being contradicted was made. The duty to disclose shall be ongoing. Items include:

1. Statements of all opinions expressed and the basis and reason for each opinion.

2. Identification of the information relied upon in forming the opinion.

3. Tables, charts or other exhibits to be used as a summary of data or in support of experts.

4. Qualifications of the expert, including a curriculum vitae and a bibliography.

5. A listing of all cases the expert has been involved with in the past four years.

Witness, Documents, and Exhibits Disclosure. The plan requires that in every civil case filed on or after February 1, 1992, at least 30 days prior to trial (or other date by order), the parties must disclose certain information regarding witnesses, documents, and exhibits. Any objections regarding the use of designated deposition testimony under Fed.R.Civ.P. 32(a) or the admissibility of other materials identified must be made within 14 days of the disclosure. Failure to do so would mean that any such objections (other than those under Fed. R. Ev. 402–403) would be deemed waived absent good cause shown. The disclosure would include the name, address, and telephone of each potential witness and the identification of each document or exhibit expected to be offered at trial.

The CJRA advisory group surveyed lawyers regarding early mandatory disclosure for cases filed after the plan was adopted. Their annual report indicated:[6] "Survey results at this stage are neither a ringing endorsement, nor a condemnation, of mandatory disclosure. About half the respondents said that mandatory disclosure improved pretrial discovery, and about half said that there was no change. A majority also said that mandatory disclosure had made either no contribution or a slight contribution to easing the problems of undue cost and unnecessary delay. On the other hand, an overwhelming majority said that mandatory disclosure had no negative effects on pretrial discovery." "A majority (55%) would make mandatory disclosure a permanent part of the local rules, and an additional 23% would make mandatory disclosure a permanent part of the local rules if modifications were made." "It appears from these data that the parade of horribles predicted by some critics of mandatory disclosure has not come to pass. On the other hand, it is not clear the extent to which mandatory disclosure has improved the operation of pretrial discovery, it at all. The vast majority of respondents have had little experience with mandatory disclosure."[7]

Differences Between Plan and Advisory Group Recommendations: None.

Differences Between Plan and Implementation: None reported. The December 1993 amendments to Federal Rule of Civil Procedure 26(a)(1) concerning mandatory initial disclosure have *not* been adopted in this district.[8] However, the local rule requires mandatory disclosure that is more extensive than that specified in Rule 26(a)(1).

CJRA POLICY 5: CERTIFY GOOD FAITH EFFORT BEFORE FILING DISCOVERY MOTION

Policy Before CJRA Plan

Pursuant to Standing Order 6 and Civil Rule 3(f), attorneys must certify a good faith effort to resolve disputes before filing discovery motions.

CJRA Plan Implementation

Approved Plan: There was no discussion in plan of this principle because the concept had already been implemented by local rule.

Differences Between Plan and Advisory Group Recommendations: None.

Differences Between Plan and Implementation: None reported.

---

[6]Wesely et al. (1994), pp. 5–6.

[7]"Indeed, nearly 40% state that they have had no experience with mandatory disclosure, even though their cases were clearly governed by the Plan."

[8]Stienstra (1995).

CJRA POLICY 6: ALTERNATIVE DISPUTE RESOLUTION PROGRAMS

Policy Before CJRA Plan

The district has had in place for a number of years a program of compulsory court-annexed arbitration in cases where the amount in controversy is $100,000 or less. In 1991, 11 percent of the cases filed were referred to arbitration.

CJRA Plan Implementation

Approved Plan: Features of the ADR program will include:

1. A continuation of the Court Annexed Arbitration program (pursuant to Local Arbitration Rule, amended February 1, 1991). All claims for money damages (except Social Security, tax matters, prisoners' civil rights, and constitutional rights cases) involving $100,000 or less will be sent to arbitration. Dissatisfied parties may obtain trial de novo, but if the result is less favorable for the requesting party than the arbitration award, that party would pay the arbitrator's fee, unless in forma pauperis). The panel would consist of a single arbitrator unless a party requested three. In 1993, 10 percent of the cases filed were referred to arbitration.

2. A program of Early Neutral Evaluation is established. It uses as evaluators a panel of attorneys who are experts in various types of civil cases. The evaluators are to be approved by the court, but serve pro bono. The court would refer cases for evaluation and recommendation as well as for identification of the primary issues in dispute, exploration of settlement possibilities, assistance with the discovery plan, and case assessment. The evaluation is non-binding. The program is considered experimental and will be reviewed on a regular basis.

3. Magistrate judges play a significant role in pre-trial civil case management, including early settlement efforts. This role for magistrate judges in pretrial management and settlement is considered to be part of the court's CJRA efforts, although the plan itself does not elaborate on this.   In addition, upon consent of the parties, the court may refer cases to a magistrate judge for an "early, firm trial date."[9]

4. Settlement Conferences are to be convened before a judicial officer in every case, unless the assigned judge deems them to be unwarranted.

5. Special Masters may be appointed by the assigned judge pursuant to Fed.R.Civ.P. 53.

6. A program of court-annexed mediation is established with a panel approved by the court to serve as mediators. Litigants may either choose from this panel, engage a separate mediator, or seek assistance from any reputable ADR organization. The parties pay the mediators' fees. The program is considered experimental and will be reviewed on a regular basis.

---

[9]Sifton (1996) amends the CJRA plan to delete the paragraph that indicates, upon consent of the parties, that the court may refer cases to a magistrate judge for an "early, firm trial date."

7. To increase awareness of the availability of alternatives to trial, counsel will receive a pamphlet describing the various ADR mechanisms. If appropriate, the judicial officer will also advise litigants of possible litigation alternatives at the initial pretrial conference.[10]

8. The court will appoint an administrator to supervise the various ADR programs. The responsibilities of this position will include educating bench and bar regarding ADR, as well as oversight of the programs, finding volunteers, certification, training and monitoring.

Differences Between Plan and Advisory Group Recommendations: None.

Differences Between Plan and Implementation: Court-annexed mediation and ENE were slow to catch on in this district, but referrals began to pick up following efforts of the ADR administrator to educate the bench and bar on the potential benefits. Most ADR referrals have come from district judges. Magistrate judges, however, have been reluctant to refer matters to mediation in part because of the added costs to the parties and in part because, under the Standing Orders, magistrate judges have been handling settlement discussions early in the proceedings. ENE, on the other hand, has started to expand but in a different way from that envisioned by the advisory group and in the plan. Judicial officers have begun referring matters to ENE at the end of discovery rather than at the outset of discovery. This practice developed because many civil cases, although trial-ready, could not be reached by the assigned judge because of that judge's criminal calendar. Knowing that these cases were at a standstill and that the parties are not charged for the evaluator's services, judicial officers have referred some of these matters to ENE, hoping that the process may lead to settlement. Thus, *early* neutral evaluation was shifting to *late* neutral evaluation. The ADR administrator has reported a recent trend to making ENE referrals earlier in the case, thereby making ENE truly *early* neutral evaluation. The number of ADR referrals to ENE and mediation combined between June 30, 1992 and April 24, 1995 was 233, of which 83 settled, 72 returned unsettled, and 78 were still pending.[11] As of June 30, 1996, 444 cases have been referred to ADR, 148 cases have settled, and 136 were returned unsettled (160 cases were pending).[12]

OPTIONAL CJRA TECHNIQUES

The CJRA indicates that each court shall consider and may include the following five litigation management techniques:[13]

I.   Requiring that counsel jointly present a discovery/case management plan at the initial pretrial conference:

---

[10]The district no longer distributes an ADR pamphlet.

[11]Letter from Edwin Wesely, Chair, Committee on Civil Litigation, E.D.N.Y., to RAND, May 18, 1995.

[12]Letter from Edwin Wesely, Chair, Committee on Civil Litigation, E.D.N.Y., to RAND, August 19, 1996.

[13]28 U.S.C. § 473(b).

The plan incorporates Standing Order 3(b) which requires the parties to confer on a possible scheduling order prior to the initial scheduling conferences. The plan does not specifically address case management plans. Accordingly, the requirements of Fed.R.Civ.P. 26(f) requiring the parties to meet and confer regarding a plan for discovery is in effect.

II.   **Requiring that each party be represented at each pretrial conference by an attorney with authority to bind that party:**

This requirement, contained in Fed.R.Civ.P. 16(c), is incorporated by reference into the plan.

III.   **Requiring the signature of the attorney *and* the party for all requests for discovery extensions or postponements of trial:**

The plan specifies that this issue be an item on the pretrial agenda..

IV.   **Offering a Neutral Evaluation program:**

The plan provides for this. See the discussion under **CJRA Policy 6.**

V.   **Requiring the attendance of party representatives with authority to bind to be present or available by telephone at settlement conferences:**

This requirement, contained in Fed.R.Civ.P. 16(c), is incorporated by reference into the plan.

OTHER POLICIES ADOPTED IN CJRA PLAN

Approved Plan:

1. Trial Practices.

   a) Expert Witnesses. In bench trials, the court may order that direct testimony be submitted in writing, and that only cross-examination be done live. Also, expert testimony may be taken by deposition. Further, the court may take experts' testimony out of the normal order of proof, if it would avoid delay or facilitate understanding.

   b) Jury Selection. The assigned judge may determine the extent of attorney participation, including submission of written questions to the court for prospective juror.

   c) Bench Trials are to be encouraged and cases will be given a date certain for trial if the parties consent to trial by a magistrate judge.[14]

---

[14]Sifton (1996) amends the CJRA Plan to delete the paragraph that indicates, upon consent of the parties, that the court may refer cases to a magistrate judge for an "early, firm trial date."

d) The court may require parties to file a pretrial statement of stipulated facts, and facts in dispute.

e) Objections to documentary evidence will be made by motions in limine, when such evidence has been designated at least 10 days prior to trial.

f) Exhibits (except those used for impeachment or rebuttal) shall be marked prior to trial.

g) The court may order that direct testimony be submitted in writing.

2. Other Discovery Rules.

a) Fed.R.Civ.P. 30(b)(4) requests for recording depositions by non-stenographic means are to be presumptively granted.

3. Sanctions.

a) Parties seeking sanctions under Fed.R.Civ.P. 11 must give notice to the violator at the time of violation, and may move for sanctions only if the conduct in question did not cease. Rule 11 motions must be made by a separate application and may not simply be appended to other motions.

4. Attorney's Fees.

a) Common Fund Cases. In the court's discretion, fees may be awarded on a percentage basis if the matter settles early and without significant attorney time having been expended. The percentage shall be calibrated to encourage early settlements. In cases that settle after significant attorney time is expended, the fee shall be based on a percentage of recovery. Attorneys, however, shall submit time records; and the lodestar method shall serve as a guideline.

b) Statutory Fee Cases. Plaintiff's attorney's fee applications and documentary support (number of hours, work performed) should be directed to defendants within 30 days of entry of final judgment. Portions of the award that are not contested are to be paid promptly, and disputed matters are to be referred to the court. The fee award should approximate actual fees charged in non-statutory fee matters. The court should use the rate that the plaintiff's attorney charges private clients in non-contingent matters since this would be a presumptive indicator of a reasonable rate.

Differences Between Plan and Advisory Group Recommendations: None.

Differences Between Plan and Implementation: None reported.

OVERVIEW OF PILOT PROGRAM IN NEW YORK, SOUTHERN DISTRICT

OVERVIEW OF IMPLEMENTED CJRA PLAN

The CJRA advisory group's report[1] stated that the civil docket of the district did not appear to be burdened by excessive delay (although the number of pending civil cases had recently increased). Magistrate judges, overburdened with current responsibilities, should be used differently. A survey of lawyers and judges suggested that excessive cost was at times occasioned by discovery practices. Motion practice need not lead to increased cost if pre-argument conferences are used effectively. However, the high level of judicial vacancies is the factor most responsible for delay in case disposition. The advisory group recommended: early judicial management of civil cases; a differential case management system under which judges could assign cases to Expedited, Standard, and Complex tracks; mandatory disclosure requirements and mandatory mediation for all Expedited cases; mandatory mediation for a random sample of the Standard and Complex track cases; and several refinements in pretrial procedures (such as holding Case Management Conferences covering several topics, and setting firm deadlines for pretrial).

The CJRA plan[2] adopted by the Court indicated that the docket showed an expanding number of pending cases and increasing delay in holding trials. Delay arose in part because of the provisions of the Speedy Trial Act, and in part because of unfilled judicial vacancies (7 out of 28 authorized judgeships). The docket showed no other excessive delay. The plan generally adopted the recommendations of the advisory group in principle, but did not specify the detail in the plan itself. Those details, usually consistent with the advisory group's detailed recommendations, were published in early 1993 by the court in a "guide" to the CJRA plan.[3]

---

[1]Sweet et al. (1991). The advisory group consisted of two judges and public- and private-sector attorneys who practiced regularly in the district as well as a lay member of the community. It sent a questionnaire to the judges of the court and 3,000 practicing attorneys (completed by 505 attorneys) and also conducted a detailed analysis of approximately 2,000 closed cases.

[2]United States District Court for the Southern District of New York (1991) (hereinafter referred to as the plan).

[3]United States District Court for the Southern District of New York (1993).

The first annual assessment of the CJRA plan indicated that, with the exception of mediation, "the plan has not had any significant impact on the conduct of civil litigation in the Southern District of New York." [4] Two major factors contributed to this result: the pressure created by chronic judicial vacancies and the need to attend to the criminal docket limit the amount of time the court can devote to civil trials; and, with the exception of mediation, the case management techniques embodied in the plan were consistent with the established practices of the court. An assessment of whether cost and delay have been affected cannot be done until more experience is accumulated under the plan and more data are collected. The court has also implemented standardized discovery in prisoner pro se cases, and moved forward on technological improvements.

The second annual assessment by the CJRA Advisory Group recommended substantial changes. Regarding differential case management tracks, the advisory group "believes that the case designation process has not served a useful purpose and should be terminated. Given the current case load and the variety of cases within each judge's docket, classification of a small portion as expedited has served no useful purpose and is unlikely to do so in the future." [5] It pointed out that complex cases will always be treated differently on an ad hoc basis by judges, and that only 15 percent of all cases filed in 1993 were ever given a track designation by the court. In a random sample of 55 expedited track cases, 64 percent of the lawyers were not aware of the automatic disclosure requirement of the plan, and "no trial setting was made within the first year in 43, and only 4 trial dates were set at the initial case management conference as the Plan provides."[6] The failure to designate track assignment has had the unfortunate side effect of limiting the flow of cases to mediation, because the track designation is the trigger point for mediation referral. Consequently, the advisory group recommended a new referral process for mediation. After 120 days of a case being filed, the judge will receive a notice from the CJRA staff attorney advising that a mediation session for the case has been scheduled, unless the judge advises otherwise (if this new process were to create an overwhelming caseload for mediators, then a system would be developed for adjusting the number of cases referred). The court adopted the advisory group's recommendation and eliminated the track system from its plan in mid-1995.

CJRA POLICY 1: DIFFERENTIAL CASE MANAGEMENT

Policy Before CJRA Plan

Case management was a matter of judicial discretion.

---

[4]Sweet et al. (1994), p. 2.

[5]Sweet et al. (1995), pp. 2–3.

[6]Sweet et al. (1995), pp. 2–3.

CJRA Plan Implementation

Approved Plan: The plan calls for:

1. A simplified case assignment system and a differential case management system for "Complex," "Standard," and "Expedited" cases.

2. Designation to case track is to be made by the judge based upon "Case Information Statements" filed by the parties, or by a determination made at a Case Management Conference. Designation of the track is made by the judge after the initial Case Management Conference.

3. In Expedited cases, defined categories of relevant documents will be produced automatically, discovery will be limited, and trial will be set within one year of service of the complaint unless good cause is shown. An expedited case is one which is relatively simple, where it is believed that there will be no more than two depositions per party, where documents to be exchanged are clear-cut in nature and relatively small in volume, where the use of interrogatories will be minimal, where there will be little or no motion practice, and where relatively little judicial supervision is needed. All expedited cases will be in a program of mandatory court-annexed mediation (see the **CJRA Policy 6** discussion below).

4. Complex and Standard cases will have a Case Management Plan developed at the Case Management Conference. It is anticipated that the Standard category will be the largest, and it shall include those cases which the parties do not believe can be tried within one year of filing *but* which do not involve an unusually large number of parties, complex issues, or anticipated discovery disputes and motions. In Standard and Complex cases, voluntary court-annexed ADR mechanisms will be discussed at the Case Management Conference. Two thirds of Standard and Complex cases, randomly selected, will be assigned to the mandatory mediation program.

Differences Between Plan and Advisory Group Recommendations: The advisory group recommended the establishment of formal guidelines for track designation. It also suggested procedures whereby a party could argue against an Expedited classification and a definition of the scope of the automatic discovery to be produced in Expedited cases. The plan largely left these issues to the discretion of the judge, although the guide to the plan issued by the court in January 1993 provided more details that address the advisory group's concerns.

Differences Between Plan and Implementation: The plan has been implemented in general, but in practice only 15 percent of all cases filed in 1993 were ever given a track designation by the court, and about one percent were classified as complex. Further, in a random sample of 55 expedited track cases, "no trial setting was made within the first year in 43, and only 4 trial dates were set at the initial case management conference as the Plan provides."[7] RAND's interviews with judges suggested that the track assignment usually did not influence how the case was managed, and

---

[7]Sweet et al. (1995), pp. 2–3.

that certain judges were making track assignments while other judges were not. Since not all judges were making track assignments, this means that any observed differences between track and non-tracked cases in terms of cost or time or satisfaction may be due to the judges who made track assignments, rather than due to the track policy itself. The district eliminated the track system in mid-1995. The intent of the plan in the area of mediation has not yet been fully realized because mediation referral only occurs when and if a track designation is made by the judge. Since the final case track designation does not occur until the Case Management Conference, and since in practice most cases were not assigned to tracks, a significant number of cases either did not get to mediation at all or were assigned to mediation after normal pretrial activities were well under way.

CJRA POLICY 2: EARLY AND ONGOING CONTROL OF PRETRIAL BY JUDICIAL OFFICER

Policy Before CJRA Plan

Pre-motion conferences were already used by most judges. The Court also offered litigants the option of a trial before a magistrate judge or a senior judge if the assigned judge was not available on a timely basis.

CJRA Plan Implementation

Approved Plan: The plan calls for:

1. Early judicial case management in all cases.

2. An initial Case Management Conference and a Case Management Plan:

   a) An initial Case Management Conference should be held in all cases within 120 days of filing the complaint.

   b) A Case Management Plan and schedule will be developed for Complex and Standard cases at the Case Management Conference. The Court and counsel shall address all necessary topics including:

      i) The identification and simplification of the principal issues in contention.

      ii) Definition of necessary discovery and its sequence (including an identification of the parties with knowledge of facts and relevant documents).

      iii) Dispositive motions.

      iv) Joinder of additional parties.

      v) Counterclaims.

      vi) Settlement and ADR possibilities. In Standard and Complex cases, there should be one conference specifically devoted to settlement, and this should occur within one year of filing the complaint.

      vii) Reference to the designated magistrate judge.

viii)   Dates for future conferences or other procedures for continuing judicial oversight.

ix)   Setting of the trial date.

3. Role for magistrate judges:

a) A magistrate judge shall be assigned by the clerk for all non-Expedited cases, but this shall not constitute an automatic reference of the case to the magistrate judge.

b) The assigned judge may authorize the magistrate judge to handle pre-trial discovery issues and other items. The advisory group and the court will monitor and evaluate the role of the magistrate judge.

4. Trial Dates:

a) Non-Expedited cases should have a firm trial date set as early as reasonable but no later than 18 months from filing, unless the court certifies that good cause exists to do otherwise.

5. Motion Practice:

a) Pre-motion conferences shall be considered where advisable.

b) Motions should be decided with reasonable promptness.

c) Motions not decided within 60 days of final submissions should be reported to the clerk by each judicial officer, and a quarterly report shall be circulated to all members of the Court. A statistical summary shall be delivered to advisory group.

6. Docket Workload:

a) The court should consider steps, including assignment and reassignment of cases, to ensure timely judicial attention to the docket.

7. Discovery Practice:

a) A discovery plan should be formulated at the initial Case Management Conference.

b) The Court should adopt standardized guidelines for deposition practice, interrogatories, requests for documents, and discovery of experts.

c) Discovery disputes should, after good faith resolution efforts by the parties, be resolved on oral motion or on the basis of a letter submission (two double spaced pages maximum). The Court should resolve letter applications as promptly as possible.

d) Sanctions for failure to comply with discovery obligations should be imposed where appropriate.

e) Appeals from discovery rulings by magistrate judges on discretionary issues are disfavored and judges should not hesitate to award sanctions for frivolous appeals.

8. Prisoner Pro Se Practice:

   a) The Court should establish guidelines, including provisions for certain items of standardized discovery, to insure prompt and appropriate disclosure.

Differences Between Plan and Advisory Group Recommendations: The advisory group had called for reducing the load of magistrate judges by eliminating assignments such as dispositive motions, Social Security appeals, and habeas corpus petitions, and reducing the number of assignments of motions to dismiss pro se cases. The advisory group also called for:

1. Hiring additional attorneys in the pro se office.

2. Assigning all pro se cases from the same plaintiff to a single magistrate judge.

3. Requiring attorneys attending the Case Management Conference to be authorized to enter into stipulations.

4. Delineating other issues for the Case Management Conference (including bifurcation, applications for recusal or disqualification, amendments to pleadings, discovery proceedings, special proceedings for management, and possible infringement of substantive rights).

5. Requiring an additional status conference for Standard cases if there has not been a trial within 18 months of service of the answer.

6. If the assigned judge cannot try the case within two months of the scheduled date, reassigning the case to another judge for the purposes of trial with a two-case credit if given to an active judge; if no other judge is available, the case would be returned to original judge.

7. Requiring a proposed plan of discovery in all non-Expedited cases to be filed within 30 days for the first responsive pleading with a conference 30 days later.

8. Putting a 10 day ceiling on the time in which discovery disputes would receive a ruling (would allow the magistrate judge to handle if not in 10 days).

9. If the party appealing a magistrate judge's discovery ruling does not obtain a more favorable result, requiring the party to reimburse the fees and costs of the victorious party.

10. Adopting rules comparable to the Eastern District of New York's Standing Orders.

Differences Between Plan and Implementation: None are reported. However, several elements of the plan are advisory, which leaves implementation of many issues in the hands of the assigned judge. The extent to which individual judges have embraced the plan's provisions cannot yet be determined.

A new Local Rule 48 was adopted on November 18, 1993, to set deadlines for responding to standardized discovery in defined classes of prisoner litigation.

CJRA POLICY 3: MORE INTENSIVE MANAGEMENT OF COMPLEX CASES

Policy Before CJRA Plan

On average, the court estimates that there are 33 complex cases on the docket of each judge. Many judges considered that they already followed the advisory group's suggested practices for complex cases.

CJRA Plan Implementation

Approved Plan: Creates a "Complex" case category. The management of these cases is individualized by the judge and there is little explicit difference between Complex and Standard cases in the plan's recommendations regarding case management.

Differences Between Plan and Advisory Group Recommendations: The advisory group had indicated that in complex cases there should be a presumption that each of the issues that could possibly be raised at a Case Management Conference should be addressed (this would fulfill the expectation of early, active, and meaningful judicial oversight in complex cases). In complex cases, the advisory group also recommended continuing case management conferences, greater use of special masters, and use of a Case Statement in RICO cases.

Differences Between Plan and Implementation: None reported.

CJRA POLICY 4: EXCHANGE OF DISCOVERY INFORMATION

Policy Before CJRA Plan

Discovery procedures and control were a matter of judicial discretion.

CJRA Plan Implementation

Approved Plan: The only mention of mandatory discovery is for Expedited cases in which "defined categories of relevant documents will be produced automatically," but the plan itself does not define those categories. The court's published guide to the plan indicates plaintiffs must provide all documents relevant to the subject matter of the complaint, and defendants must provide all documents relevant to the subject matter of the answer. A document is relevant if it either (1) supports the material averments of the pleading or (2) contradicts or otherwise makes less probable the material averments of the pleading.

Differences Between Plan and Advisory Group Recommendations: The advisory group defined the scope of the automatic discovery to be produced in Expedited cases and would have had the automatic disclosure be a two-year pilot program. The court's guide to the plan, issued after the plan was adopted, closely follows the advisory groups recommendation for which documents should be disclosed in Expedited cases.

Differences Between Plan and Implementation: None reported. However, relatively few cases have been assigned to the expedited track and hence few have been subject to this disclosure requirement. In a random sample of 55 expedited track cases, 64 percent of the lawyers were not aware of the automatic disclosure requirement of the plan.[8] The December 1993 amendments to Federal Rule of Civil Procedure 26(a)(1) concerning mandatory initial disclosure are *not* in effect in this district.[9]

CJRA POLICY 5: CERTIFY GOOD FAITH EFFORT BEFORE FILING DISCOVERY MOTION

Policy Before CJRA Plan

Local Civil Rule 3(f) required good faith consultation to resolve the discovery dispute.

CJRA Plan Implementation

Approved Plan: Discovery disputes should, after good faith efforts at resolution by the parties, be resolved on oral motion or on the basis of a letter submission.

Differences Between Plan and Advisory Group Recommendations: The advisory group supports the then proposed amendments to F.R.Civ.P. 26(c) and 37 and suggests that Local Rule 3(f) would be more effective if incorporated into the Rule 16 order.

Differences Between Plan and Implementation: None reported.

CJRA POLICY 6: ALTERNATIVE DISPUTE RESOLUTION PROGRAMS

Policy Before CJRA Plan

Since September 1984, the district has had a pilot program utilizing the services of the American Arbitration Association. Judges could, with consent of the parties, refer cases to the AAA for a conference to discuss possible use of ADR techniques. Counsel were required to attend the conference. 162 cases were referred through January of 1991 and of those, 49 proceeded to ADR (using arbitration, mediation, or a combination).

CJRA Plan Implementation

Approved Plan: The court proposed:

1. A two year program of mandatory court-annexed mediation for all Expedited cases with certain exclusions for specific natures of suit, and for a two-thirds random sample of Standard and Complex civil cases. The White Plains office was ex-

---

[8]Sweet et al. (1995), pp. 2–3.
[9]Stienstra (1995).

cluded. The court will establish a pool of attorneys to serve as mediators on a voluntary basis (qualifications to be established by the court, with credit for pro bono work to be given). Mediators each receive two days training, and are assigned at random to cases. Mediation referral can occur only after the Case Management Conference and then only if the judge assigns the case to a management "track." Other court activities on the case are not stayed during the mediation process. Cases that do not have a track assignment are not referred to mediation.

2. In Standard and Complex cases, voluntary court-annexed arbitration and other voluntary ADR mechanisms shall be discussed at the Case Management Conference. The court's published guide to the plan indicates that cases eligible for mediation are those wherein money damages only are being sought, excluding Social Security cases, tax matters, prisoners' civil rights cases, and pro se cases.

3. The advisory group will monitor and assess the effectiveness of ADR mechanisms.

Differences Between Plan and Advisory Group Recommendations: None, except in the level of detail of the discussion. The advisory group: called for at least one person to oversee the Special Mediator Program (raise filing fees to cover the cost) and an ADR administrator; would have randomly designated two-thirds of all civil cases seeking money damages (excluding Social Security, tax, prisoner's civil rights, pro se, and U.S. defendant intentional torts cases) to the mandatory mediation program (would allow volunteering if not selected); described in detail the qualifications of mediators and the actual execution of the mediation program (timing, where to take place, confidentiality, control groups and evaluation, sanctions, etc.); recommended that mediation not be held later than 150 days after last responsive pleading and that the an ADR administrator choose a mediator within 10 days of referral; recommended that the court provide for other voluntary ADR options including Early Neutral Evaluations, mini-trials, and summary jury/non-jury trials. The Court adopted these recommendations, with some refinement, in its guide to the CJRA plan that was issued in early 1993.

Differences Between Plan and Implementation: The plan has been implemented as written. However, the intent of the plan in the area of mediation has not yet been fully realized because mediation referral only occurs when and if a track designation is made by the judge, and only 15 percent of the cases filed in 1993 ever got a track designation. Since the final case track designation does not occur until the Case Management Conference, and since in practice not all cases are being assigned to tracks, a significant number of cases either do not get to mediation at all or are assigned to mediation after normal pretrial activities are well under way. Consequently, the advisory group in its annual report recommended a new referral process for mediation. 120 days after a case is filed, the judge will receive a notice from the CJRA staff attorney advising that a mediation session for the case has been scheduled unless the judge advises otherwise (if this new process were to create an overwhelming caseload for the 217 mediators, then a system would be developed for adjusting the number of cases referred).

The Court hired a CJRA Staff Attorney to implement the mediation program called for in the plan. In the time period from August 27, 1992 to February 16, 1995, 1453 cases were eligible for mediation. Of the 1453, 445 either were placed in a non-mediation control group or settled prior to mediation referral. Of the 1008 cases with a mediation session scheduled, 519 were concluded and the remainder had no report of conclusion of the mediation. Of the 519 with concluded mediation reports, 414 reported all issues were settled. Typical mediation sessions were 3 to 4 hours in length. In the future, due to lack of CJRA funding to train sufficient new mediators, the total number of mediation referrals will probably be limited to about 500 per year (2 or 3 per mediator).

OPTIONAL CJRA TECHNIQUES

The CJRA indicates that each court shall consider and may include the following five litigation management techniques:[10]

I.   Requiring that counsel jointly present a discovery/case management plan at the initial pretrial conference:

The plan requires that a discovery plan be formulated at the initial Case Management Conference. The December 1993 amendments to Federal Rule of Civil Procedure 26 are *not* in effect in this district.

II.   Requiring that each party be represented at each pretrial conference by an attorney with authority to bind that party:

There was no discussion regarding this technique.

III.   Requiring the signature of the attorney *and* the party for all requests for discovery extensions or postponements of trial:

There was no discussion regarding this technique.

IV.   Offering a Neutral Evaluation program:

There was no discussion regarding this technique.

V.   Requiring the attendance of party representatives with authority to bind to be present or available by telephone at settlement conferences:

There was no discussion regarding this technique.

OTHER POLICIES ADOPTED IN CJRA PLAN

Approved Plan:

1. Requesting authorization for additional magistrate judges.

---

[10]28 U.S.C. § 473(b).

2. Commencing a program of modernizing all existing facilities and assuring that the new courthouse be able to support:

   a) Real-time reporting and facilities (computer access, graphic image processing, etc.).

   b) Fax filing.

   c) Telephone- and video-conferencing.

   d) Suitable attorney workspace.

   e) Other technological advances mentioned in advisory group report.

Differences Between Plan and Advisory Group Recommendations: The advisory group recommended reducing the number of case type choices on the civil case cover sheet. However, this is a system-wide document, and changes to it would require action by the Administrative Office of the U.S. Court and possibly the Judicial Conference.

Differences Between Plan and Implementation: None reported. Electronic access to docket information, telephone conferencing, communications with counsel by fax, and videotaping of court proceedings have all become a standard part of judicial administration in the district. No network exists linking personal computers throughout the courthouse.

OVERVIEW OF PILOT PROGRAM IN OKLAHOMA, WESTERN DISTRICT

OVERVIEW OF IMPLEMENTED CJRA PLAN

The CJRA Advisory Group concluded that the court is delivering efficient and timely services, and viewed its recommendations as "fine tuning procedures that could improve what is already an efficient and cost and delay sensitive court system."[1]

The court's CJRA plan "accepts and adopts" the recommendations of the Advisory Group.[2] After the CJRA Pilot Program implementation, cases for which Rule 16 conferences are required are tracked and actively managed using a detailed schedule of about 20 event dates. The new special track contains fewer than 10 cases per year that are designated at the Rule 16 conference as requiring specialized or more intensive management. The new standard track contains all other cases. Mandatory exchange of information early in the case is new and includes identification of expert witnesses, all documents and data that are likely to bear significantly on any claim or defense, insurance, and exchange of a privilege log. The district has a new formally structured voluntary mediation program with about 150 cases per year, in addition to its preexisting mandatory arbitration program. The plan was implemented in January 1992, with the exception of the mediation program, which was implemented in April 1992 after development of the formal structure to support the program.

The 1992 Annual Assessment indicated that the provisions of the Plan "have not detracted from the efficient operation of the Western District court and have added some procedures that have contributed to the Court continuing its high level of competent and efficient administration of justice." No recommendations for change were made.[3]

The 1993 Annual Assessment indicates that the plan promotes economy and efficiency. It included a survey of judicial officers and courtroom deputies that found all

---

[1]Bradford et al. (1991), p. 59. The 13-person committee was chaired by a lawyer, met as a whole four times, and also worked separately in subcommittees. The reporter was the Clerk of Court, and judges were ex-officio/non-voting members. The Advisory Group interviewed judicial officers, and conducted a survey of about 200 lawyers and litigants.

[2]United States District Court for the Western District of Oklahoma (1991), p. 2.

[3]Bradford et al. (1995), pp. 8–9; and letter to Judges Thompson and West, July 1, 1993.

the judges indicating that because they really adopted or "codified" what they were doing prior to CJRA, the impact of the plan on the court and the judges is "de minimus." Courtroom deputies said the main impact that they can see is on the attorneys and changes expected of them in their practice. [4]

The 1994 and 1995 Annual Assessments both indicated that it continues to appear that the CJRA plan "promotes efficiency and economy and therefore, satisfies the purpose of the CJRA."[5]

CJRA POLICY 1: DIFFERENTIAL CASE MANAGEMENT

Policy Before CJRA Plan

The following types of cases were exempt from an initial Rule 16 scheduling conference by Local Rule: Prisoner cases, Social Security appeals, and other administrative reviews. In addition, government collection cases, foreclosure, and bankruptcy appeals usually did not have a Rule 16 scheduling conference. All other cases had a Rule 16 conference and were individually managed by judicial officers.

CJRA Plan Implementation

Approved Plan: Same as before CJRA Plan for cases without Rule 16 scheduling conference. Plan created five formal tracks with differential case management procedures, as outlined below. Initial scheduling conferences generally will not be held for the first three categories of cases.

1. Prisoner petitions: This includes prisoner petitions for writs of habeas corpus pursuant to 28 U.S.C. §2241 and §2254, motions/complaints pursuant to 28 U.S.C. §1331 and §2255, motions pursuant to Fed. R. Crim. P. 35 and civil rights complaints pursuant to 42 U.S.C. §1983. These cases are referred to a magistrate judge for a report and recommendation.

2. Social Security: Cases seeking review of a denial of Social Security benefits by the Secretary of Health and Human Services. These cases are referred to a magistrate judge for a report and recommendation.

3. Asbestos: These are transferred to the Multi-District-Litigation judge in Pennsylvania.

4. Special track: Cases designated at the Status/Scheduling Conference as requiring specialized or more intensive management because of their complexity, urgency, number of parties, number of claims or defenses, volume of evidence, extensive discovery, other factors requiring extensive pretrial preparation and management, or otherwise at the court's discretion. Management is the same as standard track except for individual case management plan and perhaps additional conferences.

---

[4]Bradford et al. (1995), pp. 8–9.

[5]Heaton et al. (1996), p. 16; and Bradford et al. (1996), p. 15.

The number of cases designated as special track has been fewer than 10 per year, and the court indicates that before CJRA those cases would have gotten similar special treatment without the track designation.

5. Standard track: All other cases not designated at the status/scheduling conference as requiring assignment to any other track shall be handled in accordance with the standard practices and procedures of the court as governed by Fed. R. Civ. P. 16 and Local Court Rule 17.

Differences Between Plan and Advisory Group Recommendations: While the Advisory Group did not formally recommend a track system, noting that the court already systematically treated cases on an individual basis, the court adopted a track system to differentially manage special and standard cases. This was seen by the court as formalizing existing practice.

Differences Between Plan and Implementation: None reported.

CJRA POLICY 2: EARLY AND ONGOING CONTROL OF PRETRIAL BY JUDICIAL OFFICER

Policy Before CJRA Plan

An initial status/scheduling conference and a mandatory settlement conference with a magistrate judge when the case appears on the published trial docket are held in civil cases. Generally final pretrial conferences are held only as requested. Lawyers jointly prepare detailed status report before initial conference, and detailed schedule is set at initial conference with about 20 dates, including trial date within 18 months. Local Rule limits discovery to 30 interrogatories and 30 requests for admission.

CJRA Plan Implementation

Approved Plan: Same as before for standard cases. For special-track cases a case management plan, more active judicial management, and perhaps additional conferences are required. Court intends to more actively encourage consent to Magistrate Judges for all purposes, and the volume of such consents has risen from less than 10 per year to over 50 in 1992 (see Differences Between Plan and Implementation for more recent developments).

Differences Between Plan and Advisory Group Recommendations: The Advisory Group suggested that non-jury trials be set for a firm date certain rather than at the end of a jury term, and that rulings on pending dispositive motions should be made promptly. The adopted plan was silent on these issues.

Differences Between Plan and Implementation: Technical changes were made in the wording of the Local Rule for the status/scheduling conference (minor technical clarifications made in the definition of a couple of the events, and the scheduled sequence of a couple of events). In April 1994, the local rules were amended to limit interrogatories and requests for admission to 25 each. The court has had to impose a moratorium on referrals of consent cases to Magistrate Judges because of their overwhelming prisoner litigation caseload.[6]

CJRA POLICY 3: MORE INTENSIVE MANAGEMENT OF COMPLEX CASES

Policy Before CJRA Plan

Individualized case management.

CJRA Plan Implementation

Approved Plan: Similar to before, except formalized. The required case management plan is to include identification of lead and liaison counsel with responsibilities of each, suggestions for maintaining confidentiality, description and sequencing of discovery, timetable for class issues if class action, timetable for dispositive motions, proposals regarding adding parties, bifurcation, and other subjects bearing on the administration of the case such as a special master to administer discovery. Fewer than 10 cases per year receive this special treatment.

Differences Between Plan and Advisory Group Recommendations: None.

Differences Between Plan and Implementation: None reported.

CJRA POLICY 4: EXCHANGE OF DISCOVERY INFORMATION

Policy Before CJRA Plan

No formal policy.

CJRA Plan Implementation

Approved Plan: Prior to the status/scheduling conference each party shall, without awaiting a discovery request, disclose to all other parties: identity of expert witnesses and summary of their testimony, general description of all documents and data "that are likely to bear significantly on any claim or defense,"[7] existence of insurance agreement(s), and exchange of a privilege log listing documents for which a privilege is asserted. Moreover, each party is under continuing obligation to supplement or correct such disclosures, with each supplement or disclosure to be signed by at least one attorney of record. Court may impose sanctions if this requirement is not observed. Local Rule 17 was amended June 15, 1993 and clarified that the disclosure should include the name of "any witness who is known at the time to be likely to bear significantly on any claim or defense."

Differences Between Plan and Advisory Group Recommendations: None.

---

[6] Letter from Chief Judge David L. Russell to RAND, April 5, 1995.

[7] United States District Court for the Western District of Oklahoma (1991), § 4.1.

Differences Between Plan and Implementation: None reported. The recent amendments to Federal Rule of Civil Procedure 26(a)(1) concerning mandatory initial disclosure are not in effect in this district.[8]

CJRA POLICY 5: CERTIFY GOOD FAITH EFFORT BEFORE FILING DISCOVERY MOTION

Policy Before CJRA Plan

Counsel must meet face to face and confer in good faith before filing discovery motion (Local Rule 14E) unless one is from out of state, in which case they must confer by telephone; counsel must certify effort when filing discovery motion.

CJRA Plan Implementation

Approved Plan: Same as before CJRA.

Differences Between Plan and Advisory Group Recommendations: None.

Differences Between Plan and Implementation: None reported.

CJRA POLICY 6: ALTERNATIVE DISPUTE RESOLUTION PROGRAMS

Policy Before CJRA Plan

Settlement conference is mandatory, usually shortly before trial, with magistrate judge who specializes in these conferences. Formally structured non-binding arbitration program is mandatory for some cases and voluntary for other cases. Local Rule 43 has mandatory assignment to non-binding arbitration for cases with money damages (only) not exceeding $100,000 in which U.S. is not a party and in which non-monetary relief is judged insubstantial, or in certain cases in which the United States is a party (e.g., Federal Tort Claims Act money only cases not exceeding $100,000). Lawyers certify that case does not exceed $100,000 or judge may determine. Administrative review cases, prisoner, U.S. constitutional rights cases, and 28 U.S.C. §1343 cases are excluded from mandatory arbitration. Local Rule 17(I) also permits mediation and summary jury trials. Approximately 150 cases per year are referred to mandatory arbitration and about 50 volunteer. Although the magistrate judge-hosted settlement conference was and is the most frequently used settlement tool, with that and the use of mandatory arbitration and the summary jury trial in the 1980's prior to the CJRA, ADR and settlement procedures became a part of doing business in this district.

---

[8]Stienstra (1995).

CJRA Plan Implementation

Approved Plan: Same as before CJRA, plus a formally structured voluntary mediation program with about 150 cases per year. Local Rule 46 provides for certification of trained mediators, maintenance of lists of mediators with information about each, a mediation clerk to administer the program, payment of the mediator by the parties, discussion of referral to mediation at the Rule 16 conference (it is on the standard form used by all judges for that conference, and an ADR staff member attends those conferences), the method of selection of the mediator and timing of the mediation "at the earliest practical time," provision of information to the mediator in advance, confidentiality, and a notice to the court of the results of the mediation. The referral to mediation usually occurs at the Rule 16 conference and the mediation takes place 30 to 60 days later. The average session lasts about 5 hours, with parties splitting the mediator's typical fee of $500 to $750. The volume of arbitration referrals dropped slightly (to 177 in 1993) after the mediation program was introduced.

Differences Between Plan and Advisory Group Recommendations: None.

Differences Between Plan and Implementation: The formally structured program was authorized as of January 1992, and actually began referring cases to mediation in April 1992 (due to the time necessary to set up the formal program structure and certify mediators).

OPTIONAL CJRA TECHNIQUES

The CJRA indicates that each court shall consider and may include the following five litigation management techniques:[9]

I.   **Requiring that counsel jointly present a discovery/case management plan at the initial pretrial conference:**

Plan requires counsel to confer and jointly prepare a Status Report prior to the Status/Scheduling Conference. Matters to be discussed are outlined in detail in Appendix 1, "Status Report/Final Pretrial Order Form," in the Plan. While discovery per se is not one of the required items in the standard report form, discovery deadlines and the like are to be discussed at the Conference. Advisory Report indicated that the Group felt that the current Rule 17 largely satisfied this technique but that more detail in case management would likely lead to increased expenses to parties through added attorney's fees.

II. **Requiring that each party be represented at each pretrial conference by an attorney with authority to bind that party:**

Plan requires counsel with authority to commit co-counsel and client for all purposes to appear at the Status/Scheduling Conference. No discussion regarding at-

---

[9]28 U.S.C. § 473(b).

tendance at other pretrial conferences. Advisory Report indicated that technique was already effectively required by Rule 17.

III. Requiring the signature of the attorney *and* the party for all requests for discovery extensions or postponements of trial:

No discussion in Plan. Advisory Report felt this requirement to be unnecessary and cost-ineffective (indicated that lawyers already have an obligation to advise clients of the status of an action).

IV. Offering a Neutral Evaluation program:

No discussion of neutral evaluation (however, certain aspects may be found in other ADR programs). Advisory Report thought a neutral evaluation program to be a novel idea but not without expense and delay.

V. Requiring party representatives with authority to bind to be present or available by telephone at settlement conferences:

Plan requires the attendance of a person empowered to fully settle the case at the mandatory settlement conference, and the local rules that implement arbitration and mediation contain similar language.

OTHER POLICIES ADOPTED IN CJRA PLAN

Approved Plan: None.

Differences Between Plan and Advisory Group Recommendations: The Advisory Group made three recommendations for actions that are beyond the control of the District Court: (1) appointment of an additional Magistrate Judge; (2) increasing the jurisdictional amount of diversity cases; and (3) prompt processing and approval of judicial nominees by Congress.

OVERVIEW OF PILOT PROGRAM IN PENNSYLVANIA, EASTERN DISTRICT

OVERVIEW OF IMPLEMENTED CJRA PLAN

The CJRA Advisory Group indicated that "many of the procedures mandated by the Act are already in place in this court."[1] They also noted that "the most serious problem facing this court is vacancies on the bench."[2] The report made recommendations in areas where the district did not already have the CJRA-mandated procedures in place, including establishment of standard and special management tracks for differential case management, and mandatory early disclosure of certain information.

The court's CJRA plan accepts and implements the recommendations of the Advisory Group, with some minor fine tuning. After CJRA, cases with Rule 16 conferences are tracked. The special track consists of cases designated by the lawyers at the time of filing or by the judge as requiring specialized or more intensive management, and has been about 7 percent of all cases filed. The standard track contains all other cases and the district's intent is to have trial within 12 months after filing. Mandatory exchange of information early in the case includes identification of witnesses, description of all documents and data that are likely to bear significantly on any claim or defense, and insurance. A high-volume mandatory arbitration program has existed since the late 1970s. Just prior to implementation of the CJRA plan, the district started a mandatory mediation program in mid-1991 that involves hundreds of cases per year.[3] The plan was implemented December 31, 1991.

The Advisory Group's 1993 annual report indicated that the CJRA plan is "working well and we find no immediate need to suggest substitution amendments."[4] The 1994 annual report[5] also indicated no need to amend the plan at this time, and noted

---

[1]Landis et al. (1991), p. 2. The 15-person committee was chaired by a lawyer, had a law professor and former Director of the Federal Judicial Center as reporter, met as a whole 13 times, and also worked separately in subcommittees. Four judges and the Clerk of Court were ex-officio members. A public hearing was held and various litigant and other organizations were surveyed for inputs.

[2]Landis et al. (1991), p. viii.

[3]United States District Court for the Eastern District of Pennsylvania (1991).

[4]Landis et al. (1993), p. 11.

[5]Landis et al. (1994).

that the court had clarified that the early mandatory disclosure requirements did not apply to special-track cases. The 1995 annual report indicated that the program "is working well in this district" and recommended against amendment of the plan.[6] The court has extended the CJRA plan through December 1997 without amendment. The advisory group conducted an extensive survey of lawyers regarding early mandatory disclosure of information, and the results are discussed in the companion evaluation report.[7]

CJRA POLICY 1: DIFFERENTIAL CASE MANAGEMENT

Policy Before CJRA Plan

The following types of cases were exempt from an initial Rule 16 scheduling conference by Local Civil Rule 16.2: Pro se prisoner civil rights actions, habeas corpus, Social Security appeals, other administrative reviews, government collection cases, bankruptcy appeals, IRS proceedings to enforce summons, ERISA cases, arbitration-eligible cases, and actions in which no pleading or appearance has been filed on behalf of any party defendant within 120 days from the filing of the complaint. In effect, four case management tracks existed for habeas corpus, Social Security, arbitration, and asbestos cases.

CJRA Plan Implementation

Approved Plan: The four tracks that existed before the CJRA Plan were supplemented with additional tracks for standard and special (usually complex) cases. The plan created six formal tracks with differential case management procedures, as outlined below. Initial scheduling conferences generally will not be held for the first three categories of cases.

1. Habeas Corpus: Cases under 28 U.S.C. §2241—§2255 are usually assigned to a magistrate judge for report and recommendation.

2. Social Security: Review of denial of Social Security benefits are usually assigned to a magistrate judge for report and recommendation. The clerk issues a standard scheduling order within 10 days of filing.

3. Arbitration: Cases designated under Local Civil Rule 16.1 (generally cases with money damages only, not exceeding $100,000) are sent to arbitration. A Rule 16 conference is not held, but the court clerk issues a scheduling order and usually there is no judge involvement until after arbitration is completed. If the case has a de novo filing after arbitration, most judges accelerate processing of the case (to discourage filings de novo by parties just to buy time) and usually do not allow more discovery.

---

[6]Landis et al. (1996), p. 10.

[7] See Kakalik et al. (1996a).

4. Asbestos: Claims for personal injury or property damage because of asbestos exposure have their own track. In July 1991 approximately 27,000 asbestos injury claims from the entire U.S. went into Multi-District-Litigation in this district. The district also has a school property damage class action (1 case for over 30,000 claims). At Judicial Conference request, these asbestos cases are not part of the RAND evaluation.

5. Special management: Cases that do not fall into the four tracks above that are commonly referred to as complex as that term is defined in the *Manual for Complex Litigation* and that need special or intense management by the court because of one or more of the following factors: "(1) large number of parties; (2) large number of claims or defenses; (3) complex factual issues; (4) large volume of evidence; (5) problems locating or preserving evidence; (6) extensive discovery; (7) exceptionally long time needed to prepare for disposition; (8) decision needed within an exceptionally short time; and (9) need to decide preliminary issues before final disposition." It may include two or more related cases. "Complex litigation typically includes such cases as antitrust cases; cases involving a large number of parties or an unincorporated association of large membership; cases involving requests for injunctive relief affecting the operation of large business entities; patent cases; copyright and trademark cases; common disaster cases such as those arising from aircraft crashes or marine disasters; actions brought by individual stockholders; stockholder's derivative and stockholder's representative actions; class actions or potential class actions; complex commercial cases and other civil (and criminal) cases involving unusual multiplicity or complexity of factual issues."[8]

The designation of a case as special is made on a form submitted by the lawyers, and if the lawyers cannot agree or the judge disagrees, then the judge decides (but only about 2 cases per year must be assigned by the judge because of such disagreement). About 7 percent of all filings are in this special track, and the goal is to have trial within 18 months after filing.

6. Standard management: Cases that do not fall into any of the above tracks are given standard management with the goal of having a trial within 12 months of filing. Judges are not reassigning standard cases to the special track; essentially if a standard case needs more intensive management, it gets it without being relabeled as special.

Differences Between Plan and Advisory Group Recommendations: None.

Differences Between Plan and Implementation: None reported.

---

[8]United States District Court for the Eastern District of Pennsylvania (1991), § 1.02.

CJRA POLICY 2: EARLY AND ONGOING CONTROL OF PRETRIAL BY JUDICIAL OFFICER

Policy Before CJRA Plan

Local Civil Rule 16.1 indicates each case will proceed through the following pretrial steps in management: scheduling conference; submission of pretrial memoranda; other reports and conferences as judge may direct; completion of discovery; submission of final pretrial order if required; and final pretrial conference. Most judges hold scheduling conferences but some judges do scheduling orders without a conference for some of their cases. The pretrial memoranda include (stated briefly): nature of action and basis for jurisdiction; statements of fact; damages claimed; non-monetary relief sought; witnesses; schedule of exhibits; number of trial days estimated; and other comments. Trial dates are usually set at the scheduling conference, although some judges set them at a later date. Usually at least one attempt is made by the judicial officer to settle each case before trial.

Mandatory arbitration and mandatory mediation cases usually have a schedule issued by the clerk and usually have no judge involvement in the individual case prior to completion of the ADR process (the typical exception being if motions are filed).

CJRA Plan Implementation

Approved Plan: Same as before for standard track cases, except the intent is for a Rule 16 conference to be held for most cases that are not exempt by local rule, and for a date to be set at the Rule 16 conference for trial within 12 months of filing. Cases in tracks that do not require a Rule 16 conference are also to have a trial date within 12 months of filing.

Differences Between Plan and Advisory Group Recommendations: None.

Differences Between Plan and Implementation: None reported.

CJRA POLICY 3: MORE INTENSIVE MANAGEMENT OF COMPLEX CASES

Policy Before CJRA Plan

Individualized case management.

CJRA Plan Implementation

Approved Plan: Special track cases always have at least 2 conferences before the final pretrial conference; one is 30 to 60 days after filing, and a joint discovery/case management plan must be submitted before that meeting; then a settlement conference is held about 6 months after filing. Scheduling is otherwise individualized by the judge. Trial date is set at the 6 month settlement conference with the judge, not at the Rule 16 conference, and is to be within 18 months of filing. About 7 percent of all filings are assigned to this special track by the lawyers using filing forms provided by the court, or by the judge.

Before the first conference, the parties will confer and provide the court with a proposed joint discovery/case management plan, to include such items as lead counsel, deposition guidelines, protective orders, in class action cases a proposal for class discovery, a description and sequence of discovery, the possibility of dispositive motions, and bifurcation. Following this conference, the court will issue a scheduling order and set the date for the second pretrial conference for the purpose of promoting settlement. An attorney of record must attend, as well as the party or a representative of the party with authority to settle. The attorney shall provide the court a statement identifying their claims and defenses with evidentiary support. If the case fails to settle, the court will set firm trial and discovery cutoff dates and order the parties to submit a plan with proposed deadlines for remaining events (dispositive motions, designation of experts and exchange of expert reports, proposed bifurcation for discovery or trial, use of ADR, proposal for use of special master or magistrate judge for discovery issues).

Differences Between Plan and Advisory Group Recommendations: None.

Differences Between Plan and Implementation: None reported.

CJRA POLICY 4: EXCHANGE OF DISCOVERY INFORMATION

Policy Before CJRA Plan

The court had no formal policy on this, except for personal injury cases for which Local Civil Rule (rescinded July 1, 1995) said: "Counsel for all parties shall exchange copies of all reports of medical examinations of any person for whose alleged personal injuries damages are sought by any party at least ten days before the pretrial conference. A report later made, or a report of a later examination, shall be submitted to opposing counsel as soon as such report is made."

CJRA Plan Implementation

Approved Plan: Section 4:01 of the CJRA plan says each party shall, without waiting for a discovery request, disclose to all other parties the following information: names and addresses of individuals likely to have information that bears significantly on the claims and defenses, a general description of documents and data "that are likely to bear significantly on the claims and defenses," and insurance agreements. Information is to be provided within 30 days of service of answer to complaint or 30 days after written demand for early disclosure. Parties are prohibited from making discovery requests until this early disclosure information has been provided, or the date it should have been provided by is past, except with the judge's approval or by stipulation.

Differences Between Plan and Advisory Group Recommendations: Same, except the Advisory Group recommended against precluding discovery pending the mandatory disclosure of the information listed above.

Differences Between Plan and Implementation: None reported. The recent amendments to Federal Rule of Civil Procedure 26(a)(1) concerning mandatory initial disclosure are not in effect in this district.[9] The recent amendments to Federal Rules of Civil Procedure 26(a)(4), 26(f), 30(a)(2), 31(a)(2) and 33(a) also are not in effect.[10]

CJRA POLICY 5: CERTIFY GOOD FAITH EFFORT BEFORE FILING DISCOVERY MOTION

Policy Before CJRA Plan

Local Rule 26.1 indicates discovery motions must contain "a certification of counsel that the parties, after reasonable effort, are unable to resolve the dispute."

CJRA Plan Implementation

Approved Plan: Same.

Differences Between Plan and Advisory Group Recommendations: None.

Differences Between Plan and Implementation: None reported.

CJRA POLICY 6: ALTERNATIVE DISPUTE RESOLUTION PROGRAMS

Policy Before CJRA Plan

Settlement conferences usually are held with a judicial officer.

A formally structured non-binding arbitration program is mandatory for some cases and voluntary for other cases. Local Civil Rule 53.2 has mandatory assignment to non-binding arbitration, with a panel of 3 arbitrators chosen from an approved list, for cases with money damages (only) not exceeding $100,000. The following types of cases are excluded from arbitration: Social Security appeals, cases in which a prisoner is a party, cases alleging a violation of a right secured by the U.S. Constitution, and actions in which jurisdiction is based on 28 U.S.C. §1343. Analysis of 1991 dispositions indicates 1156 cases were referred to arbitration. For cases filed in 1992, the number referred was 992.

A formally structured mediation program is mandatory for certain types of cases. The program was implemented in mid-1991 just before CJRA and has an experimental design (odd docket numbers in; even numbers out) to facilitate evaluation. Local

---

[9]Stienstra (1995).

[10]United States District Court for the Eastern District of Pennsylvania (1993).

Civil Rule 53.2.1 indicates that the following types of cases are excluded from the program: Social Security cases, cases in which a prisoner is a party, cases eligible for arbitration under Local Civil Rule 53.2, asbestos cases, and any other case a judge may decide to exclude. The mediation takes place before a single pro bono mediator selected by the court from a list of approved mediators (who have all been members of the bar for at least 15 years). It typically lasts one hour and is held 3 or 4 months after filing. In 1991, 785 cases were referred to mediation.

Local Rule permits any other type of ADR.

CJRA Plan Implementation

Approved Plan: Same.

Differences Between Plan and Advisory Group Recommendations: None.

Differences Between Plan and Implementation: Some refinements were made in the mediation program after initial implementation. The district changed from 3 mediations per year per lawyer (all in one morning) to one per year per lawyer, so they can meet longer than one hour if need be. In addition, a list was developed of additional types of cases thought not to be suitable for mediation for various reasons: Declaratory judgment cases, class action cases, pro se cases, and various other types of cases[11] such as: some types of contract cases, all real property cases, some types of personal injury such as airplane, some types of civil rights cases, all forfeiture and penalty cases, all labor cases, all tax cases, all property rights cases, bankruptcy cases, and most cases involving specific statutes. As a result of using this list to exclude certain types of cases, the number of cases referred to mediation was reduced, and totaled 476 in 1992.

Effective January 1, 1995, the mediation program has been refined further by a revised Local Civil Rule 53.2.1 as follows: participation in mediator training programs is encouraged; Special Management Track and bankruptcy-related cases are excluded; the timing is to be within 60 days (up from 30 days) after the first appearance for a defendant; with certain conditions, the mediation may be postponed 30 days to enable parties to be better prepared to discuss settlement; each party is to submit a 2 page summary of the case before the mediation; and the mediation may be held open after the initial conference for up to 60 days.

OPTIONAL CJRA TECHNIQUES

The CJRA indicates that each court shall consider and may include the following five litigation management techniques:[12]

---

[11]Excluded cases have the following nature of suit codes: 130, 140–160, 210–290, 310, 315, 330, 368, 370, 371, 441, 443, 444, 510–550, 610–690, 710–791, 422–423, 810, 861–865, 870–871, 400, 410, 430, 460, 820–840, 850, 870, 875, 891–895, 900, and 950.

[12]28 U.S.C. § 473(b).

I.   **Requiring that counsel jointly present a discovery/case management plan at the initial pretrial conference:**

In cases in the Special Management Track, the parties are required to confer prior to the scheduling conference and thereafter provide the court with a proposed case management plan. No similar requirement for cases on other tracks.

II. **Requiring that each party be represented at each pretrial conference by an attorney with authority to bind that party:**

The court may, in its discretion, order that each party be represented at each pretrial conference by an attorney with the authority to bind.

III. **Requiring the signature of the attorney *and* the party for all requests for discovery extensions or postponements of trial:**

Plan accepts the Advisory Report recommendation not to implement this requirement.

IV. **Offering a Neutral Evaluation program:**

Plan accepts the Advisory Report recommendation not to create such a program. However, any judge can order, and any party can suggest, the desirability of utilizing a means of ADR other than court-annexed arbitration and mediation. Advisory Report had suggested that any assessment of the mediation program (see **CJRA Policy 6**, above) include considering whether any role exists for a supplemental program of early neutral evaluation.

V.   **Requiring party representatives with authority to bind to be present or available by telephone at settlement conferences:**

Upon notice, the court may require that representatives of the parties with authority to bind them in settlement discussions be present or available by telephone during any settlement conference. The Court-Annexed Mediation program is considered a type of "early settlement conference" and the client must be available by telephone or in person for the purpose of discussing settlement possibilities. In cases in the Special Management Track, a representative of each party with authority to settle must attend the second pretrial conference. Existing Local Civil Rule 16.1 ¶ 3 required the attendance with the authority to settle at the final pretrial conference.

OTHER POLICIES ADOPTED IN CJRA PLAN

Approved Plan: None.

Differences Between Plan and Advisory Group Recommendations: The Advisory Group made comments or suggestions for actions that are beyond the control of the District Court and/or beyond the area of civil case processing: (1) improving and expediting the process of filling judicial vacancies; (2) assessing the impact of legislative proposals on the judicial system; (3) conducting research on the relation between delay and cost in civil case processing; (4) improving lawyer sensitivity to the relation between litigation practices and procedures and cost to the litigant; (5) having litigants assume responsibility for exploring with counsel the development of litigation policies intended to achieve efficient, economical, and professionally responsible practices; (6) amending Federal Rule of Civil Procedure 4(j) to reduce the 120 days permitted from filing until service of process; and (7) improving and expediting the process of authorizing and funding magistrate judgeships.

OVERVIEW OF CJRA PROGRAM IN PENNSYLVANIA, MIDDLE DISTRICT

OVERVIEW OF IMPLEMENTED CJRA PLAN

This is a comparison district, not a pilot district, so a CJRA plan had to be implemented by December 1, 1993, and it did not have to contain the six pilot program principles. This district's plan was adopted August 19, 1993 and was effective for cases filed beginning January 1, 1994. However, given the time necessary to develop a list of mediators and train them, the mediation program was effectively implemented in early June, 1994. The plan was refined but not substantially changed in October 1994.

The CJRA Advisory Group notes that "the Middle District of Pennsylvania is operated in an efficient and effective manner," and that there is "currently no significant delay." "The Advisory Group concluded that significant changes to the current practices in the Middle District are not required. The recommendations are offered to 'fine-tune' an already efficient system."[1] The recommendations generally followed the six CJRA principles, including differential case management with tracks, early and ongoing judicial control of the pretrial process, authorization to refer appropriate cases to a range of ADR options, and encouragement of the voluntary exchange of information and cooperative discovery. The Advisory Group did not recommend early mandatory exchange of certain types of information, because it suggested waiting for the outcome of the adoption of proposed Federal Rule 26, which deals with that issue.

The court's CJRA Plan approved and adopted 15 of the 16 Advisory Group recommendations, rejecting only the recommendation that would require temporary restraining orders filed by prisoners with counsel to be assigned in all instances to a Judge rather than a Magistrate Judge. With the exception of Health and Human Services cases, prisoner, pro se parties, and U.S. Government loan cases, the Plan applies to all civil cases filed on or after January 1, 1994, and at judicial discretion

---

[1] Light et al. (1992). The 15-member committee was chaired by a lawyer, had the Clerk of Court as reporter, met as a whole nine times, and also worked in subcommittees. The Chief Judge and two Senior Judges were members. The Advisory Group interviewed judicial officers, and surveyed 167 lawyers and 123 litigants.

may apply to cases pending on that date.[2] For differential case management, four tracks were created: Fast, Expedited, Standard, and Complex. Each track has a different time to trial. From the time the new track program became operational in 1994 through October 1995, about 3/4 of the cases that had a case management conference were assigned to a track. Of those assigned to tracks, 73 percent were standard, 18 percent were complex, and 8 percent were either fast or expedited. For ADR, the following types are included: summary jury trials, a settlement officer program (which can include neutral evaluation by an outside expert), and a formally structured mediation program with trained neutral lawyer-mediators. From the time the new ADR programs became operational in 1994 through October 1995, few cases have been referred for the voluntary ADR. In that period, only one judge held any summary jury trials, only 33 cases were referred to mediation, and only 34 cases had settlement officers appointed (and none were referred for neutral evaluation by an outside expert).

The 1993 Annual Assessment indicated: "Given that the civil docket is in very good condition, the Advisory Group does not recommend any significant changes . . . ."[3]

The 1994 Annual Assessment indicated: "It remains the belief of the Advisory Group that the civil case processing practices of the Court are not in need of any major changes."[4] However, the Advisory Group recommended: "The use of Case Management Tracks could and should be increased. Likewise, increased utilization of ADR is recommended . . . ."

CJRA POLICY 1: DIFFERENTIAL CASE MANAGEMENT

Policy Before CJRA Plan

The following types of cases are exempt from an initial Rule 16 scheduling conference by Local Rule: Health and Human Services cases (Social Security appeals), prisoner, and U.S. Government loan cases. All other types of cases are managed individually.

CJRA Plan Implementation

Approved Plan: The same types of cases are exempt from an initial Rule 16 scheduling conference, and in addition all pro se party cases are exempt from CJRA Plan case management policies. All other cases have a requirement for lawyers to prepare a joint case management/discovery plan for discussion with the judge at the initial scheduling and case management conference, at which conference the judge will place the case in one of the following four case management tracks:

---

[2]United States District Court for the Middle District of Pennsylvania (1994).

[3]Light et al. (undated, using data as of the end of 1993), p. 2.

[4]Marsh et al. (undated, using data as of the end of 1994), p. 2.

1. Fast Track. A standard order is issued referring the case to a Magistrate Judge for recommendations. The order sets forth standard time frames conducive to the characteristics of the case. The court anticipates that the majority of the cases assigned to this track will be procedural type cases that are not subject to a joint case management/discovery plan. In October 1994, the Plan was refined to specify a trial date goal or time to disposition of not more than six months from the filing of the action.

2. Expedited Track. The court will issue a scheduling order setting a trial date goal of not more than 240 days from filing of the initial complaint. In October 1994, the Plan was refined to specify a trial date goal or time to disposition of not more than eight months from the filing of the action. As of October 1995, 8 percent of the 573 cases assigned to tracks at the case management conference were on this expedited track.

3. Standard Track. The court will issue a scheduling order setting a trial date goal of not more than 365 days from filing of the initial complaint. In October 1994, the Plan was refined to specify a goal of not more than 15 months rather than one year because some cases that they did not want to designate as complex were requiring up to 15 months to get ready for trial for good reasons. As of October 1995, 73 percent of the 573 cases assigned to tracks at the case management conference were on this standard track.

4. Complex Track. The court will issue a scheduling order setting a trial date goal of more than 365 days from filing of the initial complaint. In October 1994, the Plan was refined to specify a goal of not more than two years. As of October 1995, 18 percent of the 573 cases assigned to tracks at the case management conference were on this complex track.

Differences Between Plan and Advisory Group Recommendations: The Advisory Group recommends differential case management and explicitly mentions the fast track. The court's plan uses four tracks and is consistent with the intent of the Advisory Group recommendation.

Differences Between Plan and Implementation: None in principle. The implementation of the track designation process is being refined, since some cases filed after January 1, 1994 did not receive a formal track designation. From the start of the plan in 1994 through October 1995, about 3/4 of the cases that had case management conferences were given track assignments. At the end of 1995, all judges were participating in this track assignment process, and for calendar year 1995 the following track assignments were made: 0 fast; 14 expedited; 261 standard; and 76 complex. About 4 percent of 1995 civil filings were designated as complex.

CJRA POLICY 2: EARLY AND ONGOING CONTROL OF PRETRIAL BY JUDICIAL OFFICER

Policy Before CJRA Plan

Initial and final pretrial conferences are held, with at least one settlement conference with a judicial officer. Limit is 40 interrogatories or requests for admission by local rule.

CJRA Plan Implementation

Approved Plan: All cases not exempt from Rule 16 conferences have a new requirement for lawyers to prepare a joint case management plan for discussion with the judge at the initial scheduling case management conference, which is to take place within 120 days after filing of the initial complaint if possible. Lead counsel shall meet and confer in person[5] to prepare the joint case management plan and file it with the court 5 days[6] before the initial court conference. The CJRA plan contains an 11-page outline of the topics to be covered in the case management plan. Those topics include legal and factual issues, ADR, consent to Magistrate Judge, disclosures of names of people and documents and damages, description of anticipated motions, description of discovery, recommendations for limitations on each type of discovery, recommended schedule dates, and other matters. At the initial pretrial conference, the judge will discuss the items in the joint plan with the lawyers, decide on placement of the case in one of the above four tracks, establish a schedule for the case, and make any other case management decisions appropriate for the case. Local Rules were amended on January 1, 1994, to place a limit of 25 on the number of interrogatories or requests for admissions and to limit depositions to 6 hours per deponent, unless the court authorizes a longer time period.

Differences Between Plan and Advisory Group Recommendations: None, except for how the case management plan is prepared and the role of Magistrate Judges relative to certain types of prisoner cases with counsel. The Advisory Group suggested that the court propose a case management/discovery plan and that counsel respond to the draft and confirm a plan agreed upon at the initial court conference. The court's plan calls for the lawyers to jointly draft the plan before the conference. The Advisory Group recommends early and ongoing judicial control of the pretrial process including: case planning, early and firm trial dates, control of discovery, and deadlines for motions. They also recommend a pretrial/settlement conference soon after the completion of discovery. The court's plan is consistent with these recommendations, and much more specific and detailed. The only recommendation that was rejected by the court was one that would require temporary restraining orders filed by prisoners with counsel be assigned in all instances to a Judge rather than a Magistrate Judge.

---

[5]A provision for conferring on the phone if the offices are over 100 miles apart was deleted in the October 1994 refinement of the Plan.

[6]The Plan was refined in October 1994 to change the time from 14 days to 5 days before the conference.

Differences Between Plan and Implementation: None reported.

CJRA POLICY 3: MORE INTENSIVE MANAGEMENT OF COMPLEX CASES

Policy Before CJRA Plan

Individualized case management, generally with more intensive management for more complex cases.

CJRA Plan Implementation

Approved Plan: Assignment to a complex case track as noted above, with individualized case management within the complex track based on discussion of the joint case management plan prepared by the lawyers.

Differences Between Plan and Advisory Group Recommendations: None.

Differences Between Plan and Implementation: None reported.

CJRA POLICY 4: EXCHANGE OF DISCOVERY INFORMATION

Policy Before CJRA Plan

No formal policy.

CJRA Plan Implementation

Approved Plan: The court will follow the December 1993 revised F.R.Civ.P. 26.

Differences Between Plan and Advisory Group Recommendations: None. The Advisory Group recommended awaiting the outcome of the adoption of the then proposed Federal Rule 26. If the newly revised Federal Rule 26 had not been adopted, then the Advisory Group recommended the court adopt a local rule to encourage the voluntary exchange of information.

Differences Between Plan and Implementation: None reported. The December 1993 amendments to Federal Rule of Civil Procedure 26(a)(1) concerning mandatory initial disclosure are in effect in this district. [7] The Chief Judge is not aware of any complaints or motions related to this disclosure requirement.

---

[7]Stienstra (1995).

CJRA POLICY 5: CERTIFY GOOD FAITH EFFORT BEFORE FILING DISCOVERY MOTION

Policy Before CJRA Plan

Local Rule requires that "counsel for the movant in all discovery matters file with the Court ten days after filing of the respondents brief a statement certifying that he has conferred with the opposing party in an effort in good faith to resolve by agreement the issues raised by the motion."[8]

CJRA Plan Implementation

Approved Plan: The court modified the Local Rule to require the certification of a good faith effort to be filed at the time of the motion.

Differences Between Plan and Advisory Group Recommendations: None.

Differences Between Plan and Implementation: None reported.

CJRA POLICY 6: ALTERNATIVE DISPUTE RESOLUTION PROGRAMS

Policy Before CJRA Plan

A settlement conference is usually held with a judicial officer. Local rule requires a pretrial conference in every civil case, unless otherwise ordered by the court and persons with authority to settle must attend or be available by phone. Local rule also requires plaintiff to initiate and conduct a conference of all attorneys at least 5 days before the pretrial conference to discuss settlement. In addition, summary jury trials are authorized by local rule; one half-time senior judge holds them for the majority of his cases that are approaching trial. Other judges use summary jury trials or mediation or neutral evaluation, but rarely (less than 10 cases per year combined).

CJRA Plan Implementation

Approved Plan: The court adopted an array of alternatives to trial, which include summary jury trials, a settlement officer program, and mediation.

Summary Jury Trials: Currently used by one half-time Senior Judge for most of his cases that approach trial, with settlement rate of 81 percent. Plan indicates: this should be the last step before actual jury trial, gives day in court and allows counsel to ask questions of jury after verdict, and judge can limit time to present case and restrict live and/or video testimony.

Mediation: Referral of a case is at the discretion of the court; referral may be requested by the parties or recommended by the court. Mediation is with a neutral attorney who has had mandatory formal mediation training and who is selected by the

---

[8]Light et al. (1992), pp. 68–69.

judge's office.[9] The initial list of mediators has about 50, who have all received two days of training and agreed to do two pro bono mediations per year.[10] The intent is for mediation to occur after or near end of the discovery process. The primary goal is settlement. Secondary goals include improving communication among counsel and litigants; identifying facts; narrowing issues; exploring real needs and interests of the parties; having parties think creatively about resolving disputes; and increasing chances of later settlement. Services would be at reasonable and prevailing fee, paid by parties. Parties with settlement authority must attend (unless good cause and then must be available by phone).

Settlement Officer Program: Litigants and counsel meet either with a Senior Judge, a Magistrate Judge, or a neutral evaluator to discuss settlement. The judge will decide who the settlement officer will be, and Senior or Magistrate Judges will usually be used. A neutral evaluator usually will be an expert in a particular field relevant to the case whom the court, with concurrence of all parties, will appoint as the settlement officer. The neutral evaluator may work pro bono or may be paid by the parties. The primary goal is settlement. Counsel and parties with settlement authority must attend (unless good cause is shown, and then they must be available by phone). Parties may be required to submit a written evaluation before conference.

Differences Between Plan and Advisory Group Recommendations: None. The neutral evaluation recommendation is one option in the settlement officer program rather than a separate program.

Differences Between Plan and Implementation: None reported. However, from the time the new ADR programs became operational in 1994 through October 1995, few cases have been referred. In that time period, only one judge held any summary jury trials, only 33 cases were referred to mediation, and only 34 cases had settlement officers appointed (and none were referred for neutral evaluation by an outside expert). Some lawyers commented that the first case management conference is too early to make a decision on voluntary mediation and that settlement conferences with judicial officers are available as needed. Judges reportedly are not strongly encouraging the lawyers to use ADR.

OPTIONAL CJRA TECHNIQUES

The CJRA indicates that each court shall consider and may include the following five litigation management techniques:[11]

I. **Requiring that counsel jointly present a discovery/case management plan at the initial pretrial conference:**

---

[9]In October 1994 the Plan was refined to specify selection of the mediator by the judge's office, rather than being randomly selected by the Clerk's Office from list of certified mediators.

[10]In October 1994 the Plan was refined to provide for pro bono mediation, rather than having mediators paid by the parties.

[11]28 U.S.C. § 473(b).

Technique adopted. See discussion in section on **CJRA Policy 1**. The court decided to follow the December 1993 revised F.R.Civ.P. 26.

II. **Requiring that each party be represented at each pretrial conference by an attorney with authority to bind that party:**

Local Rule 16.2 requires those representatives of the parties having complete settlement authority to appear at each conference and trial, or upon approval of the court, be available by telephone.

III. **Requiring the signature of the attorney** *and* **the party for all requests for discovery extensions or postponements of trial:**

Local Rule 203.2 requires motions for continuances to be signed by counsel and client.

IV. **Offering a Neutral Evaluation program:**

Plan incorporates neutral evaluation into its Settlement Officer Program; however, primary goal would be settlement (see discussion of **CJRA Policy 6**). Advisory Report did recommend a formalized Neutral Evaluation Program with a Magistrate Judge at an early stage in the litigation.

V. **Requiring party representatives with authority to bind to be present or available by telephone at settlement conferences:**

Court adopts this technique as part of its Settlement Officer Program. Local Rule 16.2 already requires those representatives of the parties having complete settlement authority to appear at each conference and trial, or upon approval of the court, be available by telephone.

OTHER POLICIES ADOPTED IN CJRA PLAN

Approved Plan: The court shall adopt a code of professional conduct to improve lawyer collegiality and civility, and establish local training programs that facilitate bench-bar interaction through seminars.

The two CJRA positions will be continued and used to manage the implementation of the ADR and differential case management programs, and perform several other CJRA-related functions.

The court recommends that Congress review legislation prior to enactment to study its impact in regard to increasing court caseloads and changes in judicial discretion.

Differences Between Plan and Advisory Group Recommendations: None. The Advisory Group also recommended that vacant judgeships be filled in a timely fashion, but that is beyond the control of the district court.

Differences Between Plan and Implementation: None reported.

OVERVIEW OF PILOT PROGRAM IN TENNESSEE, WESTERN DISTRICT

OVERVIEW OF IMPLEMENTED CJRA PLAN

The CJRA Advisory Group indicated that the "judges are working hard but are being inundated by the criminal docket; that we can't expect to keep up with the civil docket without adding more judges, courtrooms, and support staff; that increased resources are not the only issue because the influx of drug and firearm cases is changing the whole character of the federal court system."[1] The group made several recommendations including experimenting with civil motion days, rotating criminal dockets, and ADR for civil cases. It also recommended giving courtroom deputies major case management responsibility and releasing them from most courtroom responsibilities, developing specific written procedures for the clerk's office, and increased training of clerks. Attorneys were asked to support ADR procedures, cooperate in discovery, comply with deadlines, and try cases before Magistrate Judges.

The Plan indicates: "The statute requires each pilot district to include in its plan six enumerated principles . . . . All of these principles are already utilized in this district to some degree, although their use is not uniform or documented in any formal way. Thus, the plan represents a commitment by the judges of this court to apply these principles through uniform procedures."[2] After CJRA, the judges usually set a trial date at the initial conference, and the intent is for trial to take place within 18 months of filing. The court did not adopt more-formalized tracks, but it did continue the special policies already in place for six different categories of cases that are exempt from a Rule 16 scheduling conference. The court now also encourages, through informal judicial persuasion, the voluntary exchange of information and the use of cooperative discovery devices. A rotating criminal docket has been implemented, and the role of the clerks in managing civil cases has been significantly increased. While no formally structured ADR program with a substantial volume of cases exists, the

---

[1]Cody et al. (1991) transmittal letter. The 23-person committee was chaired by a lawyer, had a law professor as reporter, met as a whole several times and also worked separately in subcommittees. One judge, one magistrate judge, and the Clerk of Court were liaison members. The Advisory Group interviewed judicial officers, a public hearing was held, and various organizations were asked for inputs. Surveys were conducted of lawyers and litigants on 80 cases.

[2]United States District Court for the Western District of Tennessee (1991), § I.

plan as implemented allows several types of ADR methods to be used. The plan was adopted December 31, 1991, and implementation proceeded over the following months. As of mid-1994, the District had requested and received more ADR information from the Advisory Group and had experimented with early neutral evaluation on a few cases. Following that experiment, the judges decided to make mediation the primary ADR method in this district. As of January 1996, a CJRA annual report had not been prepared by either the Advisory Group or the Court.

CJRA POLICY 1: DIFFERENTIAL CASE MANAGEMENT

Policy Before CJRA Plan

The following types of cases were exempt from an initial Rule 16 scheduling conference by Local Rule: Pro se prisoner petitions, Social Security appeals, bankruptcy appeals, forfeiture and penalty proceedings, and reviews of other administrative proceedings.

CJRA Plan Implementation

Approved Plan: Similar to before CJRA Plan. At the time of filing, the clerk will assign all civil cases to one of six categories, each with differential case management procedures, as outlined below. Initial scheduling conferences generally will not be held for the first five categories of cases.

1. Pro Se prisoner litigation (defined as all prisoner litigation except habeas corpus). Upon filing of first responsive pleading, the judge will issue an order requiring discovery to be completed within 4 months after order, filing of all pretrial motions within 5 months, and setting of definite trial date within 9 to 12 months of order.

2. Habeas petitions. Court will attempt to dispose of within 9 months of filing, excepting death penalty cases.

3. Bankruptcy appeals. Court will issue briefing schedule consistent with Bankruptcy Rule 8009, and attempt to dispose of within 9 months of filing.

4. U.S. debt cases. No case management is planned.

5. Social Security cases. Clerk will issue an order requiring plaintiff's brief within 30 days, defense brief in response within 21 days of plaintiff's filing, and reply brief within 10 days of defense's response. Court will also seek to dispose of such cases within 9 months of filing.

6. General civil litigation. An initial Rule 16 scheduling conference will be held, at which time the court will further categorize cases according to complexity of the case and the amount of judicial involvement required and make decisions on pretrial conferences, discovery schedules, and settlement techniques, on the basis of this initial evaluation. Each case will be assessed individually and given the appropriate degree of supervision. Other than these individualized case manage-

ment procedures, there will be no set of predetermined case management tracks within the general civil litigation category.

Local Rules were revised on January 1, 1993, and exempt the first five types of cases noted above (plus forfeiture and penalty proceedings and reviews of other administrative proceedings) from an initial Rule 16 scheduling conference. For cases exempt from the initial Rule 16 scheduling conference, the judicial management is more formalized in the CJRA plan (e.g. more-standardized schedules and stated intent to dispose of most of these types of cases within 9 months).

Differences Between Plan and Advisory Group Recommendations: None.

Differences Between Plan and Implementation: None reported.

CJRA POLICY 2: EARLY AND ONGOING CONTROL OF PRETRIAL BY JUDICIAL OFFICER

Policy Before CJRA Plan

Initial and final pretrial conferences were held, usually with one attempt to settle the case. Limit was 30 interrogatories by Local Rule. Judges usually did not set the trial date at the initial conference.

CJRA Plan Implementation

Approved Plan: Similar to before, although the plan represents a commitment by the judges of this court to apply uniform procedures and to set the trial date at the initial conference.

For cases with Rule 16 scheduling conferences (all general civil litigation cases), the court will seek to schedule the conference within 90 days instead of the required 120 days of filing, and the court will undertake the following management actions:

— plan progress of the case with counsel;

— set a firm trial date within 18 months of filing, unless the required certification is made;

— set discovery deadlines, and, if appropriate, enter orders concerning the allowable extent and scope of discovery;

— set deadlines for filing motions and a time framework for their disposition;

— encourage parties to agree to trial before a magistrate judge;

— schedule any additional status or pretrial conferences; and

— ensure timely discovery by enforcing overall schedule, referring discovery motions to a Magistrate Judge, encouraging counsel to comply in timely manner with discovery requests and motions, and imposing appropriate sanctions.

A uniform order noting the above and setting the initial Rule 16 scheduling conference was developed. Lawyers are to jointly present a discovery/case management plan at the initial pretrial conference, or explain the reasons for their failure to do so.[3]

Differences Between Plan and Advisory Group Recommendations: Since the Advisory Group recommendations are numerous, there are some differences with the CJRA plan in the details. However, in general the court's stated intentions and the Advisory Group recommendations are in agreement.

Differences Between Plan and Implementation: The uniform order setting the initial Rule 16 conference does not mention a joint discovery/case management plan.

CJRA POLICY 3: MORE INTENSIVE MANAGEMENT OF COMPLEX CASES

Policy Before CJRA Plan

Individualized case management, using the *Manual on Complex Litigation* as a reference.

CJRA Plan Implementation

Approved Plan: Similar to before, except for the initial scheduling conference changes noted above. Attorneys must be prepared at the initial conference to discuss whether the case is complex or routine and the type of case management needed, and to present a joint discovery-case management plan at the conference.

Differences Between Plan and Advisory Group Recommendations: None.

Differences Between Plan and Implementation: The uniform order setting the initial Rule 16 conference does not mention a joint discovery-case management plan.

CJRA POLICY 4: EXCHANGE OF DISCOVERY INFORMATION

Policy Before CJRA Plan

No formal policy.

CJRA Plan Implementation

Approved Plan: The court will "encourage litigants to voluntarily exchange information and to use cooperative discovery devices through informal judicial persuasion at the initial Rule 16(b) conference and at other appropriate times."[4] It will also adopt as a local rule the Memphis Bar's *Guidelines of Professional Courtesy and Conduct,* under which attorneys are expected to strive to effect cooperative discovery, avoid delaying tactics, encourage methods and practices to simplify and keep legal services

---

[3]United States District Court for the Western District of Tennessee (1991), § II(A).

[4]United States District Court for the Western District of Tennessee (1991), § I(D).

cost-effective. Local Rules were revised January 1, 1993 to incorporate *Guidelines of Professional Courtesy and Conduct.*

Differences Between Plan and Advisory Group Recommendations: None.

Differences Between Plan and Implementation: None reported. The December 1993 amendments to Federal Rule of Civil Procedure 26(a)(1) concerning mandatory initial disclosure are in effect in this district. However, the court may reconsider in the future.[5]

CJRA POLICY 5: CERTIFY GOOD FAITH EFFORT BEFORE FILING DISCOVERY MOTION

Policy Before CJRA Plan

Under Local Rule 9(f), discovery motions must be accompanied by a certificate of counsel that, after consultation between the parties, they are unable to reach agreement on the discovery motion. If counsel are in same county, face-to-face consultation is required.

CJRA Plan Implementation

Approved Plan: Same.

Differences Between Plan and Advisory Group Recommendations: None.

Differences Between Plan and Implementation: None reported.

CJRA POLICY 6: ALTERNATIVE DISPUTE RESOLUTION PROGRAMS

Policy Before CJRA Plan

A settlement conference was usually held with a judicial officer.

CJRA Plan Implementation

Approved Plan: At the initial Rule 16 conference, the court will determine what particular method of ADR should be utilized. Regardless of whether an ADR method is applied, parties will be encouraged by the court to try to reach settlement through some means, with typically at least two court-facilitated efforts to settle. The court will continue to rely heavily on settlement conferences, and may use other methods such as mini-trials, summary jury trials, and mediation. "One settlement method which the judges will utilize is early neutral evaluation, with the evaluation function performed by respected attorneys within the district who are willing to perform this

---

[5]Stienstra (1995).

task. A specific neutral evaluation plan will be developed for the formation of the panel of neutral evaluation attorneys in early 1992."[6]

Local Rule 15 effective January 1, 1993 permits settlement conference, early neutral evaluation, mini-trial, summary jury trial, or mediation.

Differences Between Plan and Advisory Group Recommendations: Similar, except the Advisory Group said neutral evaluation should be explored further, and the Plan says they will utilize neutral evaluation.

Differences Between Plan and Implementation: The court asked the Advisory Group to study neutral evaluation further, and received a report in early 1993.[7] Subsequently the court experimented with early neutral evaluation on a few cases, and as a result of that experiment decided in mid-1994 to focus their primary ADR efforts on mediation rather than early neutral evaluation. Other than settlement conferences, fewer than 50 cases per year have ADR, although the number may increase if the mediation program is developed and implemented.

OPTIONAL CJRA TECHNIQUES

The CJRA indicates that each court shall consider and may include the following five litigation management techniques:[8]

I. **Requiring that counsel jointly present a discovery/case management plan at the initial pretrial conference:**

The Plan adopted this technique, "to the extent it is not already required, by including it in a uniform notice letter for the initial Rule 16(b) conference."[9] The court subsequently decided to follow the December 1993 revised F.R.Civ.P. 26.

II. **Requiring that each party be represented at each pretrial conference by an attorney with authority to bind that party:**

Plan indicated that the court would adopt this technique by local rule and expand the similar current practice regarding authority to bind at the final pretrial conference to all conferences.

III. **Requiring the signature of the attorney *and* the party for all requests for discovery extensions or postponements of trial:**

Plan rejected this technique and indicated that the Court felt that there was no evidence that attorneys did not consult with their clients about extensions and that a requirement of party signature would slightly increase cost and delay. Advisory Re-

---

[6]United States District Court for the Western District of Tennessee (1991), § I(F).

[7]Cody (1993).

[8]28 U.S.C. § 473(b).

[9]United States District Court for the Western District of Tennessee (1991), § II(A).

port recommended that all requests for postponement of the trial be signed by the attorney after communication with the party making the request.

IV. **Offering a Neutral Evaluation program:**

The Plan did adopt an experimental program as outlined in **CJRA Policy 6**, above.

V. **Requiring party representatives with authority to bind to be present or available by telephone at settlement conferences:**

The Plan indicated that the court already required the presence or availability of party representatives at settlement conferences and would incorporate the requirement into a new local rule.

OTHER POLICIES ADOPTED IN CJRA PLAN

Approved Plan:

1. **Broader job duties for courtroom deputies.** The court plans to make courtroom deputy clerks more responsible for case management, and not to require them to be in the courtroom at all times with the judge. This is a significant change in the role of the courtroom deputy clerk in this district.

2. **Plan for rotation of the criminal docket.** Criminal cases requiring 5 trial days or less are heard only in the first two weeks of each month, and only by three of the four active judges on a rotating basis. The original judge to whom the case is assigned will handle pretrial matters and trials requiring over 5 days.

3. **Other Policies.** The Court will attempt to find more facility space, improve court administration procedures in the clerk's office, improve pro se procedures, establish time targets for all matters taken under advisement, utilize visiting judges, enforce all time limits more strictly than in the past, and have the clerk develop a system of monitoring all due dates and following up on overdue pleadings or filings.

Differences Between Plan and Advisory Group Recommendations: As with the six CJRA principles, the Advisory Group recommendations here were similar to the plan adopted by the court, but differ in the details.

Differences Between Plan and Implementation: None.

OVERVIEW OF PILOT PROGRAM IN TEXAS, SOUTHERN DISTRICT

OVERVIEW OF IMPLEMENTED CJRA PLAN

The CJRA Advisory Group concluded that the problems of cost and delay are severe, and that the principal causes of delay in this district have "nothing to do with the degree of effort made by the judges or their methods of operation." They cited the demands of the criminal dockets and indicated that the district "has simply not been given resources commensurate with its workload."[1] The Advisory Group recommended a Cost and Delay Reduction Plan that called for substantial staff increases and modifications in case management, especially in the areas of differential case management and alternative dispute resolution.

The court's CJRA plan "adopts the measures, rules, and programs . . . contained in the Advisory Group's report" with minor modification.[2] The CJRA Pilot Program plan calls for new staff attorneys to screen cases for placement in appropriate tracks, and to recommend expedited processing for appropriate cases, but this aspect of differential case management could not be implemented due to lack of staff. Pretrial management changes for standard cases were made, including: Initial conferences are to be held by all judges, at which time trial date is scheduled; counsel are to meet and prepare a joint discovery/case management plan for presentation at the initial pretrial conference; and Magistrate Judges in Houston are to have approximately 50 open civil cases apiece at all times for pretrial management. A total of 32 new staffers were requested to aid in various aspects of pretrial management, but funding was available for 3 in 1992 and 5 in 1993–1995. For 10 or 20 cases per judge only, the court requires mandatory disclosure of information on identification of witnesses, all documents and data that are likely to bear significantly on any claim or defense, damages, and insurance. The court established a new formally structured voluntary mediation program with about 300 cases per year (the program allows any type of ADR but in 1992 over 98 percent of the cases actually had mediation). The plan was implemented in January 1992.

---

[1]Reasoner et al. (1991), p. 1. The 17-person committee was chaired by a lawyer, met as a whole seven times, and also worked separately in subcommittees. The reporter and co-reporter were the Clerk of Court and a law professor, respectively, and the Chief Judge was an ex-officio member. The Advisory Group interviewed judicial officers, and a survey of lawyers and litigants for about 150 cases was conducted.

[2]United States District Court for the Southern District of Texas (1991a, 1991b, and 1992).

The first Annual Assessment indicated that implementation of many parts of the Plan was delayed indefinitely because of financial and other concerns; that the aspects of the Plan that were fully implemented appear to have had a definite impact on litigation; that numerous changes in judicial personnel had taken place; and that annual felony filings were down over 40 percent between 1990 and 1992. No changes were recommended in the Plan.[3]

The third Annual Assessment indicated that many parts of the Plan implementation continued to be delayed indefinitely because of financial and staffing concerns. Between 1990 and 1994, criminal filings declined 50 percent, while civil filings climbed 14 percent. During 1994, the role of magistrate judges in case management was significantly greater than before CJRA. Over 300 cases were referred for pretrial management and over 300 for consent trial by magistrate judges (up from 67 in 1991). About 300 cases were referred to voluntary mediation in each of 1993 and 1994, and the number is growing slightly each year. No changes were recommended in the Plan.[4]

CJRA POLICY 1: DIFFERENTIAL CASE MANAGEMENT

Policy Before CJRA Plan

The following types of cases were exempt from an initial Rule 16 scheduling conference by Local Rule: Prisoner civil rights, habeas corpus, student loan, Social Security and other administrative appeals. In addition, bankruptcy, forfeiture, and government collection cases received special processing which usually did not include a Rule 16 conference. Asbestos cases were sent to a special master, and subsequently to the Multi-District-Litigation judge in Pennsylvania.

CJRA Plan Implementation

Approved Plan: Plan calls for continuation of prior management of asbestos, government collection, and prisoner cases, and expansion of the differential case processing by adding additional categories for the remaining types of cases. Initial scheduling conferences generally will not be held for the first five categories of cases listed below.

In addition, the plan calls for the court to coordinate a team of three additional staff attorneys who would "screen and review new case filings for placement in appropriate case management tracks and perform an evaluation of individual cases eligible for expedited handling, curing any defects by recommended action early on, quickly recommending appropriate dismissal and remands."

1. Asbestos Litigation. Multi-District Litigation pretrial processing done in Pennsylvania.

---

[3]United States District Court for the Southern District of Texas (1993).

[4]United States District Court for the Southern District of Texas (1995).

2. VA and Student Loan Collection Cases. All sent to one judge for special processing.

3. Prisoner Litigation (including habeas corpus). Three staff attorneys do screening and initial processing.

4. Bankruptcy Appeals. Intent of plan is that cases are to be monitored by an additional staff attorney who will review briefs and prepare recommendations for disposition.

5. Social Security Appeals. Intent of plan is that cases are to be monitored by an additional staff attorney who will review motions and the record and prepare recommendations for disposition.

6. FDIC, RTC, FSLIC Cases. Intent of plan is that cases are to be screened by an additional staff attorney for recommendation of early disposition on remand, dismissal, or summary judgment, with cases not qualifying for early disposition referred immediately to the judge for pretrial conference.

7. Pro Se Plaintiff (Other Than Prisoner) Cases. Intent of plan is that cases are to be screened by an additional staff attorney for defects with procedural instructions being forwarded to pro se plaintiffs as necessary and preparation of proposed dismissals of frivolous complaints as appropriate.

8. Removed Cases. Intent of plan is that cases are to be reviewed by an additional staff attorney to determine the propriety of removal and recommendation regarding remand and subsequent referral to judge for pretrial conference.

9. All Other Cases (Standard). As cases are filed, counsel for plaintiff will be served with a General Order requiring that counsel meet and prepare a joint discovery/case management plan for presentation at the initial pretrial conference.

Differences Between Plan and Advisory Group Recommendations: None, except the plan notes that this screening structure is to assist the judges, and is not to restrict a judge from applying his or her case-specific processing.

Differences Between Plan and Implementation: Due to staff limitations, the court indicates that it does not have the additional staff attorneys necessary to implement the staff attorney screening, review, and recommendation portions of this differential case management for any types of cases other than those involving prisoners. An initial attempt was made to review some of the removed cases on the pleadings only, but the court found it was usually difficult to determine the propriety of removal from the pleadings alone.

CJRA POLICY 2: EARLY AND ONGOING CONTROL OF PRETRIAL BY JUDICIAL OFFICER

Policy Before CJRA Plan

Usually initial and final pretrial conferences were held, and usually one attempt was made to settle the case. Some judges did not hold Rule 16 conferences for all standard cases, and did not usually hold settlement discussions. Limit was 30 interrogatories. Judges usually did not set a trial date at initial conference.

CJRA Plan Implementation

Approved Plan: Similar, with the following exceptions: Rule 16 conferences are to be held by all judges for standard cases, at which time several dates, including trial date, are to be scheduled. In addition for each standard case, a general order requires counsel to prepare a discovery/case management plan prior to the initial pretrial conference. The court has developed a uniform order form for setting the initial conference, and a description for counsel of what is to be in the joint discovery/case management plan. That joint plan is to discuss related cases, jurisdiction, adding parties, class allegations if any, motions pending, discovery types and timing, jury demand, consent to magistrate judge, alternative dispute resolution, and trial length.

In addition, magistrate judges in Houston each are given about 50 cases at a time for all pretrial management.

Differences Between Plan and Advisory Group Recommendations: None, except Galveston division was not included in the plan for expanded use of magistrate judges for all pretrial management on a subset of cases.

Differences Between Plan and Implementation: None reported, except funding for all requested extra staff to help with pretrial case management was not provided. For example, the court asked for but did not receive one new courtroom attendant for each judge, whose role would have been to relieve the deputy clerk "case manager" from courtroom support functions.

CJRA POLICY 3: MORE INTENSIVE MANAGEMENT OF COMPLEX CASES

Policy Before CJRA Plan

Individualized management by the Judicial Officer. No formal structured "complex track."

CJRA Plan Implementation

Approved Plan: Same. Plan indicates use of *Manual for Complex Litigation* and consideration of additional conferences and bifurcation.

Differences Between Plan and Advisory Group Recommendations: None.

Differences Between Plan and Implementation: None reported.

CJRA POLICY 4: EXCHANGE OF DISCOVERY INFORMATION

Policy Before CJRA Plan

No formal policy.

CJRA Plan Implementation

Approved Plan: Each judge in largest division will order discovery to proceed under the August 1991 draft of the new Fed. Civ. P. Rule 26 for 20 cases filed in January 1992. Judges in other divisions will order this for 10 cases. That draft requires early disclosure without awaiting a discovery request of: names of individuals likely to have information that bears significantly on any claim or defense, description of documents and data that are likely to bear significantly on any claim or defense, information on damages, and insurance agreements.

Differences Between Plan and Advisory Group Recommendations: None, except plan specifies 10 rather than 20 cases in the smaller divisions.

Differences Between Plan and Implementation: None reported. The December 1993 amendments to Federal Rule of Civil Procedure 26(a)(1) concerning mandatory initial disclosure are in effect in this district.[5]

CJRA POLICY 5: CERTIFY GOOD FAITH EFFORT BEFORE FILING DIS-COVERY MOTION

Policy Before CJRA Plan

Local Rule 6 indicates that opposed motions shall contain an averment that the movant has conferred with the respondent and that counsel cannot agree about the disposition of the motion.

CJRA Plan Implementation

Approved Plan: Same.

Differences Between Plan and Advisory Group Recommendations: None.

Differences Between Plan and Implementation: None reported.

CJRA POLICY 6: ALTERNATIVE DISPUTE RESOLUTION PROGRAMS

Policy Before CJRA Plan

Settlement conference usually was held with judicial officer. Selective referral of cases to arbitration or special masters, but no formally structured ADR program.

CJRA Plan Implementation

Approved Plan: Same as before CJRA, plus ADR is to be discussed at the initial pre-trial conference and cases may be referred to mediation, mini-trial, summary jury trial, arbitration, or any other ADR program. A formally structured voluntary media-

---

[5]Stienstra (1995).

tion program was established with about 300 cases per year (the program allows any type of ADR but in 1992 over 98 percent of the cases with ADR actually had mediation rather than some other type of ADR). The plan provides for certification of trained providers, maintenance of lists of providers with information about each, a clerk to administer the program, payment of the ADR provider by the parties, discussion of referral to ADR at the Rule 16 conference, confidentiality, and a notice to the court of the results of the ADR. The typical session lasts a half day to a full day, with parties splitting the mediator's fee.

In 1994, 326 cases were referred to mediation and 3 were referred to arbitration. Mediation sessions lasted an average of about 8 hours and mediator fees averaged $1840 in total, split by the parties. Questionnaire responses to a district survey indicate that attorneys and the parties they represent usually consider mediation to be helpful and productive. ADR providers who filed forms with the court (N=440 over 3 years) indicated that about 69 percent settled as a result of the voluntary mediation.

Differences Between Plan and Advisory Group Recommendations: None.

Differences Between Plan and Implementation: The formally structured program was authorized as of January 1992, and actually began referring cases to mediation in volume in the spring of 1992 (due to the time necessary to set up and fully operationalize the program).

OPTIONAL CJRA TECHNIQUES

The CJRA indicates that each court shall consider and may include the following five litigation management techniques:[6]

I.   **Requiring that counsel jointly present a discovery/case management plan at the initial pretrial conference:**

A General Order was to be entered into every case in the "standard" track (see **CJRA Policy 1**, above) which would require counsel to meet and prepare a joint plan for presentation prior to the initial pretrial conference. The court subsequently decided to follow the December 1993 revised F.R.Civ.P. 26.

II.   **Requiring that each party be represented at each pretrial conference by an attorney with authority to bind that party:**

The Plan would implement this technique through "individual notice" by the Court requiring the attendance, at all pretrial and or settlement conferences, of an attorney who has the authority to bind.

III.   **Requiring the signature of the attorney *and* the party for all requests for discovery extensions or postponements of trial:**

---

[6] 28 U.S.C. § 473(b).

The Plan would also implement this technique through "individual notice" by the Court. The Advisory Report would have implemented a uniform policy requiring party signature (or attorney certification of reasons for inability to obtain same) regarding extensions of the discovery cutoff or postponement of trial.

IV. Offering a Neutral Evaluation program:

Neutral Evaluation was not one of the ADR methods specifically recognized in the Plan but the court "may approve any other ADR method the parties suggest or the court believes is suited to the litigation."

V. Requiring party representatives with authority to bind to be present or available by telephone at settlement conferences:

As stated above, the Plan would allow a judge, by "individual notice," to require the attendance, at all pretrial and or settlement conferences, of an attorney who has the authority to bind. However, it was not specifically stated that this authority would include the ability to agree to settlement. Within the ADR program, party representatives with authority to negotiate a settlement, and all other persons necessary to negotiate a settlement, must attend the ADR session.

OTHER POLICIES ADOPTED IN CJRA PLAN

Approved Plan

In the area of trial procedures, plan allows court to use techniques to enhance jury understanding (such as tutorial media on complex concepts, and videotaped depositions), to impose limits on the time allowed for various aspects of trial, and to limit expert witness testimony on a case-by-case basis.

Differences Between Plan and Advisory Group Recommendations: None.

Differences Between Plan and Implementation: None.

OVERVIEW OF PILOT PROGRAM IN DISTRICT OF UTAH

OVERVIEW OF IMPLEMENTED CJRA PLAN

The CJRA advisory group's[1] assessment of the docket revealed no critical cost- or time-based problems in civil case processing nor any serious deficiencies in resources other than in the Office of the Clerk (additional staff needed for administrative functions). However, the district's median times of processing civil cases and median times to move civil cases from issue to trial are 33 percent longer than the national median. Lack of adherence by counsel to schedule deadlines was cited as a contributing factor.

New legislation by Congress, delay in the process of filling judicial vacancies, and shifts in Executive Branch policies were all cited as having a negative impact on the docket. This was seen as particularly true in the area of the criminal caseload, where legislation or programs such as the Speedy Trial Act, a generally expanded federal jurisdiction, guideline sentencing, mandatory minimums, and Operation Triggerlock also have a direct and sometimes deleterious impact on civil case processing. Systemic responses such as increasing the number of judges and other resources were viewed as the best way of dealing with cost and delay. It was also recommended that the Department of Justice should delegate increased settlement authority to the U.S. Attorney.

With respect to the operations of the district court, the recommendations of the advisory group included the following: making no change in current mechanisms for differentiated case management of certain categories of cases; adopting several changes in pretrial procedure and limitations on the volume of discovery; making provision for the early exchange of certain types of information; and implementing an ADR program that was specified in detail.

---

[1]Zimmer et al. (1991) (hereinafter referred to as the advisory group report). The 12-person committee included two judges (plus 5 active or senior district judges as ex officio members and the Clerk of Court as the reporter), was coordinated by the Chief Judge, and met as a whole and in three subcommittees: Consumer, ADR, and Process. Analysis of the docket was conducted and a detailed study of about 100 closed cases was incorporated. A telephonic survey of 279 attorneys was also conducted.

The CJRA plan[2] reflected the Court's conviction that most of the CJRA principles had been part of the district's practices and procedures for many years, and that little change was therefore needed. However, the plan did make changes related to two of the six CJRA principles: First, to further promote the voluntary exchange of information, the court notice form for the initial conference was modified to advise counsel to communicate with one another prior to the pretrial conference, and to exchange relevant documents at the initial conference or indicate when they might be available; and second, the court will experiment with court-supervised mediation, arbitration, mini-trials, or summary jury trials for a limited period and evaluate the results. These changes were implemented in early 1993. The court also referred suggestions made in the advisory group report regarding modification, truncating, and limiting discovery to the Advisory Committee on Revisions to the Local Rules of Practice.

The first annual assessment noted that the CJRA plan had changed in two areas.[3] First, the discovery reform changes were in effect for only 10 months (March through December 1993), after which the court adopted all of the new federal civil rules amendments (on a provisional basis at least through March 30, 1995).[4] thus dramatically altering the procedural landscape of the civil litigation process. That 10-month period through December 1993 was reported to be insufficient to draw conclusions about the effects of the discovery reform changes. Second, an experimental voluntary "opt in" mediation and arbitration program has been put into effect. Arbitrators are paid by the court ($100 per day to each of 3 panel members), and mediators serve pro bono. In the first 27 months of the ADR program, through November 1995, 86 cases were referred to mediation (of which 19 were still pending, 7 settled before and 33 settled at the session, and 27 returned to litigation) and 10 cases were referred to arbitration (of which 1 was still pending, 3 settled before and 4 settled at the session, and 2 returned to litigation). The annual assessment indicates that the advisory group last met in December 1991 and the court does not anticipate calling any subsequent meetings. As of January 1996, no additional annual reports had been issued.

CJRA POLICY 1: DIFFERENTIAL CASE MANAGEMENT

Policy Before CJRA Plan

Orders are tailored for each case at the initial status and scheduling conference after discussing: case complexity, estimates of preparation time, target dates for filing motions, outside dates for motion hearings, and firm pretrial conference dates. Some judges set trial dates at the initial conference, and other judges set them at the

---

[2]United States District Court for the District of Utah (1991) (hereinafter referred to as the plan).

[3]United States District Court for the District of Utah (1994).

[4]After the end of the provisional period on March 30,1995, the court may extend the provisional period for another six months, or may make a determination as to which, if any, of the December 1993 revised F.R.Civ.P. it will opt out of by local rule.

final pretrial conference. Certain cases receive different handling depending on case type. The categories with different handling are:

1. *Class A*: Includes prisoner civil rights petitions, select pro se civil rights petitions (screened by the assigned district judge), DHHS cases (primarily Social Security appeals), and IRS challenges. At the time of filing, the cases are uniformly referred to a magistrate judge who handles all case-related matters and submits a report and recommendation to the assigned district judge for disposition.

2. *Class B*: Includes bankruptcy appeals (first scheduling notice comes from Clerk's Office at the time of filing), condemnation and forfeiture (receive different schedules at time of filing or when answers are received), and cases for injunctive relief (placed on fast track for hearings). Differential treatment was based upon the nature of the action.

3. *Miscellaneous*: Includes registrations of foreign judgment and notices to take depositions in this district for cases pending in other districts. These were never assigned to judicial officers (unless related motions are filed that require disposition).

CJRA Plan Implementation

Approved Plan: The court felt that differential case management has long been the district's practice. Current practice provides for fine-tuning each case and was felt to be superior to any sort of more formalized tracking system. Consequently, the plan proposed no change in current practices.

Differences Between Plan and Advisory Group Recommendations: The advisory group determined that no need currently exists for recommending modifications to the court's existing mechanisms for differential case management for certain categories of cases. Some additional differential management ideas were proposed in conjunction with the group's ADR recommendation, which is discussed below in the section on **CJRA Policy 6**.

Differences Between Plan and Implementation: None reported.

CJRA POLICY 2: EARLY AND ONGOING CONTROL OF PRETRIAL BY JUDICIAL OFFICER

Policy Before CJRA Plan

The pretrial management process is provided for in Rule 204 of the local Rules of Practice. After an issue is joined, the rule provides for an initial status and scheduling conference conducted by the assigned judge or judge-designated magistrate judge. At the conference, case complexity, preparation time estimates, target dates for filing motions and outside dates for motion hearings, and firm pretrial conference dates are discussed, fixed, and ordered. At this initial status and scheduling conference, some judges always fix a provisional trial date though others wait until the final pretrial conference. However, if the case will require a block of time of weeks or months for trial, a trial date is set early by the presiding judge. Target dates for various events are set in such a way as to bring the case automatically to the attention of the court at critical junctures. Court policy is to avoid granting continuances without a date being certain.

Two of four active judges handled their own calendaring from initial pretrial to final case disposition and referred relatively few civil matters to the magistrate judges. Two others regularly referred motions to magistrate judges, had them conduct much of the discovery and pretrial process, and relied on them for initial scheduling of events and deadlines. All judges refer prisoner civil rights complaints to the magistrate judges for processing and recommendation.

The Clerk's Office has authority to grant certain types of orders (such as initial requests for time for a limited number of pleadings). However, there were no automatic or clerk-monitored procedures to handle failure to effect timely service, deal with dormant cases, or respond to excessive requests for extensions or continuances. Intervention in all of these areas was left to the judge's discretion.

CJRA Plan Implementation

Approved Plan: The court felt that current practice already provides for early and ongoing control of the pretrial process and that matters are set for trial at an appropriate point in the life of the case. Therefore the plan called for continuation of current practice. However, the plan does contemplate supplementing the notice form used for the initial status/scheduling conference to inform counsel that they:

1. Should communicate with one another prior to the pretrial conference.

2. Should agree on a suggested schedule for case preparation.

3. Should gather and examine relevant existing documents in their client's control/possession and either produce them at the initial conference or be prepared to indicate at which date those documents can be produced.

The plan also refers advisory group recommendations for limiting discovery and for other local rules changes to the court's local rules committee for evaluation and recommendation.

Differences Between Plan and Advisory Group Recommendations: The advisory group proposed revision to local rules to require counsel to meet and develop a much more formalized discovery and scheduling plan and submit the plan to the court at least three days before the initial status and scheduling conference. Also, the advisory group would have required that the scheduling order set forth a trial date and that the trial be scheduled to occur within 18 months of filing (unless the judicial officer certifies that the case is too complex or that the criminal calendar will not permit the civil trial at that time). The group recommended that, absent stipulation or court approval, interrogatories be limited to 15, requests for admissions and documents be limited to 25, and depositions be limited to one day. Also, the group urged the Court to adopt a general internal policy of setting deadlines as early as possible for the filing of motions, conducting hearings within two weeks of briefing, and ruling on dispositive motions prior to the final pretrial conference. They also recommended that page limits on summary judgment motions be modified, and that dispositive motions not be referred to magistrate judges. Finally, it was requested that the clerk provide periodic internal deadline compliance reports.

Regarding requests for extensions, continuances, and rescheduling, the advisory group urged the Court to adopt a general policy against granting them absent unusual or exceptional circumstances and good cause. When such requests are made, the advisory group report asked that requests be ruled upon a minimum of three days prior to the scheduled deadline or proceeding date; specified that the original deadline or date remain in effect until the court rules otherwise; and required the signature of the attorney and the party on the request.

The advisory group would also have delegated certain monitoring and tracking functions to the Clerk's Office regarding scheduled due dates and overdue pleadings.

Differences Between Plan and Implementation: None reported.

CJRA POLICY 3: MORE INTENSIVE MANAGEMENT OF COMPLEX CASES

Policy Before CJRA Plan

Case complexity was taken into account at the initial status and scheduling conference (see discussion on **CJRA Policy 2** above) and the management plan for the case was established accordingly.

CJRA Plan Implementation

Approved Plan: The Court felt that the initial status and scheduling conference provided the framework for needed case management in complex as well as other cases. No change in current practices was made.

Differences Between Plan and Advisory Group Recommendations: The advisory group proposed that judicial officers be permitted to waive the recommended 18-month deadline for trials if they certify that the case is sufficiently complex.

Differences Between Plan and Implementation: None reported.

CJRA POLICY 4: EXCHANGE OF DISCOVERY INFORMATION

Policy Before CJRA Plan

Through Local Rules and judicial practice, the court already encouraged the voluntary exchange of information. Many judges required the exchange of all exhibits prior to the final pretrial conference. Most required a jointly prepared pretrial order with provisions as to witnesses and exhibits.

CJRA Plan Implementation

Approved Plan: The provisions of the plan were meant to supplement current practice rather than revise it. They included:

1. Supplementing the notice form used for the initial status/scheduling conference to inform counsel that they should gather and examine relevant existing documents in their client's control/possession and either:

   a) produce them at the initial status/scheduling conference, or

   b) indicate to the court and opposing counsel when the documents can be produced.

2. Referring the suggestions made in the advisory group report regarding modification, truncating, and limiting discovery to the Advisory Committee on Revisions to the Local Rules of Practice and asking for a report back from the Committee within four months.

Differences Between Plan and Advisory Group Recommendations: The advisory group would have also required counsel, prior to the initial status and scheduling conference, to designate prospective witnesses and to agree to the prompt production of information and documents subsequently discovered.

Differences Between Plan and Implementation: The Local Rules committee completed its work in this area in August 1992. The Court adopted their recommendations and amended Local Rules were promulgated in March 1993. Most of these changes were technical or administrative in nature and had little to do with the discovery process. This district did not opt out of the December 1993 amendments to the Federal Rules of Civil Procedure, including Rule 26(a)(1) concerning mandatory initial disclosure, and Rule 26(a)(1) was in essence used by the Court to replace the CJRA plan in this area.

CJRA POLICY 5: CERTIFY GOOD FAITH EFFORT BEFORE FILING DISCOVERY MOTION

Policy Before CJRA Plan

Local Rule 202(h) already required this type of certificate.

CJRA Plan Implementation

Approved Plan: No change to prior policy.

Differences Between Plan and Advisory Group Recommendations: None.

Differences Between Plan and Implementation: None reported.

CJRA POLICY 6: ALTERNATIVE DISPUTE RESOLUTION PROGRAMS

Policy Before CJRA Plan

Judges could conduct settlement conferences with the characteristics of mediation. Under Local Rule 204(c), settlements can be explored in either a formal or informal setting, off the record, and with a judge other than the trial judge. Senior judges were sometimes used to conduct many of these settlement conferences. Utah is one of ten districts that are test sites for voluntary arbitration, which had not been fully implemented in Utah prior to CJRA.

CJRA Plan Implementation

Approved Plan

The plan considered that the most efficient method to arrive at case resolution is the method found in traditional court processes with traditional safeguards, and indicated the court opinion that a supermarket of services available at the courthouse has a tendency to weaken rather than strengthen the litigation process. However, the court will experiment with court-supervised mediation, arbitration, mini-trials, or summary jury trials for a limited period, with the determination of the approach taken being under the discretion of the individual judge. Further, it will consider very carefully the ADR-related suggestions of the advisory group and will endeavor to provide services on an experimental basis within the first post-plan year (structured and staffed in a form to be determined).

Differences Between Plan and Advisory Group Recommendations: Specific suggestions outlined in detail in the advisory group report that the plan did not incorporate included:

1. Creating an ad hoc subcommittee to draft local rules for ADR programs. However, this was subsequently done by the court when it implemented the experimental ADR program.

2. Setting out in detail the components and procedures of a proposed ADR program. However, this was subsequently done by the court when it implemented the experimental ADR program.

3. Assigning cases to the appropriate ADR mechanism based upon a questionnaire filled out by the parties early in the life of the case.

Differences Between Plan and Implementation: A lengthy ADR Local Rule was promulgated by the Court in March 1993, along with other Local Rules amendments. An ADR committee was appointed. Operational responsibility for the ADR program was delegated by the Court to its Clerk. The Clerk prepared materials publicizing the Court's new voluntary ADR program, conducted training programs for the arbitrators and mediators, and hired an ADR Administrator to run the program. The voluntary "opt in" program focuses on non-binding arbitration and mediation. Counsel must file a certificate at least 10 days before the initial pretrial conference, indicating that they have discussed ADR with their client and whether the case is to be referred to the ADR program. Any party may subsequently opt out of the process. Judicial officers retain the option of referring cases to ADR on their own motion, and again any party may subsequently opt out. Arbitrators are paid by the court ($100 per day to each of 3 panel members), and mediators serve pro bono. The court has a list of 32 approved mediators and 38 approved arbitrators, each of whom has received training provided by the court, and has at least ten years experience as a lawyer. The average time from referral to the mediation conference is about 3 months, and to the arbitration hearing is about 7 months. Both mediation and arbitration usually involve 4 to 8 hours of meetings. Discovery is normally stayed during ADR referral. In the first 27 months of the ADR program, through November 1995, 86 cases were referred to mediation (of which 19 were still pending, 7 settled before and 33 settled at the session, and 27 returned to litigation) and 10 cases were referred to arbitration (of which 1 was still pending, 3 settled before and 4 settled at the session, and 2 returned to litigation). Thus, a total of 96 cases, or 4 percent of the eligible civil caseload,[5] was referred to ADR. The ADR program is still considered experimental.

OPTIONAL CJRA TECHNIQUES

The CJRA indicates that each court shall consider and may include the following five litigation management techniques:[6]

I.   **Requiring that counsel jointly present a discovery/case management plan at the initial pretrial conference:**

The court did not "opt out" of F.R.Civ.P. 26(f), which makes this technique a requirement after December 1993. Prior thereto, Local Rule 204 governed.[7]

II.   **Requiring that each party be represented at each pretrial conference by an attorney with authority to bind that party:**

Required by Local Rule. The court did not "opt out" of the F.R.Civ.P.

III.   **Requiring the signature of the attorney *and* the party for all requests for discovery extensions or postponements of trial:**

Considered by the court and not required by the plan.

IV.   **Offering a Neutral Evaluation program:**

---

[5]Three percent of the total civil caseload.

[6]28 U.S.C. § 473(b).

[7]The plan called for informing counsel prior to the initial status/scheduling conference that they should communicate with one another prior to the pretrial conference and agree on a suggested schedule for case preparation. The plan also indicated that for the most part the objectives of the technique were sought by the district's current Rules of Practice (effective June 1, 1991).

The court indicates this is provided for by Local Rule 204-2 "Settlement Conferences." Local Rule 204-2(a) indicates "In any case pending before this court, the assigned judge may require, or any party may at any time request, the scheduling of a settlement conference."

V.   Requiring the attendance of party representatives with authority to bind to be present or available by telephone at settlement conferences:

Provided for by Local Rule 204-2.

OTHER POLICIES ADOPTED IN CJRA PLAN

Approved Plan: None.

Differences Between Plan and Advisory Group Recommendations: None.

Differences Between Plan and Implementation: None reported.

OVERVIEW OF PILOT PROGRAM IN WISCONSIN, EASTERN DISTRICT

OVERVIEW OF IMPLEMENTED CJRA PLAN

The CJRA Advisory Group indicated that the essential elements of their recommended plan "are those which encourage and facilitate negotiated disposition, those which limit and streamline pretrial discovery, and those which call for more efficient methods of criminal case management." They were optimistic that adoption of these elements would "have a positive impact upon the disposition of civil cases."[1]

The plan adopted by the court accepted all but two of the advisory group's recommendations related to civil justice, and partially accepted the other two with significant modification. The court notes that these measures "amount only to tinkering about the periphery of the real problem adversely affecting the administration of civil justice in this district. The real problem is the enormous growth of our criminal docket."[2] The plan cuts the limit on interrogatories to 15, generally limits depositions to six hours each, and makes the requirements for dispositive motion and final pretrial papers more uniform and somewhat simpler. The intent is for trial to take place within 18 months of filing. The court did not alter the existing practice of reduced case management for six types of case categories that usually do not have scheduling conferences. The court requires the mandatory exchange of certain information in support of a party's own side before formal discovery can begin. While no formally structured ADR program was created, the plan as implemented allows several types of ADR methods to be used. Other than settlement conferences, fewer than 50 cases per year have ADR. The plan was adopted December 23, 1991, and included Local Rule changes.

As of January 1996, a CJRA Annual Report had not been issued by either the Court or the Advisory Group.

---

[1] Dawson et al. (1991), transmittal page. The 18-person committee was chaired by a lawyer, had a law professor as reporter, met as a whole several times, and also worked separately in subcommittees. One magistrate judge was a member, the Clerk of Court was an ad hoc member, and two judges attended many of the meetings. The Advisory Group interviewed judicial officers, and a survey of about 350 lawyers and an unspecified number of litigants was conducted.

[2] United States District Court for the Eastern District of Wisconsin (1991), pp. 3–4.

CJRA POLICY 1: DIFFERENTIAL CASE MANAGEMENT

Policy Before CJRA Plan

Six types of cases usually have reduced case management, are not immediately routed to the assigned judicial officer, and usually do not have initial scheduling conferences.

1. In forma pauperis requests. Upon filing, these go to a pro se law clerk for examination and recommendation.

2. Prisoner civil rights cases. After in forma pauperis review or payment of filing fee, case is monitored by pro se law clerk, and goes to Magistrate Judge for report and recommendation.

3. Habeas corpus petitions. After in forma pauperis review or payment of filing fee, the case goes to the judge for determination of whether responsive pleading is required.

4. Government collections. Cases are maintained in clerk's office and generally decided by the entry of consent order or default judgment. If contested, case goes to the judge.

5. Bankruptcy appeals. Clerk will issue briefing schedule before the file is sent to the judge.

6. Social Security cases. Clerk will issue scheduling order, and send case to Magistrate Judge for report and recommendation after motions are fully briefed.

All remaining types of cases have standard case management. An initial Rule 16 scheduling conference usually will be held.

CJRA Plan Implementation

Approved Plan: The advisory group indicated that the district already has in place a program of systematic, differential treatment of civil cases which is working satisfactorily, and made no recommendation for change. In addition to the specialized processing of certain types of cases as noted above, the court will continue to rely on scheduling conferences for management on a case-by-case basis.

Differences Between Plan and Advisory Group Recommendations: None.

Differences Between Plan and Implementation: None reported.

CJRA POLICY 2: EARLY AND ONGOING CONTROL OF PRETRIAL BY JUDICIAL OFFICER

Policy Before CJRA Plan

Initial and final pretrial conferences are held, usually with one attempt to settle the case. Limit is 35 interrogatories by Local Rule. Some judges set trial date at initial conference. Procedures for early and ongoing control of pretrial process include holding an initial Rule 16 conference that includes assessment and planning of case progress, setting early and firm trial dates with the goal of being within 18 months after filing, controlling discovery, and setting deadlines for filing motions and a schedule for disposition.

CJRA Plan Implementation

Approved Plan: The plan takes the form of revised or new Local Rules, as follows:

Local Rules 6.01 and 6.05 specify time limits and page limits for motion answer briefs and reply briefs. New summary judgment motion papers requirements have also been made uniform for all judges.

Local Rule 7.01 requires completion of discovery 30 days prior to the date on which trial is scheduled (similar wording and time limit in 1991).

Local Rule 7.03 limits interrogatories to 15 (was 35 in 1991), exclusive of mandatory discovery items and questions about the names of people with discoverable information or about the existence of documentary and physical evidence. More are allowed by stipulation or with court permission.

Local Rule 7.10 establishes new rules guiding the method of taking and the duration of depositions, which, without stipulation or an exemption from the court, are limited to 6 hours.

Local Rule 7.04 states that parties may be required to attend a preliminary pretrial conference to consider future conduct of the case and to be prepared to discuss matters enumerated in Rule 16 as well as a brief (two sentence) statement of the nature of the case, any motions contemplated, amount and time to complete further discovery, and other matters related to scheduling case for trial (similar wording in 1991).

Local Rule 7.06 says court may require parties to prepare a uniform format pretrial report, to be filed at least 10 days prior to scheduled start of trial, to contain short summary of facts (two-page maximum), statement of the issues, names and addresses of all witnesses, narrative summary of background or expert witnesses (if any), list of exhibits, designation of depositions to be read into the record, best estimate of time required to try case, and, if scheduled for jury trial, proposed voir dire questions from court, proposed instructions, and proposed verdict form, with additional requirement that counsel make a good faith effort to settle and arrive at stipulations to save trial time. Unlike 1991, the new requirements are the same for every judge. The 1991 version of rule was less specific and less detailed regarding what goes in report and each judge had his or her own more detailed requirements. This new rule simplifies what is required for some judges.

Additional procedures commit the court to make every effort to resolve all dispositive motions within 6 months of the date on which the last brief is filed.

Local Rule 8.04 expressly provides for the judicial officer, at his or her discretion, to establish reasonable time limits for the trial of all civil and criminal cases.

The plan also encourages consent to trial by magistrate judge (form says "In all likelihood, therefore, a consent will mean that this civil case will be resolve sooner and more inexpensively for the parties"), gives magistrate judges more pretrial responsibility in criminal cases (to give judges increased time for civil cases), and eliminates need for magistrate judges to prepare written decisions on the "boiler plate motions which are routinely filed in criminal cases." Effective October 1, 1992, two magistrate judges each get civil cases assigned for all pretrial. The magistrate judge caseload is 60 percent of a judge's civil caseload for pretrial.

Differences Between Plan and Advisory Group Recommendations: None of a major nature. While the wording of the local rules changes recommended by the Advisory Group sometimes have been modified before incorporation in the court's plan, the intent was generally accepted and preserved by the court in its plan.

Differences Between Plan and Implementation: None reported.

CJRA POLICY 3: MORE INTENSIVE MANAGEMENT OF COMPLEX CASES

Policy Before CJRA Plan

Individualized case management. The advisory group notes that the judges already monitor complex cases through discovery/case management conferences, and says new procedures are unnecessary.

CJRA Plan Implementation

Approved Plan: Existing individualized case management and discovery procedures are deemed sufficient for meeting this guideline. However, note that all new and revised rules of general civil case management also apply to these cases.

Differences Between Plan and Advisory Group Recommendations: None.

Differences Between Plan and Implementation: None reported.

CJRA POLICY 4: EXCHANGE OF DISCOVERY INFORMATION

Policy Before CJRA Plan

No formal policy.

CJRA Plan Implementation

Approved Plan: Local Rule 7.07 provides for mandatory exchange of discovery information, specifically mandatory interrogatories. Plaintiffs are to identify witnesses "with knowledge of any fact alleged in the complaint" and summarize facts the witness knows, to describe or produce for inspection any document "which you contend supports your claims" (rule does not mention production of information supporting other side's claims), and to identify others with subrogation interest. Defendants are to correct improper identification of defendant, identify other parties that should be named, identify witnesses "with knowledge of any fact alleged in the complaint or in the answer to the complaint" and summarize facts the witness knows, to describe or produce for inspection any document "which you contend supports your defenses" and provide information on insurance coverage. Plaintiff must provide within 30 days after defendant answer; defendant must provide within 30 days after plaintiff provides mandatory information. Both must update information if found to be wrong or incomplete. They may not do any other discovery before mandatory information has been or should have been provided.

Exemptions from this Local Rule 7.07 include reviews of administrative proceedings (including Social Security), habeas corpus, government collection cases, pro se prisoner, cases which only seek an order forcing arbitration, and "cases that are not deemed to be complex or lengthy." To qualify for this last exemption, counsel must file a declaration that the party will not take more than 3 depositions or seek answers to more than 15 interrogatories, will use not more than 10 hours of trial time to present its case, and will complete discovery within 9 months. Very few have requested this last exemption.

Local Rule 7.11 covers guidelines for the confidentiality of discovery materials.

Differences Between Plan and Advisory Group Recommendations: The Advisory Group recommended exempting appeals of administrative determinations from this disclosure requirement. The court's plan modifies this significantly by also exempting habeas corpus, government collection cases, pro se prisoner, cases which only seek an order forcing arbitration, and cases that are not deemed to be complex or lengthy (see description above in this section).

Differences Between Plan and Implementation: None reported. The recent amendments to Federal Rule of Civil Procedure 26(a)(1) concerning mandatory initial disclosure are not in effect in this district.[3]

CJRA POLICY 5: CERTIFY GOOD FAITH EFFORT BEFORE FILING DISCOVERY MOTION

Policy Before CJRA Plan

Local Rule 6.02 requires any motion for discovery or production of documents to be accompanied by a statement that, after "consultation with the opposing party and sincere efforts to resolve their differences, the parties have been unable to reach an accord."

---

[3]Stienstra (1995).

CJRA Plan Implementation

Approved Plan: Same.

Differences Between Plan and Advisory Group Recommendations: None.

Differences Between Plan and Implementation: None reported.

CJRA POLICY 6: ALTERNATIVE DISPUTE RESOLUTION PROGRAMS

Policy Before CJRA Plan

No formal policy.

CJRA Plan Implementation

Approved Plan: Local Rule 7.12 indicates that at the Rule 16 conference the judicial officer may invoke one of the following settlement procedures: settlement conference with a judge or magistrate judge, appointment of a special master, or "referral of the case for neutral evaluation, mediation, arbitration, or some other form of alternative dispute resolution procedure." Costs are to be borne by parties. All cases subject to mandatory discovery (Local Rule 7.07) will presumptively be subject to one of the settlement procedures authorized by this rule. Parties may be required to attend in person or to be available on the phone. This district does not have a formally structured ADR program, and fewer than 50 cases per year go to ADR other than settlement conferences with a judicial officer.

Differences Between Plan and Advisory Group Recommendations: The Advisory Group recommended a settlement conference before a judicial officer in all civil cases within 180 days of case filing, and suggested special masters, early neutral evaluation, or mediation if the judicial officer deems them likely to assist in reaching a settlement. The court's plan modified this significantly by not mentioning any time limit for the settlement conference or other ADR process.

Differences Between Plan and Implementation: None reported.

OPTIONAL CJRA TECHNIQUES

The CJRA indicates that each court shall consider and may include the following five litigation management techniques:[4]

I.   Requiring that counsel jointly present a discovery/case management plan at the initial pretrial conference:

No discussion of a joint presentation in the Plan. Advisory Report did not believe that adoption of this technique would reduce cost or delay.

---

[4]28 U.S.C. § 473(b).

II. **Requiring that each party be represented at each pretrial conference by an attorney with authority to bind that party:**

No discussion in the Plan. Advisory Report indicated that attorneys already are required to have the authority to bind their clients regarding matters previously identified by the court for discussion.

III. **Requiring the signature of the attorney *and* the party for all requests for discovery extensions or postponements of trial:**

No discussion in the Plan. Advisory Report did not believe that there was a problem with lack of notice to the client regarding extensions or postponements, nor did it believe that adoption of this technique would reduce cost or delay.

IV. **Offering a Neutral Evaluation program:**

The Plan requires that at the conference held pursuant to F.R.Civ.P. 16, the judicial office shall determine whether the case is an appropriate one for referral to neutral evaluation as well as other ADR programs. The Advisory Report had recommended adoption of a rule requiring a settlement conference within 180 days of commencement of the action (and such a conference could have included early neutral evaluation).

V. **Requiring party representatives with authority to bind to be present or available by telephone at settlement conferences:**

The Plan indicates that parties may be required to attend settlement conferences in person or reachable by telephone.

OTHER POLICIES ADOPTED IN CJRA PLAN

Approved Plan: None.

Differences Between Plan and Advisory Group Recommendations: The Advisory Group made comments or suggestions for actions that are beyond the control of the District Court and/or beyond the area of civil case processing: (1) using more experienced attorneys to represent criminal defendants and increasing their compensation; (2) criminal sentencing guidelines impose effort and delay that may outweigh their benefits; (3) appointment of two additional Magistrate Judges; (4) appointment of two additional District Judges; and (5) existing criminal caseload statistics do not reflect the actual workload in this district.

Alliegro, Suzanne, et al., "Beyond Delay Reduction: Using Differentiated Case Management," *The Court Manager*, Winter, Spring, and Summer, 1993.

Beall, George, Chair, et al., *Report of the Advisory Group of the United States District Court for the District of Maryland Appointed Under the Civil Justice Reform Act of 1990*, Baltimore, Maryland, May 12, 1993.

Bowden, Jeanne J., and Trammell E. Vickery, *Annual Assessment of the Condition of the Court's Docket, July 1, 1991–June 30, 1992*, United States District Court, Northern District of Georgia, Atlanta, Georgia, April 1, 1993.

Bradford, Peter B., Chair, et al., *Report of the Advisory Group of the United States District Court for the Western District of Oklahoma Appointed Under the Civil Justice Reform Act of 1990*, Oklahoma City, Oklahoma, October 21, 1991.

Bradford, Peter B., Chair, et al., *Annual Assessment Under the Civil Justice Reform Act of 1990*, Oklahoma City, Oklahoma, 1993.

Bradford, Peter B., Chair, et al., *Annual Assessment Under the Civil Justice Reform Act of 1990 for the Year 1993*, Oklahoma City, Oklahoma, January 1995.

Bradford, Peter, Chair, et al., *Annual Assessment Under the Civil Justice Reform Act of 1990 for the Year 1994*, Oklahoma City, Oklahoma, June 1996.

The Brookings Institution, *Justice for All: Reducing Costs and Delay in Civil Litigation, Report of a Task Force*, Washington, D.C,. 1989.

Cavanagh, Edward D., reporter, E.D.N.Y. Advisory Group, "Feedback Conference with E.D.N.Y. Judges and Magistrate Judges—November 16, 1992," Brooklyn, New York, memorandum, November 18, 1992.

Chapper, Joy A., et al., *Attacking Litigation Costs and Delay*, American Bar Association, Chicago, Illinois, 1984.

Cody, W. J. Michael, Chair, et al., *Report of the Civil Justice Reform Act Advisory Group for the United States District Court for the Western District of Tennessee*, Memphis, Tennessee, September 26, 1991.

Cody, W. J. Michael, Chair, et al. *Memorandum to Judge Julia Gibbons Re: Early Neutral Evaluation Recommendation,* Civil Justice Reform Act Advisory Group, Memphis, Tennessee, February 2, 1993.

Dawson, John R., Chair, et al., *Civil Justice Reform Act of 1990, Report and Proposed Plan of the Advisory Group of the United States District Court for the Eastern District of Wisconsin,* Milwaukee, Wisconsin, December 1991.

Dunworth, Terence, and Nicholas M. Pace, *Statistical Overview of Civil Litigation in Federal Courts,* RAND, R-3885-ICJ, Santa Monica, California, 1990.

The Federal Courts Study Committee, *Report of the Federal Courts Study Committee,* Washington, D.C., 1990.

Goldstein, Steven M., Chair, et al., *Report of the Civil Justice Reform Act Advisory Committee of the Northern District of Florida,* Tallahassee, Florida, October 12, 1993.

Hawse, Lionel A., Chairman, et al., *Annual Report of the Advisory Group of the United States District Court for the Eastern District of Kentucky Appointed Under the Civil Justice Reform Act of 1990,* Lexington, Kentucky, December 1, 1995.

Heaton, Joe L., Chair, et al., *Annual Assessment Under the Civil Justice Reform Act of 1990 for the Year 1995,* Oklahoma City, Oklahoma, June 1996.

Hensler, D. R., *What We Know and Don't Know About Court-Administered Arbitration,* RAND, N-2444-ICJ, Santa Monica, California, 1986.

Hensler, D. R., *Does ADR Really Save Money? The Jury's Still Out,* RAND, RP-327, 1994. (Reprinted from *The National Law Journal,* April 11, 1994.)

Herndon, Henry N., Chair, et al., *Final Report from the Advisory Group Appointed Pursuant to the Civil Justice Reform Act of 1990 to the United States District Court for the District of Delaware,* Wilmington, Delaware, October 1, 1991.

Herndon, Henry N., Chair, et al., *First Assessment Report of the Advisory Group Pursuant to the Civil Justice Reform Act of 1990 to the United States District Court for the District of Delaware,* Wilmington, Delaware, September 14, 1994.

House Committee Report 101-732, Committee on the Judiciary, U.S. House of Representatives, Washington, D.C., September 1, 1990.

Kakalik, James S., and Nicholas M. Pace, *Costs and Compensation Paid in Tort Litigation,* RAND, R-3391-ICJ, Santa Monica, California, July 1986.

Kakalik, J., T. Dunworth, L. Hill, D. McCaffrey, M. Oshiro, N. Pace, and M. Vaiana, *An Evaluation of Judicial Case Management Under the Civil Justice Reform Act,* RAND, MR-802-ICJ, Santa Monica, California, 1996a.

Kakalik, J., T. Dunworth, L. Hill, D. McCaffrey, M. Oshiro, N. Pace, and M. Vaiana, *An Evaluation of Mediation and Early Neutral Evaluation Under the Civil Justice Reform Act,* RAND, MR-803-ICJ, Santa Monica, California, 1996b.

Landis, Robert M., Chair, et al., *Report of the Advisory Group of the United States District Court for the Eastern District of Pennsylvania Appointed Under the Civil Justice Reform Act of 1990,* Philadelphia, Pennsylvania, August 1, 1991.

Landis, Robert M., Chair, et al., *Annual Report of the Advisory Group of the United States District Court for the Eastern District of Pennsylvania Appointed Under the Civil Justice Reform Act of 1990,* Philadelphia, Pennsylvania, June 1993.

Landis, Robert M., Chair, et al., *Annual Report of the Advisory Group of the United States District Court for the Eastern District of Pennsylvania Appointed Under the Civil Justice Reform Act of 1990,* Philadelphia, Pennsylvania, December 1994.

Landis, Robert M., Chair, et al., *Annual Report of the Advisory Group of the United States District Court for the Eastern District of Pennsylvania Appointed Under the Civil Justice Reform Act of 1990,* Philadelphia, Pennsylvania, June 1996.

Light, Terry W., Chair, et al., *Report of the Advisory Group of the United States District Court for the Middle District of Pennsylvania Appointed Under the Civil Justice Reform Act of 1990,* Harrisburg, Pennsylvania, December 1, 1992.

Light, Terry W., Chair, et al., *1993 Docket Assessment of the Advisory Group to the United States District Court for the Middle District of Pennsylvania Appointed Under the Civil Justice Reform Act of 1990* (undated).

Lind, E. A., R. J. MacCoun, P. A. Ebener, W.L.F. Felstiner, D. R. Hensler, J. Resnik, and T. R. Tyler, *The Perception of Justice: Tort Litigants' Views of Trial, Court-Annexed Arbitration, and Judicial Settlement Conferences,* RAND, R-3708-ICJ, Santa Monica, California, 1989.

Marsh, Lucille, Chair, et al., *1994 Docket Assessment of the Advisory Group to the United States District Court for the Middle District of Pennsylvania Appointed Under the Civil Justice Reform Act of 1990* (undated).

McGarr, Frank J., Chair, et al., *Civil Justice Reform Act Advisory Group Final Report, United States District Court for the Northern District of Illinois,* Chicago, Illinois, August 1993.

McGarr, Frank J., Chair, et al., Civil Justice Reform Act Advisory Group for the United States District Court of the Northern District of Illinois, *Annual Assessment for the Year 1994,* Chicago, Illinois, March 1995.

Meierhoefer, Barbara S., *Court-Annexed Arbitration in Ten District Courts,* Federal Judicial Center, Washington, D.C., 1990.

Mullenix, L., "The Counter-Reformation in Procedural Justice," *Minnesota Law Review,* Vol. 77, 1992.

Plapinger, E., and M. Shaw, *Court ADR: Elements of Program Design,* Center for Public Resources, New York, 1992.

Plapinger, E., et al., *Judge's Deskbook on Court ADR,* Center for Public Resources, New York, 1993.

President's Council on Competitiveness, *Agenda for Civil Justice Reform in America*, Washington, D.C., 1991.

Rauma, David, and Carol Krafka, *Voluntary Arbitration in Eight Federal District Courts: An Evaluation*, Federal Judicial Center, Washington, D.C., 1994.

Reasoner, Harry M., Chair, et al., *Report and Plan: Civil Justice Reform Act Advisory Group of the United States District Court for the Southern District of Texas*, Houston, Texas, October 18, 1991,

Report of the Advisory Group of the United States District Court for the Central District of California Pursuant to the Civil Justice Reform Act of 1990, Los Angeles, California, 1993.

Report of the Civil Justice Reform Act of 1990 Advisory Group for the District of Arizona, Phoenix, Arizona, 1993.

Resnik, J., "Many Doors? Closing Doors? Alternative Dispute Resolution and Adjudication," *Ohio State Journal of Dispute Resolution*, Vol. 10, No. 2, 1995.

Robel, L., *Grass Roots Procedure: Local Advisory Groups and the Civil Justice Reform Act of 1990*, 59 Brooklyn L. R. 879, 1993.

Rolph, E. S., *Introducing Court-Annexed Arbitration: A Policymaker's Guide*, RAND, R-3167-ICJ, 1984.

Rolph, E. S., and E. Moller, *Evaluating Agency Alternative Dispute Resolution Programs: A User's Guide to Data Collection and Use*, RAND, MR-534-ACUS/ICJ, 1995.

Sander, F., *Emerging ADR Issues in State and Federal Courts*, American Bar Association, Chicago, Illinois, 1991.

Savage, Joe, Chairman, et al., *Report of the United States District Court for the Eastern District of Kentucky, Civil Justice Reform Act Advisory Committee*, Lexington, Kentucky, September 1, 1993.

Savage, Joe, Chairman, et al., *Annual Report of the Advisory Group of the United States District Court for the Eastern District of Kentucky Appointed Under the Civil Justice Reform Act of 1990*, Lexington, Kentucky, September 1994.

Segal, Richard A., Chair, et al., *Report of the Civil Justice Reform Act of 1990 Advisory Group for the District of Arizona*, Phoenix, Arizona, June 1993.

Senate Committee Report 101-416, Committee on the Judiciary, August 3, 1990, p. 12 (quoting remarks of Chairman Joseph Biden, June 26, 1990, p. 8).

Sifton, Charles P., Chief Judge, United States District Court, Eastern District of New York, *Administrative Order 96-01*, January 3, 1996.

Smaltz, Donald C., Chair, et al., *Report of the Advisory Group of the United States District Court for the Central District of California Pursuant to the Civil Justice Reform Act of 1990*, Los Angeles, California, March 19, 1993.

Steiner, Robert G., Chair, et al., *Report of the Advisory Committee to the Federal District Court for the Southern District of California as Required by the Civil Justice Reform Act of 1990 ("Biden Bill")*, San Diego, California, September 19, 1991.

Stienstra, Donna, *Implementation of Disclosure in United States District Courts, with Specific Attention to Courts' Responses to Selected Amendments to Federal Rule of Civil Procedure 26*, Federal Judicial Center, Washington, D.C., March 24, 1995.

Stienstra, Donna, and Thomas E. Willging, *Alternatives to Litigation: Do They Have a Place in the Federal District Courts?* Federal Judicial Center, Washington, D.C., 1995.

Sweet, The Honorable Robert W., Chair, et al., *Report and Recommendations of the Southern District of New York Civil Justice Reform Act Advisory Group*, New York, November 1, 1991.

Sweet, The Honorable Robert W., Chair, et al., *First Annual Assessment of the Southern District of New York Civil Justice Reform Act Advisory Group*, New York, January 27, 1994.

Sweet, The Honorable Robert W., Chair, et al., *Second Annual Assessment of the Southern District of New York Civil Justice Reform Act Advisory Group*, New York, 1995.

United States District Court for the Central District of California, *Civil Justice Expense and Delay Reduction Plan*, Los Angeles, California, December 1, 1993.

United States District Court for the District of Arizona, *1993 Annual Report*, Phoenix, Arizona, undated.

United States District Court for the District of Arizona, *Civil Justice Expense and Delay Reduction Plan*, Phoenix, Arizona, undated.

United States District Court for the District of Arizona, *Assessment of Civil Justice Expense and Delay Reduction Plan*, Phoenix, Arizona, March 1995.

United States District Court for the District of Delaware, *Civil Justice Expense and Delay Reduction Plan*, Wilmington, Delaware, undated.

United States District Court for the District of Delaware, Report of the Chief Judge, *United States Courts of the Third Circuit 1994 Annual Report*, Wilmington, Delaware, 1995.

United States District Court for the District of Maryland, *Civil Justice Expense and Delay Reduction Plan for the United States District Court for the District of Maryland*, Baltimore, Maryland, December 1, 1993.

United States District Court for the District of Utah, *Civil Justice Expense and Delay Reduction Plan*, Salt Lake City, Utah, December 30, 1991.

United States District Court for the District of Utah, *Assessment of the District of Utah Civil Justice Reform Act Plan and its Implementation*, Salt Lake City, Utah, September 1994.

United States District Court for the Eastern District of Kentucky, *Order Adopting Civil Justice Expense and Delay Reduction Plan*, Lexington, Kentucky, October 21, 1993.

United States District Court for the Eastern District of New York, *Civil Justice Expense and Delay Reduction Plan*, Brooklyn, New York, December 17, 1991

United States District Court for the Eastern District of Pennsylvania, *Civil Justice Expense and Delay Reduction Plan*, Philadelphia, Pennsylvania, December 31, 1991.

United States District Court for the Eastern District of Pennsylvania, *Standing Order re: 1993 Amendments to Federal Rules of Civil Procedure*, Philadelphia, Pennsylvania, December 1, 1993.

United States District Court for the Eastern District of Wisconsin, *Civil Justice Expense and Delay Reduction Plan*, Milwaukee, Wisconsin, December 23, 1991.

United States District Court for the Middle District of Pennsylvania, *Civil Justice Reform Act of 1990 Expense and Delay Reduction Plan*, Harrisburg, Pennsylvania, September 1993 (Revised 10/1/94).

United States District Court for the Northern District of Florida, *Civil Justice Expense and Delay Reduction Plan of the United States District Court for the Northern District of Florida Pursuant to the Civil Justice Reform Act of 1990*, November 19, 1993.

United States District Court for the Northern District of Georgia, *Civil Justice Expense and Delay Reduction Plan Pursuant to the Civil Justice Reform Act of 1990*, December 17, 1991.

United States District Court for the Northern District of Illinois, *C.J.R.A. Delay and Expense Reduction Plan*, November 15, 1993.

United States District Court for the Northern District of Indiana, *Report of the Advisory Group on the Reduction of Cost and Delay in Civil Cases*, South Bend, Indiana, October 24, 1991a.

United States District Court for the Northern District of Indiana, *Civil Justice Expense and Delay Reduction Plan*, South Bend, Indiana, December 31, 1991b.

United States District Court for the Northern District of Indiana, *Annual Report*, South Bend, Indiana, 1994.

United States District Court for the Southern District of California, *Delay and Cost Reduction Plan Adopted by the District Court, Southern District of California*, San Diego, California, October 7, 1991.

United States District Court for the Southern District of California, *CJRA Annual Assessment of the United States District Court for the Southern District of California*, San Diego, California, March 1994.

United States District Court for the Southern District of California, *CJRA Annual Assessment*, San Diego, California, October 1995.

United States District Court for the Southern District of New York, *Civil Justice Expense and Delay Reduction Plan*, New York, New York, December 12, 1991.

United States District Court for the Southern District of New York, *Guide to the Southern District of New York Civil Justice Expense and Delay Reduction Plan*, New York, New York, January 1993.

United States District Court for the Southern District of Texas, *Cost and Delay Reduction Plan Under the Civil Justice Reform Act of 1990*, Houston, Texas, October 24, 1991a.

United States District Court for the Southern District of Texas, *Order No. 91-30 Re: Provisional Implementation of Cost and Delay Reduction Plan*, Houston, Texas, December 31, 1991b.

United States District Court for the Southern District of Texas, "Amendment to the Southern District CJRA Plan," memorandum, Houston, Texas, February 4, 1992

United States District Court for the Southern District of Texas, *Report on the Impact of the Cost and Delay Reduction Plan Adopted by the United States District Court for the Southern District of Texas*, Houston, Texas, April 6, 1993.

United States District Court for the Southern District of Texas, *Report on the Impact of the Cost and Delay Reduction Plan Adopted by the United States District Court for the Southern District of Texas, 1994*, Houston, Texas, 1995.

United States District Court for the Western District of Kentucky, *Civil Justice Expense and Delay Reduction Plan*, Louisville, Kentucky, November 30, 1993.

United States District Court for the Western District of Oklahoma, *Civil Justice Expense and Delay Reduction Plan*, Oklahoma City, Oklahoma, December 31, 1991.

United States District Court for the Western District of Tennessee, *Civil Justice Expense and Delay Reduction Plan*, Memphis, Tennessee, December 31, 1991.

Vickery, Trammell E., Chair, et al., Report of the Advisory Group of the United States District Court for the Northern District of Georgia Appointed Under the Civil Justice Reform Act of 1990, September 30, 1991.

Wesely, Edwin J., Chair, et al., *Final Report to Honorable Thomas C. Platt, Chief Judge*, Civil Justice Reform Act Advisory Group, Brooklyn, New York, December 9, 1991.

Wesely, Edwin J., Chair, et al., *Annual Report of the CJRA Advisory Group to the Eastern District of New York to the Honorable Thomas C. Platt, Chief Judge*, Civil Justice Reform Act Advisory Group, Brooklyn, New York, January 25, 1994.

Westberry, R. Kent, Chairman, et al., *Civil Justice Reform Act Advisory Committee Report, United States District Court for the Western District of Kentucky,* Louisville, Kentucky, October 1993.

Wilkinson, J., *Donovan Leisure Newton & Irvine ADR Practice Book,* John Wiley & Sons, New York, 1993.

Zimmer, Markus B., committee reporter, et al., *Report of the United States District Court for the District of Utah Civil Justice Reform Act Advisory Committee,* Salt Lake City, Utah, December, 1991.

OUTCOMES

General

Carroll, S. J., with N. M. Pace, *Assessing the Effects of Tort Reforms*, R-3554-ICJ, 1987. $7.50.

Galanter, M., B. Garth, D. Hensler, and F. K. Zemans, *How to Improve Civil Justice Policy*, RP-282. (Reprinted from *Judicature*, Vol. 77, No. 4, January/February 1994.) Free.

Hensler, D. R., *Trends in California Tort Liability Litigation*, P-7287-ICJ, 1987. (Testimony before the Select Committee on Insurance, California State Assembly, October 1987.) $4.00.

_____ , *Researching Civil Justice: Problems and Pitfalls*, P-7604-ICJ, 1988. (Reprinted from *Law and Contemporary Problems*, Vol. 51, No. 3, Summer 1988.) $4.00.

_____ , *Reading the Tort Litigation Tea Leaves: What's Going on in the Civil Liability System?* RP-226. (Reprinted from *The Justice System Journal*, Vol. 16, No. 2, 1993.) Free.

_____ , *Why We Don't Know More About the Civil Justice System—and What We Could Do About It*, RP-363, 1995. (Reprinted from *USC Law*, Fall 1994.) Free.

Hensler, D. R., and E. Moller, *Trends in Punitive Damages: Preliminary Data from Cook County, Illinois, and San Francisco, California*, DRU-1014-ICJ, 1995. Free.

Hensler, D. R., M. E. Vaiana, J. S. Kakalik, and M. A. Peterson, *Trends in Tort Litigation: The Story Behind the Statistics*, R-3583-ICJ, 1987. $4.00.

Hill, P. T., and D. L. Madey, *Educational Policymaking Through the Civil Justice System*, R-2904-ICJ, 1982. $4.00.

Lipson, A. J., *California Enacts Prejudgment Interest: A Case Study of Legislative Action*, N-2096-ICJ, 1984. $4.00.

Moller, E., Trends in Punitive Damages: Preliminary Data from California, DRU-1059-ICJ, 1995. Free.

Shubert, G. H., *Some Observations on the Need for Tort Reform*, P-7189-ICJ, 1986. (Testimony before the National Conference of State Legislatures, January 1986.) $4.00.

_____ , *Changes in the Tort System: Helping Inform the Policy Debate*, P-7241-ICJ, 1986. $4.00.

Jury Verdicts

Carroll, S. J., *Jury Awards and Prejudgment Interest in Tort Cases*, N-1994-ICJ, 1983. $4.00.

Chin, A., and M. A. Peterson, *Deep Pockets, Empty Pockets: Who Wins in Cook County Jury Trials*, R-3249-ICJ, 1985. $10.00.

Dertouzos, J. N., E. Holland, and P. A. Ebener, *The Legal and Economic Consequences of Wrongful Termination*, R-3602-ICJ, 1988. $7.50.

Hensler, D. R., *Summary of Research Results on the Tort Liability System*, P-7210-ICJ, 1986. (Testimony before the Committee on Commerce, Science, and Transportation, United States Senate, February 1986.) $4.00.

Hensler, D. R., and E. Moller, *Trends in Punitive Damages: Preliminary Data from Cook County, Illinois, and San Francisco, California*, DRU-1014-ICJ, 1995. Free.

MacCoun, R. J., *Getting Inside the Black Box: Toward a Better Understanding of Civil Jury Behavior*, N-2671-ICJ, 1987. $4.00.

_____ , *Experimental Research on Jury Decisionmaking*, R-3832-ICJ, 1989. (Reprinted from *Science*, Vol. 244, June 1989.) $4.00.

_____ , *Inside the Black Box: What Empirical Research Tells Us About Decisionmaking by Civil Juries*, RP-238, 1993. (Reprinted from Robert E. Litan, ed., *Verdict: Assessing the Civil Jury System*, The Brookings Institution, 1993.) Free.

_____ , *Is There a "Deep-Pocket" Bias in the Tort System?* IP-130, October 1993. Free.

_____ , *Blaming Others to a Fault?* RP-286. (Reprinted from *Chance*, Vol. 6, No. 4, Fall 1993.) Free.

_____ , *Improving Jury Comprehension in Criminal and Civil Trials*, CT-136, July 1995. Free.

Moller, E., *Trends in Punitive Damages: Preliminary Data from California*, DRU-1059-ICJ, 1995. Free.

_____ , *Trends in Civil Jury Verdicts Since 1985*, MR-694-ICJ, 1996. $15.00.

Peterson, M. A., *Compensation of Injuries: Civil Jury Verdicts in Cook County*, R-3011-ICJ, 1984. $7.50.

_____ , *Punitive Damages: Preliminary Empirical Findings*, N-2342-ICJ, 1985. $4.00.

_____ , *Summary of Research Results: Trends and Patterns in Civil Jury Verdicts*, P-7222-ICJ, 1986. (Testimony before the Subcommittee on Oversight, Committee on Ways and Means, United States House of Representatives, March 1986.) $4.00.

_____ , *Civil Juries in the 1980s: Trends in Jury Trials and Verdicts in California and Cook County, Illinois*, R-3466-ICJ, 1987. $7.50.

Peterson, M. A., and G. L. Priest, *The Civil Jury: Trends in Trials and Verdicts, Cook County, Illinois, 1960–1979*, R-2881-ICJ, 1982. $7.50.

Peterson, M. A., S. Sarma, and M. G. Shanley, *Punitive Damages: Empirical Findings*, R-3311-ICJ, 1987. $7.50.

Selvin, M., and L. Picus, *The Debate over Jury Performance: Observations from a Recent Asbestos Case*, R-3479-ICJ, 1987. $10.00.

Shanley, M. G., and M. A. Peterson, *Comparative Justice: Civil Jury Verdicts in San Francisco and Cook Counties, 1959–1980*, R-3006-ICJ, 1983. $7.50.

_____ , *Posttrial Adjustments to Jury Awards*, R-3511-ICJ, 1987. $7.50.

Costs of Dispute Resolution

Dunworth, T., and J. S. Kakalik, *Preliminary Observations on Implementation of the Pilot Program of the Civil Justice Reform Act of 1990*, RP-361, 1995. (Reprinted from *Stanford Law Review*, Vol. 46, No. 6, July 1994.) Free.

Hensler, D. R., *Does ADR Really Save Money? The Jury's Still Out*, RP-327, 1994. (Reprinted from *The National Law Journal*, April 11, 1994.) Free.

Hensler, D. R., M. E. Vaiana, J. S. Kakalik, and M. A. Peterson, *Trends in Tort Litigation: The Story Behind the Statistics*, R-3583-ICJ, 1987. $4.00.

Kakalik, J. S., and A. E. Robyn, *Costs of the Civil Justice System: Court Expenditures for Processing Tort Cases*, R-2888-ICJ, 1982. $7.50.

Kakalik, J. S., and R. L. Ross, *Costs of the Civil Justice System: Court Expenditures for Various Types of Civil Cases*, R-2985-ICJ, 1983. $10.00.

Kakalik, J. S., P. A. Ebener, W. L. F. Felstiner, and M. G. Shanley, *Costs of Asbestos Litigation*, R-3042-ICJ, 1983. $4.00.

Kakalik, J. S., P. A. Ebener, W. L. F. Felstiner, G. W. Haggstrom, and M. G. Shanley, *Variation in Asbestos Litigation Compensation and Expenses*, R-3132-ICJ, 1984. $7.50.

Kakalik, J. S., and N. M. Pace, *Costs and Compensation Paid in Tort Litigation*, R-3391-ICJ, 1986. $15.00.

_____ , *Costs and Compensation Paid in Tort Litigation*, P-7243-ICJ, 1986. (Testimony before the Subcommittee on Trade, Productivity, and Economic Growth, Joint Economic Committee of the Congress, July 1986.) $4.00.

Kakalik, J. S., E. M. King, M. Traynor, P. A. Ebener, and L. Picus, *Costs and Compensation Paid in Aviation Accident Litigation*, R-3421-ICJ, 1988. $10.00.

Kakalik, J. S., M. Selvin, and N. M. Pace, *Averting Gridlock: Strategies for Reducing Civil Delay in the Los Angeles Superior Court*, R-3762-ICJ, 1990. $10.00.

Kakalik, J. S., T. Dunworth, L. A. Hill, D. McCaffrey, M. Oshiro, N. M. Pace, and M. E. Vaiana, *Just, Speedy, and Inexpensive? An Evaluation of Judicial Case Management Under the Civil Justice Reform Act*, MR-800-ICJ, 1996. $8.

Kakalik, J. S., T. Dunworth, L. A. Hill, D. McCaffrey, M. Oshiro, N. M. Pace, and M. E. Vaiana, *Implementation of the Civil Justice Reform Act in Pilot and Comparison Districts*, MR-801-ICJ, 1996. $20.

Kakalik, J. S., T. Dunworth, L. A. Hill, D. McCaffrey, M. Oshiro, N. M. Pace, and M. E. Vaiana, *An Evaluation of Judicial Case Management Under the Civil Justice Reform Act*, MR-802-ICJ, 1996. $20.

Kakalik, J. S., T. Dunworth, L. A. Hill, D. McCaffrey, M. Oshiro, N. M. Pace, and M. E. Vaiana, *An Evaluation of Mediation and Early Neutral Evaluation Under the Civil Justice Reform Act*, MR-803-ICJ, 1996. $20.

Lind, E. A., *Arbitrating High-Stakes Cases: An Evaluation of Court-Annexed Arbitration in a United States District Court*, R-3809-ICJ, 1990. $10.00.

MacCoun, R. J., E. A. Lind, D. R. Hensler, D. L. Bryant, and P. A. Ebener, *Alternative Adjudication: An Evaluation of the New Jersey Automobile Arbitration Program*, R-3676-ICJ, 1988. $10.00.

Peterson, M. A., *New Tools for Reducing Civil Litigation Expenses*, R-3013-ICJ, 1983. $4.00.

Priest, G. L., *Regulating the Content and Volume of Litigation: An Economic Analysis*, R-3084-ICJ, 1983. $4.00.

DISPUTE RESOLUTION

Court Delay

Adler, J. W., W. L. F. Felstiner, D. R. Hensler, and M. A. Peterson, *The Pace of Litigation: Conference Proceedings*, R-2922-ICJ, 1982. $10.00.

Dunworth, T., and J. S. Kakalik, *Preliminary Observations on Implementation of the Pilot Program of the Civil Justice Reform Act of 1990*, RP-361, 1995. (Reprinted from *Stanford Law Review*, Vol. 46, No. 6, July 1994.) Free.

Dunworth, T., and N. M. Pace, *Statistical Overview of Civil Litigation in the Federal Courts*, R-3885-ICJ, 1990. $7.50.

Ebener, P. A., *Court Efforts to Reduce Pretrial Delay: A National Inventory*, R-2732-ICJ, 1981. $10.00.

Kakalik, J. S., M. Selvin, and N. M. Pace, *Averting Gridlock: Strategies for Reducing Civil Delay in the Los Angeles Superior Court*, R-3762-ICJ, 1990. $10.00.

_____ , *Strategies for Reducing Civil Delay in the Los Angeles Superior Court: Technical Appendixes*, N-2988-ICJ, 1990. $10.00.

Kakalik, J. S., T. Dunworth, L. A. Hill, D. McCaffrey, M. Oshiro, N. M. Pace, and M. E. Vaiana, *Just, Speedy, and Inexpensive? An Evaluation of Judicial Case Management Under the Civil Justice Reform Act*, MR-800-ICJ, 1996. $8.

Kakalik, J. S., T. Dunworth, L. A. Hill, D. McCaffrey, M. Oshiro, N. M. Pace, and M. E. Vaiana, *Implementation of the Civil Justice Reform Act in Pilot and Comparison Districts*, MR-801-ICJ, 1996. $20.

Kakalik, J. S., T. Dunworth, L. A. Hill, D. McCaffrey, M. Oshiro, N. M. Pace, and M. E. Vaiana, *An Evaluation of Judicial Case Management Under the Civil Justice Reform Act*, MR-802-ICJ, 1996. $20.

Kakalik, J. S., T. Dunworth, L. A. Hill, D. McCaffrey, M. Oshiro, N. M. Pace, and M. E. Vaiana, *An Evaluation of Mediation and Early Neutral Evaluation Under the Civil Justice Reform Act*, MR-803-ICJ, 1996. $20.

Lind, E. A., *Arbitrating High-Stakes Cases: An Evaluation of Court-Annexed Arbitration in a United States District Court*, R-3809-ICJ, 1990. $10.00.

MacCoun, R. J., E. A. Lind, D. R. Hensler, D. L. Bryant, and P. A. Ebener, *Alternative Adjudication: An Evaluation of the New Jersey Automobile Arbitration Program*, R-3676-ICJ, 1988. $10.00.

Resnik, J., *Managerial Judges*, R-3002-ICJ, 1982. (Reprinted from the *Harvard Law Review*, Vol. 96:374, December 1982.) $7.50.

Selvin, M., and P. A. Ebener, *Managing the Unmanageable: A History of Civil Delay in the Los Angeles Superior Court*, R-3165-ICJ, 1984. $15.00.

Alternative Dispute Resolution

Adler, J. W., D. R. Hensler, and C. E. Nelson, with the assistance of G. J. Rest, *Simple Justice: How Litigants Fare in the Pittsburgh Court Arbitration Program*, R-3071-ICJ, 1983. $15.00.

Bryant, D. L., *Judicial Arbitration in California: An Update*, N-2909-ICJ, 1989. $4.00.

Ebener, P. A., and D. R. Betancourt, *Court-Annexed Arbitration: The National Picture*, N-2257-ICJ, 1985. $25.00.

Hensler, D. R., *Court-Annexed Arbitration in the State Trial Court System*, P-6963-ICJ, 1984. (Testimony before the Judiciary Committee Subcommittee on Courts, United States Senate, February 1984.) $4.00.

_____ , *Reforming the Civil Litigation Process: How Court Arbitration Can Help*, P-7027-ICJ, 1984. (Reprinted from the *New Jersey Bell Journal*, August 1984.) $4.00.

_____ , *What We Know and Don't Know About Court-Administered Arbitration*, N-2444-ICJ, 1986. $4.00.

_____ , *Court-Ordered Arbitration: An Alternative View*, RP-103, 1992. (Reprinted from *The University of Chicago Legal Forum*, Vol. 1990.) Free.

_____ , *Science in the Court: Is There a Role for Alternative Dispute Resolution?* RP-109, 1992. (Reprinted from *Law and Contemporary Problems*, Vol. 54, No. 3, Summer 1991.) Free.

_____ , *Does ADR Really Save Money? The Jury's Still Out*, RP-327, 1994. (Reprinted from *The National Law Journal*, April 11, 1994.) Free.

_____ , *A Glass Half Full, a Glass Half Empty: The Use of Alternative Dispute Resolution in Mass Personal Injury Litigation*, RP-446, 1995. (Reprinted from *Texas Law Review*, Vol. 73, No. 7, June 1995.) Free.

Hensler, D. R., A. J. Lipson, and E. S. Rolph, *Judicial Arbitration in California: The First Year*, R-2733-ICJ, 1981. $10.00.

_____ , *Judicial Arbitration in California: The First Year: Executive Summary*, R-2733/1-ICJ, 1981. $4.00.

Hensler, D. R., and J. W. Adler, with the assistance of G. J. Rest, *Court-Administered Arbitration: An Alternative for Consumer Dispute Resolution*, N-1965-ICJ, 1983. $4.00.

Kakalik, J. S., T. Dunworth, L. A. Hill, D. McCaffrey, M. Oshiro, N. M. Pace, and M. E. Vaiana, *An Evaluation of Mediation and Early Neutral Evaluation Under the Civil Justice Reform Act*, MR-803-ICJ, 1996. $20.

Lind, E. A., *Arbitrating High-Stakes Cases: An Evaluation of Court-Annexed Arbitration in a United States District Court*, R-3809-ICJ, 1990. $10.00.

Lind, E. A., R. J. MacCoun, P. A. Ebener, W. L. F. Felstiner, D. R. Hensler, J. Resnik, and T. R. Tyler, *The Perception of Justice: Tort Litigants' Views of Trial, Court-Annexed Arbitration, and Judicial Settlement Conferences*, R-3708-ICJ, 1989. $7.50.

MacCoun, R. J., *Unintended Consequences of Court Arbitration: A Cautionary Tale from New Jersey*, RP-134, 1992. (Reprinted from *The Justice System Journal*, Vol. 14, No. 2, 1991.) Free.

MacCoun, R. J., E. A. Lind, D. R. Hensler, D. L. Bryant, and P. A. Ebener, *Alternative Adjudication: An Evaluation of the New Jersey Automobile Arbitration Program*, R-3676-ICJ, 1988. $10.00.

MacCoun, R. J., E. A. Lind, and T. R. Tyler, *Alternative Dispute Resolution in Trial and Appellate Courts*, RP-117, 1992. (Reprinted from *Handbook of Psychology and Law*, 1992.) Free.

Moller, E., E. S. Rolph, P. Ebener, *Private Dispute Resolution in the Banking Industry*, MR-259-ICJ, 1993. $13.00.

Resnik, J. Many Doors? Closing Doors? Alternative Dispute Resolution and Adjudication, RP-439, 1995. (Reprinted from The Ohio State Journal on Dispute Resolution, Vol. 10, No. 2, 1995.) Free.

Rolph, E. S., *Introducing Court-Annexed Arbitration: A Policymaker's Guide*, R-3167-ICJ, 1984. $10.00.

Rolph, E. S., and D. R. Hensler, *Court-Ordered Arbitration: The California Experience*, N-2186-ICJ, 1984. $4.00.

Rolph, E. S., and E. Moller, *Evaluating Agency Alternative Dispute Resolution Programs: A Users' Guide to Data Collection and Use*, MR-534-ACUS/ICJ, 1995. $13.00.

Rolph, E. S., E. Moller, and L. Petersen, *Escaping the Courthouse: Private Alternative Dispute Resolution in Los Angeles*, MR-472-JRHD/ICJ, 1994. $15.00.

Special Issues

Kritzer, H. M., W. L. F. Felstiner, A. Sarat, and D. M. Trubek, *The Impact of Fee Arrangement on Lawyer Effort*, P-7180-ICJ, 1986. $4.00.

Priest, G. L., *Regulating the Content and Volume of Litigation: An Economic Analysis*, R-3084-ICJ, 1983. $4.00.

Priest, G. L., and B. Klein, *The Selection of Disputes for Litigation*, R-3032-ICJ, 1984. $7.50.

Resnik, J., *Managerial Judges*, R-3002-ICJ, 1982. (Reprinted from the *Harvard Law Review*, Vol. 96:374, December 1982.) $7.50.

_____, *Failing Faith: Adjudicatory Procedure in Decline*, P-7272-ICJ, 1987. (Reprinted from the *University of Chicago Law Review*, Vol. 53, No. 2, 1986.) $7.50.

_____, *Due Process: A Public Dimension*, P-7418-ICJ, 1988. (Reprinted from the *University of Florida Law Review*, Vol. 39, No. 2, 1987.) $4.00.

_____, *Judging Consent*, P-7419-ICJ, 1988. (Reprinted from the *University of Chicago Legal Forum*, Vol. 1987.) $7.50.

_____, *From "Cases" to "Litigation,"* RP-110, 1992. (Reprinted from *Law and Contemporary Problems*, Vol. 54, No. 3, Summer 1991.) Free.

_____, *Whose Judgment? Vacating Judgments, Preferences for Settlement, and the Role of Adjudication at the Close of the Twentieth Century*, RP-364, 1995. (Reprinted from *UCLA Law Review*, Vol. 41, No. 6, August 1994.) Free.

AREAS OF LIABILITY

Auto-Accident Litigation

Abrahamse, A., and S. J. Carroll, *The Effects of a Choice Auto Insurance Plan on Insurance Costs*, MR-540-ICJ, 1995. $13.00.

———, *The Effects of Proposition 213 on the Costs of Auto Insurance in California*, IP-157, September 1996. Free.

Carroll, S. J., and A. Abrahamse, *The Effects of a Proposed No-Fault Plan on the Costs of Auto Insurance in California*, IP-146, March 1995. Free.

———, *The Effects of a Proposed No-Fault Plan on the Costs of Auto Insurance in California: An Updated Analysis*, January 1996. Free.

Carroll, S. J., and J. S. Kakalik, *No-Fault Approaches to Compensating Auto Accident Victims*, RP-229, 1993. (Reprinted from *The Journal of Risk and Insurance*, Vol. 60, No. 2, 1993.) Free.

Carroll, S. J., A. Abrahamse, and M. E. Vaiana, *The Costs of Excess Medical Claims for Automobile Personal Injuries*, DB-139-ICJ, 1995. $6.00.

Carroll, S. J., J. S. Kakalik, N. M. Pace, and J. L. Adams, *No-Fault Approaches to Compensating People Injured in Automobile Accidents*, R-4019-ICJ, 1991. $20.00.

Carroll, S. J., and J. S. Kakalik, with D. Adamson, *No-Fault Automobile Insurance: A Policy Perspective*, R-4019/1-ICJ, 1991. $4.00.

Hammitt, J. K., *Automobile Accident Compensation, Volume II, Payments by Auto Insurers*, R-3051-ICJ, 1985. $10.00.

Hammitt, J. K., and J. E. Rolph, *Limiting Liability for Automobile Accidents: Are No-Fault Tort Thresholds Effective?* N-2418-ICJ, 1985. $4.00.

Hammitt, J. K., R. L. Houchens, S. S. Polin, and J. E. Rolph, *Automobile Accident Compensation: Volume IV, State Rules*, R-3053-ICJ, 1985. $7.50.

Houchens, R. L., *Automobile Accident Compensation: Volume III, Payments from All Sources*, R-3052-ICJ, 1985. $7.50.

MacCoun, R. J., E. A. Lind, D. R. Hensler, D. L. Bryant, and P. A. Ebener, *Alternative Adjudication: An Evaluation of the New Jersey Automobile Arbitration Program*, R-3676-ICJ, 1988. $10.00.

O'Connell, J., S. J. Carroll, M. Horowitz, and A. Abrahamse, *Consumer Choice in the Auto Insurance Market*, RP-254, 1994. (Reprinted from the *Maryland Law Review*, Vol. 52, 1993.) Free.

O'Connell, J., S. J. Carroll, M. Horowitz, A. Abrahamse, and D. Kaiser, *The Costs of Consumer Choice for Auto Insurance in States Without No-Fault Insurance*, RP-442, 1995. (Reprinted from *Maryland Law Review*, Vol. 54, No. 2, 1995.) Free.

Rolph, J. E., with J. K. Hammitt, R. L. Houchens, and S. S. Polin, *Automobile Accident Compensation: Volume I, Who Pays How Much How Soon?* R-3050-ICJ, 1985. $4.00.

Asbestos

Hensler, D. R., *Resolving Mass Toxic Torts: Myths and Realities*, P-7631-ICJ, 1990. (Reprinted from the *University of Illinois Law Review*, Vol. 1989, No. 1.) $4.00.

_____ , *Asbestos Litigation in the United States: A Brief Overview*, P-7776-ICJ, 1992. (Testimony before the Courts and Judicial Administration Subcommittee, United States House Judiciary Committee, October 1991.) $4.00.

_____ , *Assessing Claims Resolution Facilities: What We Need to Know*, RP-107, 1992. (Reprinted from *Law and Contemporary Problems*, Vol. 53, No. 4, Autumn 1990.) Free.

_____ , *Fashioning a National Resolution of Asbestos Personal Injury Litigation: A Reply to Professor Brickman*, RP-114, 1992. (Reprinted from *Cardozo Law Review*, Vol. 13, No. 6, April 1992.) Free.

Hensler, D. R., W. L. F. Felstiner, M. Selvin, and P. A. Ebener, *Asbestos in the Courts: The Challenge of Mass Toxic Torts,* R-3324-ICJ, 1985. $10.00.

Kakalik, J. S., P. A. Ebener, W. L. F. Felstiner, and M. G. Shanley, *Costs of Asbestos Litigation*, R-3042-ICJ, 1983. $4.00.

Kakalik, J. S., P. A. Ebener, W. L. F. Felstiner, G. W. Haggstrom, and M. G. Shanley, *Variation in Asbestos Litigation Compensation and Expenses*, R-3132-ICJ, 1984. $7.50.

Peterson, M. A., *Giving Away Money: Comparative Comments on Claims Resolution Facilities*, RP-108, 1992. (Reprinted from *Law and Contemporary Problems*, Vol. 53, No. 4, Autumn 1990.) Free.

Peterson, M. A., and M. Selvin, *Resolution of Mass Torts: Toward a Framework for Evaluation of Aggregative Procedures*, N-2805-ICJ, 1988. $7.50.

_____ , *Mass Justice: The Limited and Unlimited Power of Courts*, RP-116, 1992. (Reprinted from *Law and Contemporary Problems*, No. 3, Summer 1991.) Free.

Selvin, M., and L. Picus, *The Debate over Jury Performance: Observations from a Recent Asbestos Case*, R-3479-ICJ, 1987. $10.00.

Aviation Accidents

Kakalik, J. S., E. M. King, M. Traynor, P. A. Ebener, and L. Picus, *Costs and Compensation Paid in Aviation Accident Litigation*, R-3421-ICJ, 1988. $10.00.

_____ , *Aviation Accident Litigation Survey: Data Collection Forms*, N-2773-ICJ, 1988. $7.50.

King, E. M., and J. P. Smith, *Computing Economic Loss in Cases of Wrongful Death*, R-3549-ICJ, 1988. $10.00.

_____ , *Economic Loss and Compensation in Aviation Accidents*, R-3551-ICJ, 1988. $10.00.

_____ , *Dispute Resolution Following Airplane Crashes*, R-3585-ICJ, 1988. $7.50.

Executive Summaries of the Aviation Accident Study, R-3684, 1988. $7.50.

Employment

Dertouzos, J. N., E. Holland, and P. A. Ebener, *The Legal and Economic Consequences of Wrongful Termination*, R-3602-ICJ, 1988. $7.50.

Dertouzos, J. N., and L. A. Karoly, *Labor-Market Responses to Employer Liability*, R-3989-ICJ, 1992. $7.50.

Environment: California's Clean-Air Strategy

Dixon, L. S., and S. Garber, *California's Ozone-Reduction Strategy for Light-Duty Vehicles: Direct Costs, Direct Emission Effects and Market Responses*, MR-695-ICJ, 1996. $13.00.

———, *Economic Perspectives on Revising California's Zero-Emission Vehicle Mandate*, CT-137, March 1996. $5.00.

Dixon, L. S., S. Garber, and M. E. Vaiana, *California's Ozone-Reduction Strategy for Light-Duty Vehicles: An Economic Assessment*, MR-695/1-ICJ, 1996. $15.00.

———, *Making ZEV Policy Despite Uncertainty: An Annotated Briefing for the California Air Resources Board*, DRU-1266-1-ICJ, 1995. Free.

Environment: Superfund

Acton, J. P., *Understanding Superfund: A Progress Report*, R-3838-ICJ, 1989. $7.50.

Acton, J. P., and L. S. Dixon with D. Drezner, L. Hill, and S. McKenney, *Superfund and Transaction Costs: The Experiences of Insurers and Very Large Industrial Firms*, R-4132-ICJ, 1992. $7.50.

Dixon, L. S., *RAND Research on Superfund Transaction Costs: A Summary of Findings to Date*, CT-111, November 1993. $5.00.

_____ , *Fixing Superfund: The Effect of the Proposed Superfund Reform Act of 1994 on Transaction Costs*, MR-455-ICJ, 1994. $15.00.

_____ , *Superfund Liability Reform: Implications for Transaction Costs and Site Cleanup*, CT-125, 1995. $5.00.

Dixon, L. S., D. S. Drezner, and J. K. Hammitt, *Private-Sector Cleanup Expenditures and Transaction Costs at 18 Superfund Sites*, MR-204-EPA/RC, 1993. $13.00.

Reuter, P., *The Economic Consequences of Expanded Corporate Liability: An Exploratory Study*, N-2807-ICJ, 1988. $7.50.

Medical Malpractice

Danzon, P. M., *Contingent Fees for Personal Injury Litigation*, R-2458-HCFA, 1980. $4.00.

_____ , *The Disposition of Medical Malpractice Claims*, R-2622-HCFA, 1980. $7.50.

_____ , *Why Are Malpractice Premiums So High—Or So Low?* R-2623-HCFA, 1980. $4.00.

_____ , *The Frequency and Severity of Medical Malpractice Claims*, R-2870-ICJ/HCFA, 1982. $7.50.

_____ , *New Evidence on the Frequency and Severity of Medical Malpractice Claims*, R-3410-ICJ, 1986. $4.00.

_____ , *The Effects of Tort Reform on the Frequency and Severity of Medical Malpractice Claims: A Summary of Research Results*, P-7211, 1986. (Testimony before the Committee on the Judiciary, United States Senate, March 1986.) $4.00.

Danzon, P. M., and L. A. Lillard, *The Resolution of Medical Malpractice Claims: Modeling the Bargaining Process*, R-2792-ICJ, 1982. $7.50.

_____ , *Settlement Out of Court: The Disposition of Medical Malpractice Claims*, P-6800, 1982. $4.00.

_____ , *The Resolution of Medical Malpractice Claims: Research Results and Policy Implications*, R-2793-ICJ, 1982. $4.00.

Kravitz, R. L. , J. E. Rolph, K. A. McGuigan, *Malpractice Claims Data as a Quality Improvement Tool: I. Epidemiology of Error in Four Specialties*, N-3448/1-RWJ, 1991. $4.00.

Lewis, E., and J. E. Rolph, *The Bad Apples? Malpractice Claims Experience of Physicians with a Surplus Lines Insurer*, P-7812, 1993. $4.00.

Rolph, E. S., *Health Care Delivery and Tort: Systems on a Collision Course?* Conference Proceedings, Dallas, June 1991, N-3524-ICJ, 1992. $10.00.

Rolph, J. E., *Some Statistical Evidence on Merit Rating in Medical Malpractice Insurance*, N-1725-HHS, 1981. $4.00.

_____ , *Merit Rating for Physicians' Malpractice Premiums: Only a Modest Deterrent*, N-3426-MT/RWJ/RC, 1991. $4.00.

Rolph, J. E., R. L. Kravitz, and K. A. McGuigan, *Malpractice Claims Data as a Quality Improvement Tool: II. Is Targeting Effective?* N-3448/2-RWJ, 1991. $4.00.

Williams, A. P., *Malpractice, Outcomes, and Appropriateness of Care*, P-7445, May 1988. $4.00.

Product Liability

Dunworth, T., *Product Liability and the Business Sector: Litigation Trends in Federal Courts*, R-3668-ICJ, 1988. $7.50.

Eads, G., and P. Reuter, *Designing Safer Products: Corporate Responses to Product Liability Law and Regulation*, R-3022-ICJ, 1983. $15.00.

_____ , *Designing Safer Products: Corporate Responses to Product Liability Law and Regulation*, P-7089-ICJ, 1985. (Reprinted from the *Journal of Product Liability*, Vol. 7, 1985.) $4.00.

Garber, S., *Product Liability and the Economics of Pharmaceuticals and Medical Devices*, R-4285-ICJ, 1993. $15.00.

Hensler, D. R., *Summary of Research Results on Product Liability*, P-7271-ICJ, 1986. (Statement submitted to the Committee on the Judiciary, United States Senate, October 1986.) $4.00.

_____ , *What We Know and Don't Know About Product Liability*, P-7775-ICJ, 1993. (Statement submitted to the Commerce Committee, United States Senate, September 1991.) $4.00.

Moller, E., *Trends in Civil Jury Verdicts Since 1985*, MR-694-ICJ, 1996. $15.00.

Peterson, M. A., *Civil Juries in the 1980s: Trends in Jury Trials and Verdicts in California and Cook County, Illinois*, R-3466-ICJ, 1987. $7.50.

Reuter, P., *The Economic Consequences of Expanded Corporate Liability: An Exploratory Study*, N-2807-ICJ, 1988. $7.50.

Workers' Compensation

Darling-Hammond, L., and T. J. Kniesner, *The Law and Economics of Workers' Compensation*, R-2716-ICJ, 1980. $7.50.

Victor, R. B., *Workers' Compensation and Workplace Safety: The Nature of Employer Financial Incentives*, R-2979-ICJ, 1982. $7.50.

Victor, R. B., L. R. Cohen, and C. E. Phelps, *Workers' Compensation and Workplace Safety: Some Lessons from Economic Theory*, R-2918-ICJ, 1982. $7.50.

MASS TORTS AND CLASS ACTIONS

Hensler, D. R., *Resolving Mass Toxic Torts: Myths and Realities*, P-7631-ICJ, 1990. (Reprinted from the *University of Illinois Law Review*, Vol. 1989, No. 1.) $4.00.

_____ , *Asbestos Litigation in the United States: A Brief Overview*, P-7776-ICJ, 1992. (Testimony before the Courts and Judicial Administration Subcommittee, United States House Judiciary Committee, October 1991.) $4.00.

_____ , *Assessing Claims Resolution Facilities: What We Need to Know*, RP-107, 1992. (Reprinted from *Law and Contemporary Problems*, Vol. 53, No. 4, Autumn 1990.) Free.

_____ , *Fashioning a National Resolution of Asbestos Personal Injury Litigation: A Reply to Professor Brickman*, RP-114, 1992. (Reprinted from *Cardozo Law Review*, Vol. 13, No. 6, April 1992.) Free.

Hensler, D. R., W. L. F. Felstiner, M. Selvin, and P. A. Ebener, *Asbestos in the Courts: The Challenge of Mass Toxic Torts*, R-3324-ICJ, 1985. $10.00.

Hensler, D. R., M. A. Peterson, *Understanding Mass Personal Injury Litigation: A Socio-Legal Analysis*, RP-311, 1994. (Reprinted from *Brooklyn Law Review*, Vol. 59, No. 3, Fall 1993.) Free.

Kakalik, J. S., P. A. Ebener, W. L. F. Felstiner, G. W. Haggstrom, and M. G. Shanley, *Variation in Asbestos Litigation Compensation and Expenses*, R-3132-ICJ, 1984. $7.50.

Kakalik, J. S., P. A. Ebener, W. L. F. Felstiner, and M. G. Shanley, *Costs of Asbestos Litigation*, R-3042-ICJ, 1983. $4.00.

Peterson, M. A., *Giving Away Money: Comparative Comments on Claims Resolution Facilities*, RP-108, 1992. (Reprinted from *Law and Contemporary Problems*, Vol. 53, No. 4, Autumn 1990.) Free.

Peterson, M. A., and M. Selvin, *Resolution of Mass Torts: Toward a Framework for Evaluation of Aggregative Procedures*, N-2805-ICJ, 1988. $7.50.

_____ , *Mass Justice: The Limited and Unlimited Power of Courts*, RP-116, 1992. (Reprinted from *Law and Contemporary Problems*, Vol. 54, No. 3, Summer 1991.) Free.

Selvin, M., and L. Picus, *The Debate over Jury Performance: Observations from a Recent Asbestos Case*, R-3479-ICJ, 1987. $10.00.

Dixon, L. S., D. S. Drezner, and J. K. Hammitt, *Private-Sector Cleanup Expenditures and Transaction Costs at 18 Superfund Sites*, MR-204-EPA/RC, 1993. $13.00.

TRENDS IN THE TORT LITIGATION SYSTEM

Galanter, M., B. Garth, D. Hensler, and F. K. Zemans, *How to Improve Civil Justice Policy*, RP-282. (Reprinted from *Judicature*, Vol. 77, No. 4, January/February 1994.) Free.

Hensler, D. R., *Trends in California Tort Liability Litigation*, P-7287-ICJ, 1987. (Testimony before the Select Committee on Insurance, California State Assembly, October 1987.) $4.00.

_____ , *Reading the Tort Litigation Tea Leaves: What's Going on in the Civil Liability System?* RP-226. (Reprinted from *The Justice System Journal*, Vol. 16, No. 2, 1993.) Free.

Hensler, D. R., M. E. Vaiana, J. S. Kakalik, and M. A. Peterson, *Trends in Tort Litigation: The Story Behind the Statistics*, R-3583-ICJ, 1987. $4.00.

ECONOMIC EFFECTS OF THE LIABILITY SYSTEM

General

Carroll, S. J., A. Abrahamse, M. S. Marquis, and M. E. Vaiana, *Liability System Incentives to Consume Excess Medical Care*, DRU-1264-ICJ, 1995. Free.

Johnson, L. L., *Cost-Benefit Analysis and Voluntary Safety Standards for Consumer Products*, R-2882-ICJ, 1982. $7.50.

Reuter, P., *The Economic Consequences of Expanded Corporate Liability: An Exploratory Study*, N-2807-ICJ, 1988. $7.50.

Product Liability

Dunworth, T., *Product Liability and the Business Sector: Litigation Trends in Federal Courts*, R-3668-ICJ, 1988. $7.50.

Eads, G., and P. Reuter, *Designing Safer Products: Corporate Responses to Product Liability Law and Regulation*, R-3022-ICJ, 1983. $15.00.

_____ , *Designing Safer Products: Corporate Responses to Product Liability Law and Regulation*, P-7089-ICJ, 1985. (Reprinted from the *Journal of Product Liability*, Vol. 7, 1985.) $4.00.

Garber, S., *Product Liability and the Economics of Pharmaceuticals and Medical Devices*, R-4285-ICJ, 1993. $15.00.

Hensler, D. R., *Summary of Research Results on Product Liability*, P-7271-ICJ, 1986. (Statement submitted to the Committee on the Judiciary, United States Senate, October 1986.) $4.00.

_____ , *What We Know and Don't Know About Product Liability*, P-7775-ICJ, 1993. (Statement submitted to the Commerce Committee, United States Senate, September 1991.) $4.00.

Peterson, M. A., *Civil Juries in the 1980s: Trends in Jury Trials and Verdicts in California and Cook County, Illinois*, R-3466-ICJ, 1987. $7.50.

Wrongful Termination

Dertouzos, J. N., E. Holland, and P. A. Ebener, *The Legal and Economic Consequences of Wrongful Termination*, R-3602-ICJ, 1988. $7.50.

Dertouzos, J. N., and L. A. Karoly, *Labor-Market Responses to Employer Liability*, R-3989-ICJ, 1992. $7.50.

COMPENSATION SYSTEMS

System Design

Darling-Hammond, L., and T. J. Kniesner, *The Law and Economics of Workers' Compensation*, R-2716-ICJ, 1980. $7.50.

Hammitt, J. K., R. L. Houchens, S. S. Polin, and J. E. Rolph, *Automobile Accident Compensation: Volume IV, State Rules*, R-3053-ICJ, 1985. $7.50.

Hammitt, J. K., and J. E. Rolph, *Limiting Liability for Automobile Accidents: Are No-Fault Tort Thresholds Effective?* N-2418-ICJ, 1985. $4.00.

Hensler, D. R., *Resolving Mass Toxic Torts: Myths and Realities*, P-7631-ICJ, 1990. (Reprinted from the *University of Illinois Law Review*, Vol. 1989, No. 1.) $4.00.

_____ , *Assessing Claims Resolution Facilities: What We Need to Know*, RP-107, 1992. (Reprinted from *Law and Contemporary Problems*, Vol. 53, No. 4, Autumn 1990.) Free.

King, E. M., and J. P. Smith, *Computing Economic Loss in Cases of Wrongful Death*, R-3549-ICJ, 1988. $10.00.

Peterson, M. A., and M. Selvin, *Resolution of Mass Torts: Toward a Framework for Evaluation of Aggregative Procedures*, N-2805-ICJ, 1988. $7.50.

Rolph, E. S., *Framing the Compensation Inquiry*, RP-115, 1992. (Reprinted from the *Cardozo Law Review*, Vol. 13, No. 6, April 1992.) Free.

Victor, R. B., *Workers' Compensation and Workplace Safety: The Nature of Employer Financial Incentives*, R-2979-ICJ, 1982. $7.50.

Victor, R. B., L. R. Cohen, and C. E. Phelps, *Workers' Compensation and Workplace Safety: Some Lessons from Economic Theory*, R-2918-ICJ, 1982. $7.50.

Performance

Abrahamse, A., and S. J. Carroll, *The Effects of a Choice Auto Insurance Plan on Insurance Costs*, MR-540-ICJ, 1995. $13.00.

Carroll, S. J., and A. Abrahamse, *The Effects of a Proposed No-Fault Plan on the Costs of Auto Insurance in California*, IP-146, March 1995. Free.

Carroll, S. J., and J. S. Kakalik, *No-Fault Approaches to Compensating Auto Accident Victims*, RP-229, 1993. (Reprinted from *The Journal of Risk and Insurance*, Vol. 60, No. 2, 1993.) Free.

Carroll, S. J., A. Abrahamse, and M. E. Vaiana, *The Costs of Excess Medical Claims for Automobile Personal Injuries*, DB-139-ICJ, 1995. $6.00.

Carroll, S. J., A. Abrahamse, M. S. Marquis, and M. E. Vaiana, *Liability System Incentives to Consume Excess Medical Care*, DRU-1264-ICJ, 1995. Free.

Carroll, S. J., J. S. Kakalik, N. M. Pace, and J. L. Adams, *No-Fault Approaches to Compensating People Injured in Automobile Accidents*, R-4019-ICJ, 1991. $20.00.

Carroll, S. J., and J. S. Kakalik, with D. Adamson, *No-Fault Automobile Insurance: A Policy Perspective*, R-4019/1-ICJ, 1991. $4.00.

Hensler, D. R., M. S. Marquis, A. Abrahamse, S. H. Berry, P. A. Ebener, E. G. Lewis, E. A. Lind, R. J. MacCoun, W. G. Manning, J. A. Rogowski, and M. E. Vaiana, *Compensation for Accidental Injuries in the United States*, R-3999-HHS/ICJ, 1991. $20.00.

_____ , *Compensation for Accidental Injuries in the United States: Executive Summary*, R-3999/1-HHS/ICJ, 1991. $4.00.

_____ , *Compensation for Accidental Injuries: Research Design and Methods*, N-3230-HHS/ICJ, 1991. $15.00.

King, E. M., and J. P. Smith, *Economic Loss and Compensation in Aviation Accidents*, R-3551-ICJ, 1988. $10.00.

O'Connell, J., S. J. Carroll, M. Horowitz, and A. Abrahamse, *Consumer Choice in the Auto Insurance Market*, RP-254, 1994. (Reprinted from the *Maryland Law Review*, Vol. 52, 1993.) Free.

O'Connell, J., S. J. Carroll, M. Horowitz, A. Abrahamse, and D. Kaiser, *The Costs of Consumer Choice for Auto Insurance in States Without No-Fault Insurance*, RP-442, 1995. (Reprinted from *Maryland Law Review*, Vol. 54, No. 2, 1995.) Free.

Peterson, M. A., *Giving Away Money: Comparative Comments on Claims Resolution Facilities*, RP-108, 1992. (Reprinted from *Law and Contemporary Problems*, Vol. 53, No. 4, Autumn 1990.) Free.

Peterson, M. A., and M. Selvin, *Mass Justice: The Limited and Unlimited Power of Courts*, RP-116, 1992. (Reprinted from *Law and Contemporary Problems*, Vol. 54, No. 3, Summer 1991.) Free.

Rolph, J. E., with J. K. Hammitt, R. L. Houchens, and S. S. Polin, *Automobile Accident Compensation: Volume I, Who Pays How Much How Soon?* R-3050-ICJ, 1985. $4.00.

SPECIAL STUDIES

Hensler, D. R., and M. E. Reddy, *California Lawyers View the Future: A Report to the Commission on the Future of the Legal Profession and the State Bar*, MR-528-ICJ, 1994. $13.00.

Merz, J. F., and N. M. Pace, *Trends in Patent Litigation: The Apparent Influence of Strengthened Patents Attributable to the Court of Appeals for the Federal Circuit*, RP-426, 1995. (Reprinted from *Journal of the Patent and Trademark Office Society*, Vol. 76, No. 8, August 1994.) Free.

An annotated bibliography, CP-253 (12/96), provides a list of RAND publications in the civil justice area through 1996 To request the bibliography or to obtain more information about the Institute for Civil Justice, please write the Institute at this address: The Institute for Civil Justice, RAND, 1700 Main Street, P.O. Box 2138, Santa Monica, California 90407-2138, or call (310) 393-0411, x6916.